LIFE–WORK OF LOUIS KLOPSCH

LIFE-WORK

OF

LOUIS KLOPSCH

ROMANCE OF A MODERN
KNIGHT OF MERCY

BY

CHARLES M. PEPPER

WITH NUMEROUS ILLUSTRATIONS

Send your ships with corn and wheat,
Bid our starving thousands eat.

. . . At his command
Corn-bearing ships to famine lands set sail —
Our country's banners flying at the mast.

THE CHRISTIAN HERALD
New York

A FOREWORD

I FIRST met Louis Klopsch on a bright day in August, 1882. I was just out of college and had come to New York to offer my services to one of the great journals on Park Row. There had been doubt in my mind as to whether I should give my assistance to Mr. Dana of the Sun or Mr. Hurlburt of the World or Mr. Bennett of the Herald or Mr. Jones of the Times. That doubt no longer existed, for none of these gentlemen had been willing to consider my talents, or even to let me hear the sound of their voices.

I was well out of hope and courage when I called at 92 White Street, agreeably with the request of Louis Klopsch, then the proprietor of a trade journal. I showed him my letters.

"What salary do you expect?" he asked.

"I would begin at ten dollars a week," I said.

"You may try the work, and if your services are satisfactory, I'll start you at fifteen a week," he answered.

With this generous act he came into my life. To my mind it was princely, magnificent; and I do remember well that it was good business. It gave me the key-note of his character. Next day I turned in my first copy. I recall how it amused and delighted him. His recognition was not less generous than his pay.

We were friends from that day, and in the twenty-

*seven years of life that remained to him I was to see
Louis Klopsch under most of the moods and circumstances that come to men. I never saw him refuse an
appeal for help or turn a deaf ear to the voice of trouble.
The vilest man who walked the streets could halt his
hurried step and engage his thought and get a meal
ticket on a plea of hunger. The man who worked for
him faithfully was his brother. The troubles of that
man were a part of the troubles of Louis Klopsch. His
money and his great talents went beyond all reasonable
generosity in his behalf.*

*"Find out how much you owe and I'll see what I
can do for you," I have often heard him say to such
men, as a prelude to a plan of financing their debts.*

*He was constantly taking upon himself the burdens
of other men and just for the love of making them happy.
He lifted mortgages, paid life insurance premiums,
and took up notes by way of meeting the emergencies
of those he knew.*

*I remember a time in my own business life, when
reverses had come. He sent a substantial check, all
unsolicited, having heard that I was in need of help,
and he said: "If you're ever able to return this money,
all right. If not — all right."*

*But he was in no sense "easy," as they put it these
days. No man ever had keener eyes or a surer judgment
of men. There may be those who cherish a secret
notion that they had fooled him in one way or another;
but it was they who were fooled — not Louis Klopsch.
I do not remember to have come in contact with any
mind so keen, so alert, so penetrating in the affairs
that engaged his thought. He was thoroughly modern*

*in his spirit. He was profoundly religious, but free
of bigotry. His religion was full of joy — so full
that to certain old-fashioned folk it suggested effusive-
ness. He was, indeed, very human, but he was also
very true and genuine. He fought the good fight with
a brave and merry heart. He gave and forgave and
helped and loved and did as he would be done by. He
was quite as prompt in the debts of business as in the
debts of charity. He loved little children, especially
those of the poor, and his chief recreation was drawn
from the happiness that he gave them. That overflow
of joy and gratitude at Mont-Lawn and the Bowery
Mission were the food of his spirit.*

*I have said that he was modern. There was a wel-
come and, as I am inclined to think, a new note in his
religion. Mainly he preached with bread; he prayed
with human kindness; he blessed with wheat and corn.
His best missionaries were loaded ships; his happiness
was in mitigated pain. His week-day was as holy
as his Sabbath, his office as consecrated as his church,
his note of hand as binding as his creed, his business
as sacred as his religion. He was a new and a great
preacher.*

IRVING BACHELLER.

CONTENTS

CONTENTS

CONTENTS

ILLUSTRATIONS

LIFE–WORK OF LOUIS KLOPSCH

LIFE-WORK OF LOUIS KLOPSCH

CHAPTER I

EARLY ACTIVITIES

AMERICAN OPPORTUNITY EMBRACED BY YOUNG KLOPSCH — "GOOD MORNING"
TO THE BUSINESS WORLD — BUYS A PRINTING OFFICE — PIONEER IN PIC-
TORIAL JOURNALISM — APTITUDE SHOWN — SYNDICATING REV. T. DEWITT
TALMAGE'S SERMONS — TRIP TO EUROPE AND THE HOLY LAND — PURCHASE
OF "THE CHRISTIAN HERALD" — THE CHOSEN INSTRUMENT OF A NOBLE
AMBITION — FIRST FIVE YEARS REVIEWED.

THE early struggles of successful men are
familiar chapters. By some instinct they
seek the field in which their abilities will
find the sphere of action to which they are best
adapted. America has been the land of opportunity
for hosts of those who, born abroad, have left
the country of their birth in early youth and in the
New World have realized their ambitions. Others
have been born and brought up in this favored
country, while some have come to it at such an early
age that they may almost be considered as native
born.

Louis Klopsch, though born in Germany, was
essentially an American boy. His young life was
spent in New York and vicinity. Opportunity lay
all around him, but he did not wait for it to come
to him. He sought it. He soon drifted into various
advertising and publishing enterprises. Always it
was the new idea which appealed to him.

1

Just out of his teens in the early seventies he saluted the reading public with *Good Morning*, a four-page publication, the size of *The Christian Herald*, printed upon high-grade tinted paper, with excellent selections of reading matter suited to the family, issued weekly. He found a great sale for this paper amongst retail dealers in dry goods, boots and shoes, groceries, drugs, etc., who would purchase one or more thousand copies for distribution in the immediate neighborhood of their stores. Each retail dealer was privileged to have his own advertisement appear in the copies he purchased. With about a hundred retail dealers as customers he could readily afford to permit each to have his wish gratified in distributing the paper to his neighbors.

Possessed of a very active brain, publishing became his forte. His great aim and ambition ran in the channel of the printing and publishing business.

He had worked up a plan for a special publication which he believed would prove a success. Being fundless he sought out one who had befriended him on similar occasions, and with his aid he in the latter part of the Centennial year issued the first numbers of the *Daily Hotel Reporter;* and through it he began to get a solid footing, finally purchasing a printing office.

Some years after this he met the friend who had stood by him in the past, related his circumstances, and impressed this friend with the fact that he was not unmindful of the former kind acts nor of his financial indebtedness to him; that he hoped soon to liquidate it, and also remarked that if he could send any printing to this man's printing office he would gladly do it and it could apply on the old account.

Shortly after this conversation his old patron dropped into the office and informed Mr. Klopsch that one to whom he was personally indebted desired to have a law case printed, having lost a suit which was to be appealed, and it required several thousand dollars' worth of printing. Mr. Klopsch agreed to do the printing, but after taking account of stock—that is, type and finances—found himself up against a stone wall; yet, resourceful in thought and plan, he hit upon a solution. As the work would more than three times cover the amount of his indebtedness, if the party requiring the printing would upon submission of proofs of each one hundred pages advance one-third in cash, he would be enabled to purchase the necessary type and print the law case, and out of the other two-thirds the total indebtedness would be wiped out. And it was done, showing a new way to pay old debts.

This incident proves the honesty of purpose with which he was imbued. And up to the time of his passing away he never lost an opportunity of practically showing his appreciation of his old standby, who doubly benefited by this transaction, for he was enabled to wipe out an old score of debt to his friend for whom the printing was done.

At the same time he engaged in various enterprises which called forth the exertions of his powers of impressing people with his business capacity. In later years he was accustomed to speak of an incident when he was hard pressed by the tightness of business.

"I remember," he said, "that when I was editing an album and doing an advertising business, things were dreadfully dark; there was absolutely nothing in sight, and I was somewhat discouraged; but such moods never lasted long with me, and I quickly made up my mind to make business. I took my last thirty dollars — it was all I had in ready cash — bought a new suit, necktie, and hat, got shaved, and had my boots blacked. Then I went out and made things hum, turning in more business than I had done in many a day. I learned from this and other similar experiences the importance of putting on a good front in business, and of what great value to a young man was his personal appearance and neatness in making an impression upon those he comes in contact with in business. I never forgot that experience."

Pictorial journalism was one of the features of young Klopsch's early activities. With his intuitive perception of what the great masses of people wanted, he saw that the picture appealed to them in connection with reading matter. At that period mechanical processes for illustrating newspapers were in a backward state of development. The illustrations in the daily journals, which now form so marked a feature, were almost unknown. Occasionally some enterprising journal would reproduce the portrait of a distinguished person, usually in connection with an obituary. Young Klopsch saw that readers wanted to see how people of note looked and that it was not necessary to wait until they were dead in order to reproduce their portraits. He accordingly established the *Pictorial Associated Press*, which began in a small way by supplying cuts of men and women who were in the public eye, and this business he enlarged until the development of mechanical processes enabled the leading journals to provide themselves with their own means of illustration. Many of the ideas which they followed were due to the initiative of Mr. Klopsch and the *Pictorial Associated Press* which he controlled.

An incident which illustrated his views of business relations occurred during these early years when he was experimenting with various publications. A place on one of them became vacant. The work was of a fixed character, at a fixed salary. A young man, who afterward achieved reputation, was at that time walking the streets of New York in search of employment. He heard of an opening on the Klopsch publication, and in his anxiety to obtain work, went to the proprietor and offered to take the place at a smaller salary than had previously been paid. Mr. Klopsch refused the offer. "That work," he said, "is worth so much a week, and we have been paying so much as salary. If you can perform it satisfactorily, you are entitled to have the full salary. If you can't do it to suit us, your services won't be cheap at the rate you offer, because we won't want you at all. Suppose you start in, and we will give you the full salary. But if we find you incompetent, we won't keep you."

The offer was gratefully accepted. The young man

performed the duties of the position satisfactorily
until his talents gave him an opening in another
direction. It was characteristic of young Klopsch's
business principles, which he carried through his
later life, that he was always ready to pay full value
for services rendered.

In his business activities as a young man, Mr.
Klopsch did not neglect the evangelical work to
which he gave the best of his mature manhood.
He was attracted to the Brooklyn Tabernacle, of
which the Rev. T. DeWitt Talmage was the pastor.
They were thrown together, and a warm friendship
sprang up. Dr. Talmage's methods were considered
sensational, but the message he delivered from the
pulpit he had to deliver in his own way. That it
was an acceptable message was shown by the multitudes who thronged the Tabernacle to hear him.

The daily newspapers of New York Monday
mornings usually contained a report of his sermon,
and these reports were sometimes republished by
other newspapers, but they had no general circulation. Mr. Klopsch saw that a vast audience beyond
the confines of the Brooklyn Tabernacle were eager
to read, if they could not hear, Dr. Talmage's sermons regularly. He conceived the plan of syndicating them to several hundred papers. At that time
this means of supplying large numbers of readers
with the same material had not come into general
use. Mr. Klopsch first broached the suggestion to
Dr. Talmage and obtained his consent. Then he
took it up with newspapers large and small all over
the world. Some were doubtful, and others indifferent, but the majority were glad to have the oppor-

tunity of offering their readers the weekly sermon as delivered in the Brooklyn Tabernacle, furnished in advance so that it could be published the day following its delivery.

The syndicating of the Talmage sermons was gradually developed until it became one of Mr. Klopsch's most important business enterprises. It began in 1885.

At this period, Mr. Klopsch was beginning to make an impression on the publishing world. His energy, ability, and determination to succeed overcame every obstacle and commanded the good-will, respect, and support of all with whom he came in contact. His industry and his fidelity to business engagements helped him to win his way to higher success. He had started out without a dollar of capital, and the limitation of funds at his command restricted somewhat his enterprises, but gradually he was able to give his energies broader scope.

Mr. Klopsch, as a development of the syndication of the Talmage sermons, proposed to the famous divine a trip to Europe and to the Holy Land. Dr. Talmage consented, and Mr. Klopsch accompanied him. The trip was made in 1889. Dr. Talmage preached in many places abroad, and these sermons when published in the United States met with great favor.

Mr. Klopsch often spoke of this visit to the Holy Land as one of the most enjoyable experiences of his life. It was the fulfillment of a desire that he had cherished from boyhood. In letters to his friends he gave his impressions in his own vivid manner.

During this trip abroad, Mr. Klopsch matured plans that had long been working in his mind. He spent some time in England in conference with the Rev. Michael Baxter, the owner of *The Christian Herald*. This popular British weekly had a large circulation in the United Kingdom. An edition was also published in New York for American readers. The American edition had much in it of value, but Mr. Klopsch thought that if it could be dedicated more especially to readers of the United States, its usefulness would become greater. Besides, he had certain ideas of his own which he wanted to carry out. After some negotiations with Dr. Baxter, the arrangement was made by which he took the management of *The Christian Herald* in New York, and subsequently bought it outright, so that it became his sole property, and his cherished ambition was realized. At that time it had a circulation of about 30,000, which was considered good for a religious journal. Mr. Klopsch told some of his associates that the circulation could be brought up to a quarter of a million. This seemed a wild notion in view of the limitations with which religious journals were supposed to be surrounded. But before his death, twenty years later, Mr. Klopsch's judgment was amply vindicated.

On his return to New York, when he found himself in full control of *The Christian Herald*, Mr. Klopsch arranged to relinquish his other newspaper publications, and thereafter his energies were devoted solely to the paper and to the publishing business which he developed from it.

Dr. Talmage became coadjutor editor, and Mr. Klopsch began to develop his plans. He had two leading purposes in view. He determined to make *The Christian Herald* the most successful religious paper in the world, and to make it a medium of American bounty to the needy throughout the world. He had found his life-work in his chosen sphere. His views of the field of the religious newspaper were to give it a broad evangelical character and to make it co-ordinate with the secular newspaper.

An editorial which appeared a year or so after Mr. Klopsch became the owner reflected his views of the secular newspaper, as well as of the evangelical journal.

"I congratulate newspaper men," said the editorial, "on the splendor of an opportunity, but I charge them before God that they be careful to use their influence in the right direction. How grand will be the result in the last day for the man who has consecrated the printing press to high and holy objects! God will say to such a one, 'You broke off a million chains, you opened a million blind eyes, you gave resurrection to a million of the dead.'

"It is a vast responsibility that rests upon people who set type, or sit in editorial chairs. The audience is so large, the influence is so great, the results are so eternal, that I believe in the day of judgment, amid all the millions of men who will come up to render their accounts, the largest accounts will be rendered by newspaper men."

How far his ambition was to be fulfilled gradually began to be apparent. In a December issue in 1894, there was "A word about ourselves." Among other things the article said:

"So swiftly does time pass that it seems scarcely possible that five years have nearly elapsed since Dr. Talmage assumed editorial charge of *The Christian Herald*. It has been the privilege of *The Christian Herald* and its management during these five years of material prosperity to take a more active share in the great work of disseminating pure literature than has probably ever before fallen to the lot of any religious newspaper. The total expense involved in five great years of literary undertaking has been $399,000.

"Charity has formed another and hardly less prominent part of *The Christian Herald's* mission in these five years. As we regard events in retrospect, it seems to have been divinely led into a field of philanthropy so wide and so far-reaching as to impress the sympathy and co-operation of its readers in every clime. In this special field of charity, $120,000 has been expended in the aggregate.

"In the line of distinctly religious work, *The Christian Herald's* efforts have been signally blessed. Its expenditures in the various fields of Christian effort altogether aggregate a total of $530,000, or upward of $105,000 a year."

It was during these five years that Dr. Klopsch was steadily working out the plan described of making his paper the great religious journal that it has become, and at the same time the instrument of the bounty of the American people. *The Christian Herald* family grew and spread until it covered all parts of the world where the English language is read. The educational and missionary work grew in the same proportion.

CHAPTER II

RUSSIAN RELIEF

THE first of the remarkable chain of world-wide charities which Dr. Klopsch undertook was for the relief of starving millions of Russian peasants.

The vast extent of the Czar's dominions, from the frozen sea of the Arctic to the frozen sea of the Pacific, is little understood. The area is estimated at nearly nine million square miles and the population at one hundred and sixty million inhabitants.

In so extensive a region there is naturally much variety of resources, yet the chief reliance of the people is on the soil. The mass of peasantry is absolutely dependent on the crops and the conditions are such that they have little chance of saving from one season to another. They are as much of the soil as when they were serfs.

In the best of conditions the lot of the peasants is not a comfortable one, yet they are peaceful, hard-working, and make the best of their surroundings.

11

A description of Russian peasants at home by an American writer, Mrs. Isabel F. Hapgood, gives a graphic idea of their manner of existence.

Mrs. Hapgood wrote: "We visited the peasants in their cottages. The rope and moss-plugged log house stood flat on the ground, and was thatched with straw which was secured by a ladder-like arrangement of poles along the gable ends. Three tiny windows, with tinier panes, relieved the street front of the house. The entrance was on the side, from the small farmyard littered with farm implements, chickens, and manure, and enclosed with the usual fence of wattled branches. From the small ante-room, designed to keep out the winter's cold, the storeroom opened at the rear and the living-room at the front.

"The lefthand corner of the living-room as one entered was occupied by the oven made of stones and clay and whitewashed. In it the cooking was done by placing the pots among the glowing wood coals. The bread was baked when the coals had been raked out. Later still, when desired, the owners took their steam bath, more resembling a roasting, inside it, and the old people kept their aged bones warm by sleeping on top of it close to the low ceiling. Around three sides of the room ran a broad bench which served for furniture and beds. In the righthand corner, opposite the door, the great corner of honor, was the case of images, in front of which stood the rough table whereon meals were eaten. This was convenient, since the images were saluted at the beginning and end of meals with the sign of the cross and a murmured prayer. The case also contained the sacred pictures of the home."

Like every crop country Russia experiences periods of plenty, when it ships enormous quantities of grain to other countries. Then sometimes come the periods of short crops, when the richest districts do not supply enough for themselves. Such a time came in the winter of 1891–1892.

The richest agricultural region in the great Empire is the basin of the Volga. This is equal in extent and in productivity to our own Mississippi Valley. Repeated droughts and the pest of insects caused a complete crop failure in the Volga Basin and in other districts extending over sixteen provinces. Fully twenty million cultivators of the soil were affected. It was known that the crops in Russia were short, yet for months the outside world had little conception of the suffering or of the need of relief. The districts were so remote, and so little was known of the great interior of the Czar's dominions, that at first it was regarded only as an ordinary crop failure. Gradually something became known of the extent of the suffering.

Reports were received of famine refugees filling the big cities of Moscow and St. Petersburg. Something was also learned of the vigorous measures of the Russian government and accounts were received of the relief trains which were daily dispatched. Then word began to come from those who had gone among the peasantry and who were writing of what they saw. Here is a striking picture given by a correspondent of his visit with a member of a local branch of the Red Cross Society in the province of Rexan to a distressed family:

Attended by the elders of the place we went into the first miserable hut of the wretched little row that constituted the street. My friend entered unceremoniously and roughly without knocking or calling. A kind of vapor poured out of the open door, and on entering I descried through the thick atmosphere several human beings whose appearance and attitude filled me with horror. In the background stood a wrinkled hag, a handkerchief around her head. The rest of her costume, consisting of a short petticoat and leggings, was squalid and wretched to the last degree. To the right was an immense stove and over this a broad shelf, on which several frightened children were huddled together. They looked dirty and savage beyond description. There was no floor. We were standing upon the bare ground. The hut was about twenty feet square by ten feet high. A table and two benches were the only furniture the hut could boast of, and they were black with age and dirt.

Running from the door to the stove was a beam or rafter and on this were a few wretched dishes and cooking utensils. A fearful stench pervaded the hut. Cap in hand, with trembling knees, haggard cheeks and hollow eyes, stood the owner, who bade us welcome with a cringing humility and a look of mingled cunning and fear. Besides the old peasant and his wife there were two young men and their wives. I realized that three generations camped on that shelf over the stove. My guide looked around restlessly and insolently, his cap on his head, while the peasants stood uncovered.

"What bread have you?" he said. "Show us your bread."

"We have no bread. We have had nothing to eat for three days," they all sang in a sort of chorus.

"Nonsense; you have some bread."

"Not a morsel."

They looked as though they had not eaten anything for weeks, not days. We left their wretched hovel and entered

their storeroom opposite the entrance and occupying the other
side of the hut. Here were a few empty boxes, nothing else.
We went to the next barn and cattle sheds. The barn was
empty and bare. The roof had been taken down for fuel.
Some of the neighbors had nothing but the skeletons of their
barns left, and several had begun to consume the roofs of their
huts. The cattle sheds were also empty. The livestock of
the village had been reduced to a single famished-looking sheep
and a horse that was only a bag of bones.

The same picture was presented a million times
over throughout the Volga Basin and the other
famine-stricken provinces. Yet the cry for bread
was not loud. The peasants could only wait. They
did not know how to make their distress known.

Finally the people of the United States began to
realize the condition of the Russian peasantry.
When they realized it relief movements were started.
The cry for bread was met by providing cargoes of
grain and flour. One of the earliest of these cargoes
was that of the steamer *Indiana*, which carried
succor to the Black Sea port of Libau. Its officers
brought back reports of the need for further and
continued succor and of the gratitude of the Russian
people. The state of Minnesota sent a cargo of
flour on the steamer *Missouri*. The same reports
came back of the need of further relief and of the
gratitude with which the aid was received. The
citizens of Philadelphia chartered the steamer *Conemaugh*, and undertook to send a cargo of flour to
Riga.

Dr. Klopsch had heard the cry for bread. Without delay he answered it. He asked on behalf of
the readers of *The Christian Herald* permission to

send a few hundred sacks of flour, which was granted. Thereupon he made public appeal through the paper. His practical mind grasped the situation. He figured that at the prices then prevailing a barrel of sound, wholesome flour, weighing 190 pounds, could be bought for $3.50; that $10.00 would purchase nearly three barrels, the equivalent of 570 five-cent loaves of bread. Dr. Klopsch and his associates made the first contributions. Then the gifts began to flow in with steadily increasing volume, and some 5000 sacks of flour were loaded on the *Conemaugh*.

When the steamers were ready to sail ceremonies were held at the pier and the Rev. T. DeWitt Talmage invoked divine blessing upon *The Christian Herald's* gift of flour to Russia. Dr. Klopsch presided. Dr. Talmage in the course of his address said:

"There is no sadder sound on earth than a nation's cry for bread. Such a cry came up when Hamilcar besieged Utica and Titus besieged Jerusalem and the Assyrians besieged Samaria and the Spaniards besieged Leyden, and from other besieged cities where men gnawed the left arm in hunger while with the right arm they fought. But now, in time of peace, from that Russia which has been one of the richest wheat fields of all the earth comes the groan of nearly twenty million people dying for lack of food. Famine is a monster which has at some time put its paw upon almost every nation, with hot tongue lapping up the feverish blood of the starving. Through a merciful Providence the most of us have been kept from hearing in our households the unavailing cry for food. No parent's heart is stout enough calmly to hear a cry like that.

"In a land of ripe orchards and golden harvests it is an awful thing to starve. What a blessing that this Russian appeal comes at a time when our barns are full of wheat and our cribs are full of corn! We assemble here today to start the first installment of a million pounds of flour contributed from all parts of the land, through the hand of *The Christian Herald* which has been pleading this cause. Look off upon yonder sacks of flour! What do they mean? They mean life for a great multitude. They mean children given back to their parents and parents given back to their children. They mean sunshine for eyes that are closing in darkness. They mean new pulsation to hearts that are ceasing to beat. They mean prospered American homes giving salutation to agonized Russian homes. They mean the prayer of lips that are too weak to do more than whisper, answered from the throne of God, by the wave of American sympathy. They mean resurrection.

"O Thou who didst walk the Sea of Galilee when Thy disciples sailed, walk beside the *Conemaugh* as it shall plow the deep carrying this mercy from a prospered nation to an afflicted land. O Thou who holdest the wind in Thy fist, let no hurricane whelm this treasure. May the angels of Thy protection hover over the bread wagons. May the relief which is sent today be multiplied until upon all America and all Europe may come the blessing of Him who said, 'I was an hungered and ye fed me.'"

The *Conemaugh* with the first *Christian Herald*

fund shipment on board duly reached Riga and was welcomed by the Russian people as the harbinger of further relief. The cargo was found in perfect condition. A number of Russian officials and prominent citizens of Riga visited the steamer at her wharf and expressed the warmest gratitude of the Russian people for the gift from America to their suffering fellow-countrymen.

In the meantime further details of the famine conditions were received in the United States. Mr. W. C. Edgar, a public-spirited citizen of Minnesota who had gone out with the cargo of flour sent by the citizens of that state, gave an interesting account of his own observations and of the need of further aid. He brought back with him some loaves of Russian "hunger bread" on which the peasants in many of the afflicted provinces were subsisting. It had the appearance of a mixture of earth, straw, stable refuse, dry bran, and a very small modicum of bran sweepings. When baked it presented a surface so hard as almost to turn the point of a knife. It was stringy and porous, with the color of dried and blackened turf, and had the pungent odor of dog feed or tobacco. Upon this compound hundreds of thousands were subsisting. It was the bread of want and bitterness and despair, yet it was being fed daily to sick women and to tender children as their only nourishment.

About the same time an account was received of the relief work which Count Leo Tolstoi, the famous author and philanthropist, had organized. Count Tolstoi himself described the manner of giving

relief and the conditions which were met. He
wrote:

"The village of Petrovka may be said to be the
center of the famine region. It is situated some 50
miles from the nearest railway station. Towards
dusk, after 12 hours sleighing, I arrived here and
proceeded to the house of Count Lyeff Tolstoi, my
son. On the following morning I proceeded with my
son on a tour of inspection through the neighboring
villages. We visited three, where I saw more misery
than I have seen in any other district. We visited
also one of the enormous free tables established by
my son on the plan of those instituted by myself.

"The place was crowded with about fifty emaciated, sickly creatures — more like living skeletons
than sturdy peasants, as the majority of them were
before the famine came. On leaving this place a
poor woman came up to our sledge and beseeched
us with tears in her eyes to come to her cottage, as
her husband and father were dying. We went to
the cottage and found in the dimly lighted room two
men who were manifestly *in extremis*. The husband,
who a few months ago had been a fine, powerful
moujik with long beard and curly hair, was in a high
fever; and in a dark corner at his feet lay another
ghastly figure stretched out and doubled up with
pain and suffering. This was the father, a grey-
bearded old man, also dying.

"On leaving this house of death we were stopped
by a peasant, who appealed to my companion for
help and who informed us that both his father and
mother had just died of starvation.

"The next house we visited was a cottage inhabited by a dying woman with her son and three children. The owner of this wretched place was lying on a plank bed covered with a ragged quilt, while her two children were feebly playing around her. She had given all her extra food to them. And these cases were no exceptions, but were typical of many others. In almost every second house we visited half if not all of the inmates were laid up with typhus, influenza, or intestinal complaints caused by insufficient nourishment and exposure to the cold. Their deplorable condition, too, is intensified by the complete absence of either doctors or medicaments for the sick. In this district, indeed, with its population of eighty thousand, there is only one doctor, and probably half of those who die might be saved with proper medical attention."

The appeal of stories of suffering such as this to Dr. Klopsch's charitable impulses was irresistible. After the *Conemaugh* had speeded on her mission of mercy, contributions continued to come in. The vast majority of these were of small sums, many being for a dollar, some for a half dollar, some for a quarter, and some even for a nickel. A penny contribution would not be rejected. Dr. Klopsch knew that these contributions came from the heart. He knew that it was the aggregate of the small sums that must be depended on in every great demand. There were also many liberal contributions, and these were acknowledged with gratitude; and others who out of their means were able to give liberally were encouraged to do it. But, large or small, it was evident that the relief movement had taken deep hold on the constituency which now looked to *The Christian Herald* for guidance and direction.

Dr. Klopsch did not have a moment's hesitation. When the twenty-thousand-dollar mark was reached he decided to send a steamer-load of food on his own account. He chartered the steamer *Leo* for $10,000, reduced the charter price by selling the deck privileges to a lumber company for $2,500, and began to load and buy flour. He bought through the New York Chamber of Commerce and the Chicago Board of Trade, and in a remarkably short time he had 17,000 sacks of good American flour beneath the *Leo's* hatches, besides a goodly supply of medicines and delicacies for the sick. Some of the flour mills of the Northwest contributed directly.

It was in June, 1892, when the *Leo* lay at the dock with her complete cargo, amounting to about two and three-fourths million pounds of flour, and the delicacies and medicines. When the contribution of 280,000 pounds was shipped aboard the *Conemaugh* and it was apparent that there would be further contributions, Dr. Klopsch had said he would raise a million pounds. Then he increased the figures to two million pounds. But in all, as it developed, there were nearly three million pounds shipped for the starving Russian people.

When the *Leo's* cargo was ready, Dr. Klopsch decided that he would himself proceed to Russia to see to the distribution and to determine whether further help would be necessary from the American people. Accompanied by Mrs. Klopsch and the Rev. T. DeWitt Talmage, he set sail.

The *Leo's* cargo was consigned to the American Consul-General at St. Petersburg. Dr. Klopsch and Dr. Talmage reached there before the arrival of the steamer, and arranged the details for the distribution of the food. When the *Leo* arrived everything was in readiness. The Mayor and military authorities of the Russian capital prepared a splendid reception for their American guests. Everywhere were flags floating, and bunting. The Stars and Stripes were raised at the United States Legation and Consulate, and the Russian and American flags fluttered on the public buildings. Even the street cars were decorated in this manner.

The *Leo* was officially welcomed on Thursday morning, July 14th, with every possible manifestation of popular enthusiasm. The evening before news had been received from Kronstadt that the relief ship had passed that point on its way to St. Petersburg, and official invitations signed by the Mayor were hastily dispatched in different directions requesting the presence of the recipients the following morning on board the harbor police boat *St. Petersburg*, for the purpose of welcoming the American relief ship. A tremendous crowd had gathered at the quay ready to greet the American guests. As the carriage drove up with Dr. Klopsch and Mrs. Klopsch and Dr. Talmage, the cheers went up from thousands of powerful Russian throats, and these were continued as the *St. Petersburg* steamed out on her way to meet the *Leo*. On board, besides the guests of the occasion, were various officials, including the American Consul-General and the *Chargé d'Affaires.* An hour's sail brought in sight the majestic *Leo* clad in festal array with flying colors from topmast to deck.

In the afternoon the party returned to the quay. Just as the steamer was about to drop anchor, alongside the dock and parallel to the river, one hundred freight cars, elaborately festooned and each decorated with a Russian and an American flag, stood ready to receive the flour. The anchor once cast, all was bustle and excitement. From thousands of throats rang out the loud huzzas. Hats, handkerchiefs, and flags were waving in the air with rapid motion, and shrill steamboat whistles vainly contended with the great volume of human voices for supremacy.

When the gangplank was adjusted Captain Caines of the *Leo* came ashore. He was immediately surrounded by the town council and others, all in full dress and wearing their badges of office. The marshal of nobility, Count Vsevolovshky, took an elevated stand on the plank and addressing the Captain in English congratulated him on having safely made the journey with a ship laden with the tokens of sympathy and love from a distant nation. Then Mayor Prokofiero mounted the platform bearing in his hands a handsomely finished oaken box. He said: "Gentlemen, the city of St. Petersburg greets you and congratulates you on your safe arrival with the cargo presented by the generous readers of *The Christian Herald* to the inhabitants of the Russian districts now suffering from the failure of last year's harvest. Gratitude for the contributions of the Americans will set an indelible stamp on the hearts of all Russians, and will unite together two great nations in the bonds of mutual esteem and friendship. The city of St. Petersburg, the capital of all Russia, begs of you to accept these trifles in memory of this day."

When these remarks were finished the Mayor opened the case and, displaying a beautiful speaking trumpet, handed it to Captain Caines and at the same time handed to the first mate a magnificent, silver, gold-lined, old-fashioned drinking cup. The Captain and the mate were sailors and not used to making speeches in public. They were too confused to reply, but Dr. Talmage came to their rescue and made a brief speech for them.

After these ceremonies most of the crowd dispersed, but Dr. Klopsch and Count Andre Bobrinskoy, the representative of the Russian Relief Committee, remained and saw a portion of the cargo dispatched for the interior the very evening of the day of arrival. It proved much more convenient to dispatch the cargo from St. Petersburg than it would have been from Riga, since the localities most in need were thus most easily reached.

The American visitors, including Mrs. Klopsch, were honored with an official reception by the town council, which was held in the halls of the Duma. Many distinguished Russians were present. An address of thanks was read by Mayor Prokofiero, who presided. Among other things this address said:

"The Russian nation knows how to be grateful.

If hitherto during the whole period of the existence of the United States two such great nations as the Russian and the American have not only never been at enmity, but on the contrary have always sincerely wished each other power and all prosperity, then these feelings of mutual sympathy can only increase with the consciousness that these two great nations will find in each other cordial, disinterested, and sincere support and assistance in the hour of calamity. And when is true friendship to be known if not in the hour of misfortune?

"Allow us, therefore, Reverend Sirs, as the representatives of the city of St. Petersburg, to express through you our deep gratitude to the transatlantic friends of the Russian people as well as our good wishes for the continuance of the prosperity, power, freedom, and indissolubility of the United States of North America, and for the strengthening of the bond of sympathy between Russia and America."

Dr. Talmage responded to the address, and Dr. Klopsch also made a short speech. Then the party proceeded to Moscow to further superintend the distribution of the food. At Moscow the Mayor and the Prefect were equally cordial in their attentions to the Americans and in aiding the work. The gratitude of the Russian people, officials and plain citizens alike, was universal and irrepressible, appearing in many forms. Invitations were showered upon them everywhere and the generous hospitality was overpowering. When they were leaving Moscow the Mayor, in explanation of the extraordinary attention they had received, declared that were they to visit the remotest village in Russia they would meet with the same cordial reception; that it was the manner his countrymen had of expressing their gratitude for the sympathy and generosity of Americans to the Russian peasants.

Everywhere it was the same. Wherever the travelers stopped they encountered the glad welcome, if not always in words then in other forms, that gave expression to what the hearts felt but the strange tongues could not utter. The story of the *Leo*, her mission, and the Christian love and charity of those who sent her were on every Russian's lips and became household words by Russian hearths. The famine too, fortunately, was ending and in a few months the harvests were normal and the Russian peasantry were able to provide for themselves out of the products of the soil which they tilled.

An incident of Dr. Klopsch's visit to Russia in connection with the relief work which gave him much pleasure was the imperial invitation summoning him and Dr. Talmage to the Imperial Palace at Peterhof for an audience. Peterhof is on the Gulf of Finland a few miles from the capital. On arriving at the wharf they entered the court carriage that stood in waiting for them and, accompanied by an escort, proceeded to the palace. This is a two-story yellow building and is situated on high ground overlooking beautiful gardens and groves. Fountains throw their sparkling columns of spray far in the air, and the variety of flowering plants is equal to that of any garden in Europe. The grounds are laid out after the fashion of the famous gardens at Versailles, with miniature lakes, statuary, and water scenes. Peterhof is very attractive from its romantic surroundings and the art treasures it contains. In one room there are 860 historic portraits of beautiful women painted during the reign of the Empress Catherine II. It also contains a room used by Peter the Great as a study.

Cossack guards in dark uniforms, and high Russian officials, were encountered on the way. Count Bobrinskoy introduced them to the Czarevitch, that is, the Crown Prince, who was the only representative of royalty in Russia at that time. They received a most cordial greeting and expressions of the gratitude and affection which Russia felt towards the United States. The Prince asked them to bear to the American people Russia's thanks for the aid it had received in time of need. He assured them that these noble actions were ever to be remembered. Subsequently, when he became Emperor of all Russia as Czar Nicholas, he recalled the services of Dr. Klopsch, and in coöperating in other relief movements expressed the satisfaction he felt at knowing their dispenser of world charities and his methods. Dr. Klopsch on his part always recalled the pleasant impression made on him by the Czarevitch.

CHAPTER III

ARMENIA, THE MARTYR NATION

DESCRIPTION OF THIS PART OF WESTERN ASIA — AMBASSADOR BRYCE'S ACCOUNT OF MT. ARARAT — HISTORIC CHURCH — A PERSECUTED PEOPLE — MASSACRES OF 1894-95 — DR. HAMLIN'S APPEAL — ATROCITIES AT TREBIZOND — MISS KIMBALL'S STORY OF VAN — "CHRISTIAN HERALD" RELIEF STATIONS — MISS SHATTUCK AT OORFA — HEROIC ZEITOUNLIS — MISSIONARY ACKNOWLEDG-MENTS — THRILLING INCIDENTS — CARE FOR THE ORPHANS — MURDER AND PILLAGE AT ADANA IN 1909 — DR. KLOPSCH EXTENDS AID TO THE SURVIVORS.

ARMENIA has been well called the martyr nation. Though it is not now a nation in the geographical or political sense, its people have preserved their individuality, their racial unity, and everything that goes to make a nationality, for more than 2,000 years. They have also preserved many of the traits of their ancestors.

The region in Western Asia generally known as Armenia lies between the Black and the Caspian Seas and is of a mountainous character, comprising an area of 120,000 square miles. Ancient Armenia, as it was territorially understood, extended from the Tigris and the Euphrates to the southern shores of the Black Sea. In the course of centuries it has fallen to Turkey, Persia, and Russia. Most of what is known as Modern Armenia is a part of Turkey-in-Asia.

The region known as Armenia was the first part of the globe to be settled by the human race after the

flood and Mt. Ararat, where the Ark rested, still rears
its lofty crest 17,000 feet in height and overlooks
the same landscape of valley, plain, and mountain
that greeted the eyes of Noah and his companions
when they gazed upon the new risen earth after the
subsidence of the Deluge. The eminent British
statesman and scholar, James Bryce, Ambassador
at Washington, who ascended Mt. Ararat, in one of
his books gives this account:

"The only topographical reference in the Scripture narrative of the flood is to be found in the
words, Genesis, 8:4, 'In the 7th month, on the 17th
day of the month, the ark rested upon the mountains of Ararat,' which may be taken as equivalent
to 'on a mountain of (or in) Ararat.'

"The word Ararat is used in three or rather in
two other places in the Scriptures. One is in
II Kings, 19:37, and the parallel passage in Isaiah
37:38, where it is said of the sons of Sennacherib,
who had just murdered their father, that they
escaped into the land of Ararat, rendered in our
version and in the Septuagint, 'Armenia.' The
other is in Jeremiah, 51:27, 'all together against her
(i.e., Babylon) the kingdoms of Ararat, Minni and
Ashchenaz.' The question then is, what does this
Ararat denote? Clearly the Alexandrian translators
took it for Armenia; so does the Vulgate when it
renders in Genesis, 8:4, the words which we translate, 'On the mountains of Ararat' by 'super montes
Armeniae.' This narrows it a little and St. Jerome
himself helps us to narrow it still further when, in
his commentary on Isaiah, 37:38, he says that
'Ararat means the plain of the middle Araxes, which
lies at the foot of the great mountain Taurus.'

"The identification, therefore, is natural enough;

what is of more consequence is to determine how early it took place; for as there is little or no trace of an independent local tradition of the flood, we may assume the identification to rest entirely on the use of the name Ararat in the Hebrew narrative. Josephus (Ant. Jud., bk. 1, ch. 3) says that the Armenians called the place where Noah descended 'the disembarking place, for the ark being saved in that place, its remains are shown there by the inhabitants to this day,' and also quotes Nicholas of Damascus, who writes that 'In Armenia, above Minyas, there is a great mountain called Baras, upon which it is said that many who escaped at the time of the flood were saved, and that one who was carried in an ark came ashore on top of it, and that the remains of the wood were preserved for a long while. This might be the man about whom Moses, the lawgiver of the Jews, wrote.'

"Marco Polo, whose route does not seem to have led him near it, says only, in speaking of Armenia: 'Here is an exceedingly great mountain, on which it is said the Ark of Noah rested, and for this cause it is called the mountain of the Ark of Noah. The circuit of its base cannot be traversed in less than two days; and the ascent is rendered impossible by the snow on its summit, which never dissolves, but is increased by each successive fall. On the lower declivities the melted snows cause an abundant vegetation, and afford rich pastures for the cattle, which in summer resort thither from all the surrounding countries.'"

Legendary history makes Haik, the great-grandson of Noah, the first Armenian monarch. After that the country was semi-independent, then subject to Assyria, and then came under the Roman conquest. It was once part of the Greek Empire, and once a

Persian province. It was also part of the Empire of Ghengis Khan and Tamerlane. After the sixteenth century it was shared by Turks and Persians. In 1828 a strip of the Armenian territory was conquered by Russia, and this was increased by the Berlin Treaty of 1878.

It is chiefly of the Armenia that is under Turkish dominion that modern history is written. There are said to be 4,000,000 Armenians, of whom one-half are scattered over Western Asia. The inhabitants are chiefly of the genuine Armenian stock, though in the course of time there has come to be some mixture with the border races.

The Armenian tongue is of the Indo-European family of languages, but there are in fact two tongues — the literary and ecclesiastical language, known as "Old Armenian," and the ordinary spoken and written language, which is mixed with many Turkish and Persian words, and which is known as "New Armenian." In the seventeenth century there was a revival of the Armenian literature and much more became known of the history and the genius of the people through Armenian authors. The Armenians have ever shown a fondness for enlightenment. It is well known that wherever an Armenian settlement exists there a printing press will be found.

The Armenian Church is historic. Armenia was the first country which officially embraced Christianity. This was done at the beginning of the third century under Gregory the Illuminator, although some maintain that the Armenian Church was really founded as early as A.D. 34. In the sixth century the Armenian separated from the Greek Church, but the doctrines and usages closely resemble those of the Greek Church. The Armenian priesthood is hereditary. There are four patriarchs and one primate, or "Katholikos," the actual head of the Church, who resides in the monastery of Etchmiadzin, north of Mt. Ararat in Russian territory. He is elected for life by delegates from the various Armenian communities throughout the world, who come here for that purpose when a vacancy occurs, and he is the spiritual head of all believers in the Armenian creed in America, Europe, Asia, and Africa. Though differing from orthodox Christians in many respects, the fidelity with which the Armenians have retained their ancient worship has always created a feeling of brotherhood for them among Christians in all parts of the world.

The Armenians have been a persecuted people almost from the time their history begins. The Persians sought to root out Christianity. The Mohammedans time and again sought to cause them to abjure their ancient faith and frequently the waves of Moslem fanaticism have swept over them.

The most notable persecution was in the enlightened nineteenth century, when the fearful massacres of 1895 and 1896 were perpetrated. Religious fanaticism had much to do with these massacres. The political policy of the Sultan Abdul Hamid, who was then in power at Constantinople, had more to do with it; and the desire to despoil the thrifty and industrious Armenians by their lawless neighbors also was an element of savage destruction.

It was late in 1894 that the civilized world was thrilled with horror over the news that several thousand Christians in Armenia had been butchered by savage and bloodthirsty Kurds, but the real story of the awful occurrence was not known for months later and by that time the situation had become a fearful one. Turkish Armenia, the northwestern division of Kurdistan, is a great plateau of nearly 60,000 square miles, bounded on the north by the Russian frontier, on the east by Persia, on the west by the plains of Mesopotamia, and on the south by Asia Minor. In this section half of the people are Mohammedans. The Kurds lead a pastoral and predatory life, dwelling in the mountain villages. Some of these tribes are migratory, but almost all are warlike, and many are brigands pure and simple. For centuries they have oppressed the Christians. The Kurdish costumes are picturesque and nearly all the tribesmen are magnificent horsemen. Years ago the Government at Constantinople organized them as a military force, but their spirit is one that scarcely brooks the restraints of military discipline. They were always formidably armed.

It was these Kurds who filled the world with horror by their slaughter at Dalvoring and Sassoun. The first news of the deplorable plight of the Armenians and of the attack of the Kurds on the villages of Sassoun and Dalvoring came from Dr. Grace M. Kimball, an American missionary in Turkish Armenia. She sent a most vivid picture of the suffering that prevailed in the spring and summer of 1895.

Her story was corroborated by other missionaries and by the Turks themselves.

Later came fuller accounts and stories of fresh atrocities. So widespread was the want that it was written, "Many declared in bitterness of heart that there was no food in all the length and breadth of Armenia, which was long ago the Garden of Eden." Still later came sickening stories of massacres at Trebizond, Van, Erzeroum, and other places.

The city of Trebizond on the Black Sea, which was the scene of perhaps the greatest massacre — that in October 1895 — is older than Rome. The Greeks founded it 800 years before Christ. The Romans drove out the Greeks and the Emperor Trajan made Trebizond the capital of the Province of Cappadocia. Hadrian built the harbor. The Roman Emperor Justinian erected a splendid castle. Xenophon, the leader of the retreat of the 10,000 Greeks, found asylum there at the end of his famous march. The camel caravans today travel over the same route that was followed by Xenophon.

The Reverend Cyrus Hamlin, founder of Robert College, Constantinople, and known to philanthropic Christendom the world over, confirmed the worst stories of what was going on. In an interview with Dr. Klopsch in *The Christian Herald* office Dr. Hamlin said:

"I have lately finished reading two hundred letters from missionaries, a very large part of them dealing with the oppressions and sufferings of the Armenians, which were of the most frightful character. The poor creatures must have help before the winter opens in earnest or they will perish. The Armenian winter is usually very severe, the snow lying on the ground from four to six feet in depth, and the cold being intense. The whole civilized Christian world must help these people. They must be saved and assisted over the winter. They can look in no other direction for help, for there is no sympathy and assistance to be had from Turkey. Indeed the policy of the Sultan's Government is apparently dictated by a desire to efface the Armenian people altogether, at least those of them who will not accept Mohammed. When you talk sympathizingly about these people a Turk will say in surprise, 'Why do you speak in behalf of such worthless trash and try to save them? They can save themselves. All they need to do is to accept Islam, and then they are safe and out of trouble.'

"And so a Turk regards it as strange that an Armenian should refuse to purchase his life at the cost of his faith; but there are some among them who take a different view. Some of the Turkish soldiers who shared in the terrible atrocities lately perpetrated on the Armenian Christians have been stricken by remorse afterward. One soldier who had borne his part in several horrible butcheries of women and children was so troubled that he could not sleep. He had visions of his victims that ultimately drove him insane."

As news came of one massacre following another, and of the inertness, if not of the actual complicity, of the Turkish Government in the attacks, the whole Christian world became stirred. In England, where for political reasons the Ministry that was then in power had sought to shield the Turkish

Government, the indignation was voiced by the great statesman, William E. Gladstone, and relief measures were undertaken by private societies and individuals. In the United States the movement for relief was spontaneous. As usual, Dr. Klopsch and *The Christian Herald* were foremost in it. An American, Mr. W. W. Howard, who had a short time previously returned from Armenia, was made *Christian Herald* Commissioner, and started at once for Van to begin the relief work systematically.

Meantime further details of the reign of terror were received. The American missionaries who were everywhere risking their lives were constantly threatened. But they continued to do their duty. An account of the massacre at Trebizond was received in a private letter. This letter said:

Like a clap of thunder in a clear sky the thing began about 11 A.M., October 8th (1895). Unsuspecting people walking along the streets were shot ruthlessly down. Men standing or sitting at their shop doors were instantly dropped with a bullet through their heads or hearts. The aim was deadly and I heard of no wounded men. Some were slashed with swords until life was extinct. They passed through the quarters where only old men, women and children remained, killing the men and large boys, and generally permitting the women and the younger children to live. For five hours this horrid work of human butchery went on. The cracking of musketry, sometimes like a volley from a platoon of soldiers, but more often single shots from near and distant points, the crashing in of doors and the thud thud of sword blows sounded on our ears. Then the sound of musketry died away and the work of loot began. Every shop of an Armenian in the market was gutted and the victors in this cowardly and brutal work glutted themselves with spoils. The intention evidently was to impoverish and as near as possible to blot out the Armenians of this town. So far as appearance went the police and soldiers distinctly aided in this savage work. They mingled with the armed men and so far as we could see made not the least effort to check them. Apparently they took care to see that the right ones, that is Armenians, were killed; also that an offer of surrender might be made to all that were found unarmed. To any found with arms no quarter was given, but large numbers were shot down without any proffer of this kind. One poor fellow when called on to surrender thought he was called on to give up his religion and when he refused he was hacked to pieces in the presence of his wife and children. While I write the wails of the newly bereaved fall on my ears. Some in suspense wait to know the fate of their missing ones; others rejoice at greeting them again. Throngs fill the schools that are under foreign protection and the consulates. There is no telling how many have perished.

What was written of events at Trebizond was true of Van, of Erzeroum, of Bitlis, and of scores of other places.

Further reports were received from Miss Kimball, telling of the conditions and of the growing need for relief. A cry that reached every heart was the appeal of Armenia at the Christmas season of 1895 as voiced by the sympathetic pen of Mrs. Cyrus Hamlin, the wife of the veteran missionary. It was this:

> Fierce winter comes and we must die,
> Western brothers, hear our cry!
> In your ceiled houses warm,
> Safe shut in from sleet and storm,
> Help the houseless. Clothe the feet
> That must freeze in storm and sleet.
> Brothers! sisters! hear our cry,
> Winter comes, we all must die.

Free America! afar,
Show the Kaiser and the Czar
What the heart of God can teach —
How the hand of man can reach!
Send the Red Cross! Murder reigns!
Pestilence walks through our plains!
Send your ships with corn and wheat,
Bid our starving thousands eat.

In December a ray of cheer came from Miss
Kimball in acknowledging the receipt of $10,000
from *The Christian Herald* fund. "This news," she
wrote, "has given us our real Thanksgiving Day.
We are now feeding at Van about 1,500 people
daily, and are distributing clothing to these people
and hundreds of other villagers who are in the
greatest need."

But in every district there was the same tragic
story of massacre, outrage, pillage, and abduction,
monasteries sacked and Christian pastors and people butchered. In many villages of Armenia priests
were among the number who laid down their lives
as a testimony of the faith. Thousands of women
were carried away captive to become inmates of
Moslem harems. At the village of Hoh in the
Sanjak district the local magistrates promised to
protect the Christians, but when they saw villages
burning in every direction they refused to keep
their word. All the Christians were told that under
pain of death they must accept Islam. They were
assembled at the mosque, and there eighty young
men were picked out and led outside the village for
slaughter. The young women of the village were

taken to Turkish harems, and the survivors of the Christian population were scattered among other villages.

The chief *Christian Herald* relief station was at Van, but other stations were opened. Word now was received from Commissioner Howard. He wrote that the Kurds were raging up and down the country, burning villages, killing the inhabitants, committing all kinds of atrocities, and carrying off the sheep, cattle, and household property of the unfortunate people. He gave a list of the villages between the Persian border and the city of Van that had been destroyed. The traditional site of the Garden of Eden, the place that God made holy with His presence, ran with blood and resounded with the shrieks of anguish of men and women.

An account came from Oorfa of the slaughter there. It was written by Miss Corinna Shattuck, an American missionary of Dorchester, Massachusetts. She was the Christian heroine of that awful event.

Writing under date of January 24, 1896, Miss Shattuck told this story of the massacre at Oorfa:

. . . Sunday, in the early afternoon, martial music was heard and in triumphal strain. It proved a grand procession of military and civil officers and private Moslems of wealth and position viewing the streets and homes. They requested entrance to our yard and that I appear on the veranda. They expressed salaams and "begged I would not be disturbed; the proceedings did not pertain to me; I was in perfect safety." I subsided as soon as possible. They peered into windows and inquired if we had men here. Servant and guards honestly said: "No, only women and children." Was I not thankful I had hidden elsewhere the sixty men?

All day we had the smell of burning wool and cotton, bedding, etc., in the homes fired (buildings are of stone and so cannot be burned). Later, the indescribable, sickening odors from the great holocaust in the Gregorian Church, where some three thousand, having gone there Saturday night for refuge, perished. Monday the work was declared done. The Kurds and Arabs about the city were driven off by the soldiers and everywhere announcements were made that people were safe. Slowly they began to come out of their hiding-places; wells, vaults, drains, and all imaginable and unimaginable places. Some coming to me, Tuesday, had not tasted food since Saturday. They looked like corpses. Meanwhile, the authorities were dragging off the dead and burying them outside the city in long trenches. Fifteen hundred were so buried. Four days the line of Jews was seen on the brow of the hill just back of our house, lugging in sacks the bones, ashes, etc., from the church. Last of all came the clearing of wells. Some estimate that five hundred were taken out. Many wells and cisterns are very large. I know of one from which twenty-five bodies were taken. In all, our dead number five thousand, as nearly as can be estimated. Our Protestant loss, one hundred and ten. The wounded under the care of the government physician, the only doctor left, were three hundred and fifty. Many of these died. We had twenty-two here under our care, our rooms and schoolrooms being filled with the most forlorn and helpless.

Our special guards have been most faithful. We fed them regularly. They fought as for dear life that Saturday and Sunday, and kept the mob from us a distance of three doors. The mob entered our girls' schoolroom in the church yard and smashed boxes, glass, etc., but did no more in the church region. I saw a man shot down just across the street on one side, and heard the crashing, smashing of the doors all about us. I am told that the Sultan himself sent a telegram for my protection. Of course, if so, it was at the instigation of Minister

Terrell. I am thankful I am spared that I may serve; but I would willingly have died that parents might be spared to their children. The end we see not, we are in a thick cloud; but God lives and we will trust him though all expected help of man fail.

Miss Shattuck lived for many years in Oorfa after these horrors, and did the great work of her life there. She died at her home in Massachusetts in the summer of 1910.

There was one bright page in the story of Armenia's sufferings and of the massacres of defenseless people. The brave mountaineers of Zeitoun held their stronghold against every attack until the Turkish Government was compelled to grant their demands and they could look to Europe to see that the conditions were faithfully fulfilled.

Zeitoun was a fortified town in Cilicia, the fortress being 300 feet higher than the town itself. Its people were better educated and more independent than the Armenians of the interior and the Black Sea. When the peaceful Armenians of Marash and Alabash were attacked and slaughtered the Zeitounlis went to their aid. Then the Sultan sent officials to Zeitoun to disarm the people there, the usual preliminary to a massacre. The people revolted, attacked and captured the fortress, 600 soldiers surrendering to the victors. The Armenian women went to the fortress, the mosque, and other buildings, and covered them with crosses, putting the cross on the top of the mosque to show that the whole town had become Christian. The Zeitounlis held the fortress for five months. Fighting was con-

tinuous. At last there were no fewer than 11,000
Turkish soldiers engaged in the siege, while the de-
fenders numbered only 8000. The Zeitounlis garrisoned the fortress and every point of vantage, and
suffered a loss of only 80, with 75 wounded, who
died because they had no medical aid. The Turks
refused to let the Red Cross Society enter the town.

Twice the Government representatives tried to
begin negotiations, but their terms were so extrava-
gant that the people would not listen. Then the
representatives of the United Powers and the people
chose three of the chiefs who conducted the defense
to negotiate. The Sultan granted their demands.
They were promised a Christian Kimakan, or Governor, for the Zeitoun District, chosen by the representatives of the Powers, and established under
their guarantee, the people to appoint their own
police and administration — all to be Christian.

Slowly the clouds lifted in the desolated districts.
The Turkish Government was compelled by the
negligent Christian governments of Europe to cease
connivance with the massacres. In some districts
humane Turkish officials who did not sympathize
with the slaughter were no longer interfered with
in their efforts to prevent it. A letter of appreciation
came from Miss Kimball dated at Van, January 7,
1896. She wrote:

DEAR DR. KLOPSCH: I inclose financial statement and
summary of work now in hand. You will see by the inclosed
how sorely we needed your magnificent fund, and perhaps you
may be able to dimly imagine what a tremendous relief we
experienced when your telegram came very opportunely on

New Year's Day. I cannot express to you adequately our
deep gratitude to you and your co-laborers for this noble
work. Many and many a poor villager says to me, "You have
saved this province from a terrible famine." The praise be-
longs not to me, but to yourself and the generous men and
women in America and England who have thus generously
opened their hearts and purses. We are indeed the only hope
of these people for the winter. May the good work go on.

Accompanying this letter was a summary of the
relief work at Van.

A letter received by the National Armenian Relief
Committee in New York from a leading missionary
of the American Board in Constantinople gave some
interesting information regarding the relief work
generally. The missionary wrote:

The funds so far appropriated will probably maintain the
work on the present scale through the month of January. A
special industrial relief is now being carried on at Van, where
there are more than 15,000 refugees. The funds mainly come
from *The Christian Herald* of New York. The American
missionaries stationed in the provinces of Trebizond, Erzeroum,
Bitlis, Van, Harpoot, Diarbekir, Sivas, Angora, Adana, and
Aleppo are careful in making their statements, and their
private letters; and their more formal reports to the United
States Legation here have been extensively used in forming the
opinions herein expressed.

The Christian Herald continued its work of arousing the American people and of collecting subscriptions, which were promptly forwarded. It kept in
close touch with the relief stations established.
Official assurances were published that the relief
funds had reached their destination safely. When
the word came that the city of Harpoot, one of

the chief stations of the American Board of Foreign
Missions, had suffered greatly and that several thousand Armenian Christians had fallen there under
the Kurdish and Turkish swords, a further remittance was promptly sent to that point. *The Christian Herald* Commissioner kept up his active work
of organizing relief stations. By this time sixteen
of these stations were in operation. Miss Kimball
continued to write of the good work that was being
done:

" *The Christian Herald's* bakeries," she said in one letter, "are
forging along magnificently, and are the great famine break-
water to the community. Last Saturday was the Armenian
Christmas, and on the day before we made special effort to
see that as many as possible were supplied with the bare means
of existence. On that day 9,000 were actually provided for
through the different departments, and untold suffering relieved. We blessed continually the generous people who make
this work possible, and the Armenian people, though unable
even to thank their benefactors directly, still do not fail in
constant expressions of the profoundest gratitude."

The Rev. W. M. Chambers wrote from Erzeroum
acknowledging the receipt of $2,000 from *The Chris-
tian Herald* fund:

. Allow me to thank you most heartily in the name of the
thousands of suffering people here for the generous gift. We
have distributed in this city 100 mattresses and coverlets, with
a considerable amount of clothing and fuel. We are feeding
daily 2,600 persons. We issue bread tickets to each family to
be held for a week. The distress is indescribable. The gratitude of the recipients is deep and most touching.

In March 1896 came word that the crisis had passed
and that the refugees were returning to their village

homes. It was thereupon arranged that the relief
funds should be closed in April. The American
Board missionaries at Sivas, another station of *The
Christian Herald* fund, wrote expressing the thanks
of the sufferers of that section for the help extended.
In the Sivas massacres 2,000 Christians were slaughtered, homes were looted, and chapels, dwellings,
schools and even school books were burned. At
Gurun 2,000 were killed, and 250 brides and young
girls were abducted.

In March Commissioner Howard got back to New
York, after nearly six months of incessant travel,
and many perilous adventures on the Turkish border.
Although excluded from Turkey by special order of
the government at Constantinople, he was nevertheless able to do much toward aiding the relief
movement. He rescued and aided the terrified
fugitive Armenians who had fled across the snowy
mountains to Salmis and other border cities in Persia,
from the massacres in Van province; and in conjunction with the Christian missionaries at Urumia
organized a relief movement there to care for the
perishing exiles. Through his efforts the Persian
border villages were transformed into havens of
shelter and refuge for those who sought to escape
the cruel Kurdish lances or the no less savage Turkish
swords.

Further letters came telling of the suffering that
had been endured. From Cesarea the Rev. W. S.
Dodd wrote relating the incidents of a relief expedition to the adjacent village of Gigi:

"When the plunderers approached, the people fled and so saved the clothes they wore. When they returned it was hardly more than roofs that they found. I visited every house, opening flour bins, uncovering jars and taking a light into dark corners. Most of the houses consisted of two rooms, some of only one. The first room presented only four mud walls and a mud floor with a hole in the center for a fire. Around this would be gathered 5 or 10 children or adults spending their time in keeping warm. In many houses the flour bins were smashed to pieces and there was nothing to examine. When I asked them what they were going to eat tomorrow, 'God knows,' they replied; 'we borrowed this to-day; perhaps we can borrow some more tomorrow.' In the whole village there was not a single bed, hardly a thing that could be called a quilt — nothing but little heaps of rags which they treasured up carefully to spread out for the night."

One of the most touching stories of martyrdom was that contained in a letter from an Armenian farmer living at Shefik, a village near Harpoot. After telling of the ravaging and burning of the place by Kurds and Turks successively, he wrote:

"On the eighth day, as they had finished their work, they came to us who were on the banks of the stream. They killed brother Bagdogh's son and pastor Meclon, because they would not change their religion. It became night, darkness was upon us, but they came with lanterns and selected 45 young men, saying that the government wished them. Knowing what would befall them, they asked for an hour's grace. They prayed and sang, they asked forgiveness of each other, they kissed the hands of their parents and parted with tears with the expectation of never seeing each other. Taking them to a desolate place half an hour distant they were taken apart two by two and threatened with death if they would not change their religion. They all with one voice agreed upon saying boldly, 'We will not deny our religion; we are ready to die for our Saviour's love.' Only 5 succeeded in making their escape, but the remaining 40 became martyrs for the love of Jesus. My son Samuel was among the 45, but he escaped with 4 others and hid in a cave for 10 or 12 days. My youngest son, 22 years old, was killed. How heart-rending was the sight! A week before we were in our homes, comfortable, having made every preparation for the winter, and having our friends about us; but like Job we were deprived of everything — dwelling house, furniture, beds, food, clothing. With heads uncovered, feet bare, little clothing upon us, we passed from rock to rock, from mountain to mountain, with great wailing and lamentation, to find our children. Rachel weeping for her children, and would not be comforted, because they were not."

Miss Kimball, in a later statement of the condition of the relief work at Van, wrote:

"My heart aches for the ladies and little children who are accustomed to live on the abundant milk in the villages; poor little things, with nothing but crusts of dried bread to munch now. And even the supply for the nurslings gives out when the poor mothers eat only insufficient dry bread; not only from physical hardship but the mental suffering often of grief for husband or brother murdered; always for houses robbed, property destroyed, and the hopelessness for the food. I call to mind one of hundreds of similar instances, a family of refugees in a house which I can see from where I sit while writing this. The father was killed, the mother with 5 small children fled to the city and found refuge in a cold, damp stable — no beds, no fire, no food and no clothing, the thermometer below zero. The mother fell ill with fever and when my attention was called to the family the baby was simply a skeleton in the last stages of starvation, and the other children were little better. It was a real satisfaction to be able through the generosity of the people at home to send on now with fuel, clothing, beds and medicine. But, alas, one of the men came the next day for a winding sheet for the baby."

Here as always the cry of the children reached Dr. Klopsch's heart. Provision for the Armenian orphans was one of his first thoughts. In a letter from the Brussa Orphanage the question of providing for the vast number of orphans whose parents were victims in the massacre was brought up by the principal of the orphanage, Gregory Bagdasarian. He wrote:

"The Orphanage of Brussa, being the only Protestant asylum in this part of Asia Minor, has already opened its gates to the orphans of this glorious host of martyrs. The Armenian martyrs are now crowned by their Lord and Saviour, whom they would not deny. What should be done with the great number of destitutes and orphans?"

When the fund was closed and no further subscriptions were received for immediate relief work, it was found that there was a balance of a fraction under $7,000. The arrangement made was that this balance should be used for the support of orphanages at Oorfa, Harpoot, Mardin, and Van. Pledges were made which enabled the orphans to be cared for for a period of three years, while further means were taken to establish them on a more permanent basis. Much attention was given to industrial training, and the Armenian orphanages more than justified the provision made for their maintenance. Miss Shattuck wrote from Oorfa glowing accounts of what was being accomplished, and equally favorable reports were received from the other orphanages.

During the closing days of the relief fund the responses of the friends of Armenia were prompt and liberal. It was arranged that *The Christian Herald* subscriptions should be closed, and that contributions intended for Armenia should thenceforth be sent to the Rev. Dr. Creegan, of the American Board, by whom the money was cabled to the American missionaries.

The total contributions to the fund from September 4, 1895, when the first subscription was received, to June 1, 1898, when the last dollar was taken in, amounted to $63,867.98. There was hardly a mission from Van to the Bosphorus in which the readers of *The Christian Herald* were not remembered with blessings and gratitude.

Dr. Klopsch and the readers of *The Christian Herald* continued to afford relief to various districts of the Turkish Empire in later years when disasters came upon them. A liberal sum was provided for the earthquake sufferers at Constantinople, and this was distributed through Turkish sources. Erzeroum, late in 1901, suffered from an earthquake shock and some relief was necessary for the survivors.

To this *The Christian Herald* readers contributed. Bitlis suffered a severe earthquake in 1907, with much destruction of property and loss of life. Contributions were made to the survivors of this disaster.

It was in the spring of 1909, when the rule of Abdul Hamid was ending, that more massacres of Christians occurred. The scene of these horrors was the province of Adana. How far they were due to the intrigues of the Abdul Hamid régime, in order to excite the Christian world against the Young Turks who were gaining control in their long struggle for the regeneration of Turkey, and how far it was a sudden eruption of fanatical Mohammedanism, may never be fully known. But the recurrence of fanaticism was marked by the usual scenes of murder, pillage, and worse.

More than 30,000 Christians — Greeks, Syrians, and Armenians, but chiefly the latter — were slaughtered. In Adana and Tarsus the savagery was the worst. One report of the carnage at Tarsus said:

"Armenian men and women were stood up in rows, or one by one, and shot down to the applause of the Moslem multitude. Vast numbers are homeless and threatened with famine if they escape the sword. Only young Christian girls are spared and they are being bartered as if they were a new sort of currency. Children snatched from the breasts of murdered parents are being traded by their captors for arms and ammunition; and girls are sold into harems and rendered victims to even grosser horrors. The dead in the City of Adana lie in heaps, and in the Sihun River, flowing down to the Mediterranean, the bodies of women and children float thickly on the waves."

Fever and famine followed the massacres. Contagious diseases broke out among the refugees. Ambassador Leishman cabled from Constantinople that great suffering existed in the ravaged districts and an epidemic was feared owing to the unsanitary conditions caused by unburied dead.

Military law was proclaimed; the Christian Powers sought to support the Young Turks in their efforts to control the fanatics. Further massacres were stopped, but the suffering continued. The missionaries in Asiatic Turkey appealed as usual to Dr. Klopsch. The State Department in Washington in answer to a telegram from Dr. Klopsch gave full details of the work of the relief committee at Adana. Although international in character, it was largely composed of resident American missionaries headed by the American and the British Consuls. The appeal was for help for the refugees, the survivors of the horror. Turkey's new government had begun with an official investigation of the infamies, and this investigation later resulted in the punishment of many of the principals. Yet the great need was for immediate relief. This Dr. Klopsch met by a cable remittance for $5,000, soon to be followed by a second remittance of the same amount. These remittances were made in anticipation of contributions to the relief fund.

Relief work was got quickly under way, and food and medical supplies were distributed among the refugees. The officers and crews of the foreign warships greatly helped the missionaries in their humane work.

The Christian Herald received contributions and transmitted them to the scene of suffering, until the distress was passed. The Armenians, not only of Asiatic Turkey, but all over the world, and especially in the United States, showed their appreciation of its work. Many letters were received from individual Armenian survivors of the massacres and famine telling of the splendid results which were secured by the prompt relief afforded. When all was over, the Young Turks were in full control at Constantinople, and their continued supremacy in the government of the Ottoman Empire affords hope that the days of massacres of Armenian Christians are passed.

A GROUP OF INDIA FAMINE ORPHANS, SUPPORTED BY *THE CHRISTIAN HERALD*

CHAPTER IV

INDIA AND HER PEOPLE

THE HOME OF THREE HUNDRED MILLIONS — HINDUS AND MOHAMMEDANS — CAUSES OF THE GREAT FAMINES — CROP FAILURE IN 1897 — MISSIONARIES CALL FOR HELP — BISHOP THOBURN — STEAMER "EVERETT" DISPATCHED BY DR. KLOPSCH — "CHRISTIAN HERALD" REMITTANCES — TALES OF SUFFERING RELIEVED — PLAN FOLLOWED — THANKS MEMORIAL IN THE TAMIL LANGUAGE — GREETING FROM THE METHODISTS — GOOD DONE THROUGH THE FUND — ACCOUNTING FOR $400,000 — AMBASSADOR PAUNCEFOTE CONVEYS INDIA'S THANKS.

NO country in the world has a greater fascination than India, with its many races, its numerous languages, its contrasted religions, its hideous system of castes, its strange customs, and its history of destructive wars and pestilences.

There are 300,000,000 human beings in the Indian Empire. We do not realize just what India is on the map of the world, but actually it is a collection of kingdoms and peoples differing very widely in all their characteristics. A recent writer has supposed a roving traveler to enter India from the north through Cashmere and to survey the country in this manner:

Radiating east and south the traveler would perceive the snowy slopes and cool valleys of the Himalayas, the sub-mountainous districts below them, the level plains of the Punjab, the stifling sands of Sind, the arid deserts of Rajputana, the steaming valley of the Ganges Basin, the rugged highlands of Central India, the tableland of the Deccan, the garden province of Guzerat, the palm-fringed Malabar Coast, the rice fields of Burma, the rocky hinterlands of the interior of Southern India, the fertile coastal territories of Coromandel, the forested tracts of the Ghauts, Mysore, and the Wynadde, the rolling downs of Nilgherries, and the tropic glories of Travancore. He would recognize in all these varying scenes distinct countries, differing one from another in aspect and altitude, in flora and fauna, and in soil and climate as completely as do the peoples who inhabit them in race, religion, and language.

Meanwhile, our hardy traveler might have experienced vicissitudes of temperature and rainfall able to confound all his previous knowledge. For instance, at Murree in the Punjab he might have been buried under six feet of snow; in Assam, after drowning in a rainfall that exceeds 400 inches a year, the process of thawing could have been accelerated by a trip to Jacobabad in Sind, where the thermometer looks down at 130° shade; and for a dry climate Bickannis is hard to beat, seeing that twenty-four months may pass without any rain at all.

The people of India described by Bishop Heber a century ago are today as he pictured them and as they were scores of centuries ago.

The earliest record of events in the history of India is the Mahabharatha, or great war, a Sanscrit epoch written some fifteen hundred years before the birth of the Saviour. At the time it was written, settled government existed, and the arts of civilization had reached an advanced stage of development, kingdoms and governments were fully organized, and authority was handed down from father to son in settled succession. The poem illustrates the manners and customs of the time as well as the traits and usages of the people. A good deal of romance is mixed with the narrative.

At the present time, the major divisions of the people exist with little variation about as they did in the days of the Mahabharatha, except that the Mohammedans, unknown at those remote periods, have overrun the country from north to south, and from east to west. The followers of the Prophet have never merged with the Hindus. They remain to this day quite distinct and separate. The old Hindu race, with its numerous interdivisions, keeps as aloof from other races as it did four thousand years ago, a striking example of the influences of caste in keeping races apart. The minor divisions of the people and the nomadic tribes remain also as they were centuries ago.

The nature of the Indian country, so largely agricultural, makes the vast mass of the population dependent on the soil. Irrigation was a science known to the Hindus and to the Mohammedans many centuries ago. The Mahrattas of Southern India, the Rajputs in the North, and their conquerors, the Moguls, were irrigation engineers. In Southern India the dam of Madras, a solid mass of rough stones one thousand feet in length, forty to sixty feet in breadth, and fifteen to eighteen feet in depth, which stretched across the Cauvery River, is said to have been built in the second century. In the North, what is today the immense Bari-Doab Canal was the Hasli Canal of the Mogul Dynasties, which carried the water of the Ravi River to the region of Lahore, a distance of 130 miles. The inundation canals of

Multan were the work of the famous Mohammedan engineer of the 16th century, Diwar Sawn Mal.

Notwithstanding these irrigation works, India has ever been a famine-stricken land. In the ancient times they were not sufficient to guard against the droughts, and, moreover, in the vast extent of country plenty might obtain in one region and dearth in others. In modern times with the building of railways the means of relief have been augmented, for supplies can be quickly transported from one district to another. Very great improvement also has been made in the irrigation systems and the area under cultivation has been vastly extended. Nevertheless famines still come with almost distressing regularity.

In 1897 India was subjected to one of its great periodical famines. The crops were a failure in many districts. Hundreds of thousands of the natives were dying from hunger, fever, and other forms of pestilence. The whole world was appealed to for relief. The Viceroy of India formed a Government Committee in Calcutta. The Government of the United States lent its aid, and provided a ship of the Navy to carry the contributions made by the American people.

Many missionaries in India wrote to Dr. Klopsch regarding this famine, urging relief both on the grounds of humanity and as a material aid to missionary labor. A cablegram from the Viceroy stated that American aid would be most welcome. This cablegram was published in *The Christian Herald*, whose readers quickly responded. A missionary

committee was formed which included many of the
leading American and English missionaries in India,
and at the head of which was the distinguished
Bishop J. M. Thoburn. To this committee, as to
all missionary committees in subsequent work under
similar conditions, was entrusted the duty of distribution, which was carried on by systematic organization and through business-like methods.

Cash contributions, as usual ranging from sums
less than a dollar up to large checks, began to flow
in in response to *The Christian Herald* appeal. For
the week ending January 23, 1897, which covered the
first subscriptions, the total was $354.64. For the
week ending May 1, 1898, the total was $18,624.70.
The amounts continued to aggregate liberal sums
all through the year so that the cash relief which
could be transmitted was constant. Most of the
remittances were made by cable.

Another very practical measure was characteristic of Dr. Klopsch. He chartered a steamship, the
City of Everett, and proceeded to collect grain which
could be distributed among the starving natives of
India. Very liberal contributions were made and
the railroads and other transportation lines coöperated by giving cash freight refunds. When a full
cargo had been received the *City of Everett* sailed
from San Francisco with the Rev. R. G. Hobbs in
charge as the representative of *The Christian Herald.*

Word came back from many sources of the good
work that was being accomplished through the funds
which Dr. Klopsch and his constituency supplied.
The Rev. George H. Brock, a Baptist missionary of

Kaniji in the Nellore District, wrote that the suffering of the people was terrible to witness, and it was a great help to him when *The Christian Herald* sent him a remittance from the funds so generously supplied by its readers. He set the starving people to work, he and his helpers distributing the relief in 36 villages, giving money or food to the aged or sick and employing the able-bodied in digging wells and other work which would be a permanent benefit to the communities. Mr. Brock had a field of missionary labor covering over a thousand square miles, with a population of 140,000. He was assisted by 27 native preachers and helpers. Another Baptist missionary in the Nellore District, the Rev. E. Bullard, wrote expressing gratitude for the funds received indirectly from *The Christian Herald.*

The Rev. T. S. Johnson, of Jabulpur, wrote especially regarding the support of orphans and describing the method adopted in the distribution of the American grain.

The general plan adopted was first to choose a village where the inhabitants were aborigines or were known to be specially poor. The relief list of the village was scrutinized and the poorer tenants were selected. A signed ticket was then given to the tenant for a very small sum, and he was told to come to the store where the grain was kept, present his ticket, and receive dole. Tickets of different colors were issued for different quantities of grain, so that the illiterate people might know the value of their tickets and get supplied with the right amount. The cultivators were ready to walk long distances to the central store to get their supplies.

The Rev. Wm. Osborne Ballantine, of Rahuri, wrote:

From early morning till late at night the driveway past our gate is crowded — the aged, who after all their years of hardship and scarcity are now dying of starvation; mothers with little helpless children pinched with hunger; other children with neither father nor mother, their ceaseless crying ringing in my ears as I write — when I tell you of all this you will understand that we are thankful enough to the good people in the home land whose gifts you have forwarded to us. Every dollar we have received from you is regarded as a sacred trust and is used to do the utmost good possible. Thousands of lives have been saved by *The Christian Herald* fund.

The Rev. Dr. Lambert, of the Mennonite Church, who went to India as the bearer of a large sum of money contributed by the members of the Mennonite Church in America, on his return to New York called to see Dr. Klopsch and to tell of the gratitude of the people for all that *The Christian Herald* readers had done for them. One missionary wrote him that before the welcome help came the death rate in his district which nominally was under 50 in the thousand was forced by starvation up to the appalling figure of 627 in the thousand.

The Rev. Richard Winsor, the American Board's missionary at Sirur, in a letter paid an eloquent tribute to the generous work of the readers of *The Christian Herald*. He wrote:

The year of 1897 was a year of years. We were in the midst of a famine and plague. The pen of a ready writer would be needed to describe the want, suffering and wretchedness, much of which as we saw it here can never be made known. When there was not much prospect that we would be able to furnish relief the scenes began to be beyond endurance. But the splendid gifts from *The Christian Herald* and the help received from other sources nerved us and equipped us for the great work there was to do, and it has been a great work indeed. For months our whole time was given up to the work, which afforded us opportunities of becoming acquainted with the people and of putting the truth before them as nothing ever before enabled us to do. The people have been blessed, and everywhere pour out their thanks for what has been done for them.

Another acknowledgment came through the Rev. J. E. Robinson, Secretary of the Central Conference of the Methodist Episcopal Church in India. Mr. Robinson wrote:

I have great pleasure in forwarding you a copy of a resolution passed unanimously and with great cordiality at the recent central conference. I may add that in my editorial capacity numerous instances come under my notice of the grateful regard of those in this land for the good friends across the sea who write so nobly in behalf of the suffering people. Their splendid service will never be forgotten.

The resolution was as follows:

At the Biennial session of the Methodist Episcopal Church of India and Malaysia, held at Lucknow, the following resolution was unanimously passed: Resolved, — That the conference place on record its thankful acknowledgment of the sympathy and generosity with which the people of other lands have responded to the cry for aid in the Indian famine of 1897. And that we make special mention of the great help given through the agency of *The Christian Herald*, and also to the Rev. R. G. Hobbs and the Rev. George Lambert, through whose agency the ship-load of grain was distributed to the famine sufferers of India; and that we assured these gentlemen that not only was their service thankfully accepted by all who shared in their gifts but also that this exposition of international friendliness and sympathy has made a profound and pleasing impression upon the people of India both rich and poor.

WIDOWS OF THE INDIA FAMINE

ORPHAN CHILDREN OF INDIA SUPPORTED BY *THE CHRISTIAN HERALD*

Dr. Hobbs had sailed on the *City of Everett* with the corn contributed by the friends of *The Christian Herald*. Dr. Lambert had served as a member of the International Missionary Committee organized by Bishop Thoburn to distribute the fund and the corn.

On his return from India Dr. Hobbs brought from Madras an interesting document in the native language. It was written on parchment and was a marvel of delicate penmanship. Translated, it proved to be a message to the readers of *The Christian Herald*. The document was as follows:

INDIA'S DEEP GRATITUDE

THE ORPHAN HOME.
VEYASARPAUDY, MADRAS.

To Dr. Louis Klopsch, Proprietor of "The Christian Herald," and Rev. R. G. Hobbs, D.D., "The Christian Herald's" Famine Commissioner:

DEAR SIRS:

[Here follows the document in the native language, of which the following is a translation.]

[TRANSLATION.]

We, the undersigned, workers, orphans, and scholars of the Madras Tamil Mission, have been impressed with the love and generosity of the people of Great Britain and Ireland in contributing such large sums of money for the relief of the famine-stricken millions of India.

But we feel profoundly touched with that love which has prompted you to raise in America such an *enormous quantity of grain and a magnificent sum of money to feed the hungry in a foreign land like India.*

What a glorious calling to be Ambassadors of the
Lord Jesus Christ and the great American nation, in
bringing to our shores a steamer-load of grain!

Realizing, as we do, the privations and hardships of India's poor, and the comforts your cargo
of grain will bring to thousands of helpless women
and famishing children, we feel we cannot let you
leave Madras without thanking you heartily for
this labor of love, and assure you that God will
perform to you personally: (Hosea 14: 5–6).

Will you kindly remind the readers of *The Christian Herald* and your fellow-citizens in America that
by feeding India's hungry millions they shall have
the satisfaction of having fed Jesus himself. (Matt.
25: 35). If a cup of cold water given in Christ's
name will not lose its reward, will not God perform
to them (Malachai 3:10)?

We are, dear sirs, yours in Jesus,

There was also to Dr. Klopsch a message of greeting and gratitude from the Methodist Episcopal publishing house at Madras. The publishing house from which the testimonial came originated in the work of Dr. A. W. Rudisill, who went from the Baltimore Conference in 1884 as a missionary to India. He took with him a little printing press, the gift of his father, which was large enough to print only a page of 6 inches long and 4 wide. One day Dr. Rudisill set up in type John 3:16 in Tamil characters. A large number of these small pages having been printed and circulated, their usefulness was soon demonstrated, and Dr. Rudisill began to agitate for a full-fledged printing establishment. Contributions flowed in and by the end of 1886 enough money was on hand to set up a press and the necessary type in the mission house. Later a larger press was secured and an electrotyping and photo-engraving plant and a bindery were added. Employees were secured who could set type in nearly all the languages spoken in India. It was from these employees, and from the orphans in the mission house, that this tribute came:

To Louis Klopsch, Esq., Proprietor "The Christian Herald":

DEAR SIR: The Methodist Episcopal Publishing House, Madras, India, send you greetings. Although Providence has, in undeserved mercy, preserved our beautiful city from dire calamities, our hearts bleed because large portions of India suffer from famine, pestilence and earthquake.

We, therefore, the undersigned establishment of

the Methodist Episcopal Publishing House, Madras, India, hail with joy the arrival in our harbor of *The Christian Herald Ship* flying *The Christian Herald Flag*. As we look into her now empty store-rooms and reflect that they came filled with food for India's starving millions, we are overcome with amazement and gratitude at the wealth of love that prompted you to come so grandly to the help of this stricken land.

The Agent of this Press, with a full heart, is also mindful of the fact that the columns of *The Christian Herald* were thrown open a few years ago to aid the then mere beginning of what is now a many-sided and extensive Publishing House, which we dare hope, through God's blessing, may be made a power for good in India, as is *The Christian Herald* in America and other lands. The God of peace be with you.

We are, dear sir, yours cordially,

A. W. RUDISILL, Agent.

W. MILES, Assistant to Agent.

Madras, India.

The second testimonial is also signed by a number of Tamil, Telegu, Canarese, Hindustani and American employes in the binding, envelope, booklet, electrotyping, engraving and other departments of the great Madras Publishing House.

The end of the famine was told of in a letter from Bishop Thoburn received late in January, 1898. The Bishop wrote:

It is a wonderful relief to feel that the famine is practically over. Harvests in many districts are very bountiful and the people look hopeful once more; but it will be many long years before the traces of this awful visitation will wholly disappear from the country.

Some months later Dr. Klopsch was able to pub-
lish the audited statement showing the total receipts
from all sources, and particulars of the distribution through the American missionaries and by
the Interdenominational Committee of which Bishop
Thoburn was chairman, with the cost of sending out
the steamer *Everett* with a cargo of food, and also
the special fund apportioned among various missionaries for the support and education of orphans whose
parents perished in the famine.

This statement showed cash contributions received
by *The Christian Herald* amounting to $196,561.68;
cash received from the sale of grain, etc., $46,810.35;
cash freight refunds received from railroads and
transportation lines, $13,130.01. This made total
receipts from all sources of $256,502.04. In addition
the cash value in India of the *City of Everett's* cargo
was placed at $150,000. There were also over-
pledges in the special orphan fund of $3,130.72.
This meant that *The Christian Herald's* India relief
fund had amounted to more than $400,000. The
detailed account was given of the disbursements,
with the public accountant's certification that after
having carefully examined the books of *The Christian Herald* and diligently compared every voucher,
receipt, check, and stub, he had found the statement
submitted to be an accurate and true statement of
the receipts and expenditures in connection with
the India famine fund under the auspices of *The
Christian Herald*.

Official notification of the result of the Indian
famine fund work came in the form of a letter from

William R. Day, Assistant Secretary of State, to Dr. Klopsch. This letter transmitted copy of a note from the British Ambassador conveying the thanks of the Government of India to Dr. Klopsch and the people of the United States for the sympathy they had shown the sufferers from famine in India by gifts of grain and money. The letter of the British Ambassador was as follows:

WASHINGTON, D. C.

HON. JOHN SHERMAN,

Sir: I have received instructions from the Marquis of Salisbury to inform you that the Government of India desire that their grateful acknowledgment may be tendered to the Government and to the people of the United States for the generous sympathy they have shown towards the sufferers from famine in India by gifts of grain and money, and Her Majesty's Secretary of State of India wishes to associate himself cordially with these expressions of thanks. I have the honor to transmit copy of a dispatch from the Government of India with its enclosures, and to request you to be good enough to convey the thanks of Her Majesty's Government and of the Government of India to Dr. Klopsch and others, by whose exertions the grain and money were collected.

I have the honor to be, with the highest consideration, sir,

Your most obedient and humble servant,

JULIAN PAUNCEFOTE.

Accompanying the letter was a document signed by Lord Elgin, the Viceroy of India, and his official associates in the government relief work, which in giving details said:

The Government and people of India are deeply indebted to the Government of the United States for the assistance thus rendered in the mitigation of suffering from famine; and in particular to Dr. Klopsch, proprietor of the New York *Christian Herald*, and the many other persons, by whose exertions the grain and money received in India have been collected.

There was also a letter from Bishop Thoburn, in which further particulars were given of the distribution of *The Christian Herald* funds.

CHAPTER V

THE GREAT INDIA FAMINE RELIEF

WHEN FIVE MILLIONS FACED STARVATION — FUNDS CABLED BY THE "CHRISTIAN
HERALD" — SPEEDING THE RELIEF SHIP "QUITO" — PRESIDENT MC KINLEY'S
PRACTICAL SYMPATHY — DR. KLOPSCH'S VISIT TO THE STRICKEN LAND —
HIS GRAPHIC STORY OF SCENES OF SUFFERING — VIVID PEN PICTURES OF CITY
AND COUNTRY — ARRIVAL OF THE "QUITO" — CARGO DISTRIBUTED — MORE
FUNDS — MISSIONARIES' TESTIMONIALS — DR. KLOPSCH'S RETURN TO THE
UNITED STATES — SUMMARY OF RECEIPTS AND EXPENDITURES.

INDIA'S freedom from starvation was brief. It
lasted less than three years, though usually there
had been an interval of nineteen or twenty
years. But before the people had had time to
recover from the appalling suffering of 1897 and 1898
the monsoon, the rain-bringing, life-giving wind from
the south, had again failed and the crops were
withered.

In November, 1899, the existence of the famine was
officially recognized. At that time about 400,000
peasants were affected. But it spread rapidly and
in the succeeding year fertile districts which had
suffered no such visitation within a century found
that the crops were failing. The famine area was
extending with fearful rapidity. Soon there were
1,000,000 sufferers, then 2,000,000 were in need of
aid. Not long after that the figures mounted to
3,000,000 to 4,000,000, and finally there were
5,000,000 natives on the verge of starvation.

Late in 1900 letters began to reach the United

States telling of the conditions.   Every mail brought
appeals for aid.   Missionary after missionary wrote
to Dr. Klopsch reciting the ominous news, and again
asked his help in appealing to Christian people.   So
generous had been the response to the call for funds
two years previously that he felt reluctant to plead
again for the same country.   It seemed as if America
had done enough for India.   But he found it impossible to turn a deaf ear to the stories of suffering which
every mail brought him.   It was by no fault of their
own that the natives of India were bowed under a
visitation closely following on the heels of a former
calamity.   It was impossible to incur the responsibility of keeping silence in view of the reports of
distress and the earnest prayers for help that came
from the missionaries.   The facts had to be told
and the matter left in the hands of the American
people to say whether the starving women and children of whom such harrowing accounts were received
should live or die.

The confidence of the missionaries in India that
their appeal would not go unheeded was expressed
in their letters.   The pictures they drew of the conditions were convincing of the need of aid.

Before the contributions from the readers of *The
Christian Herald* could begin to be received in
appreciable amounts Dr. Klopsch cabled $5,000 to
be divided equally among five missionaries who were
named.   Four of these were Americans and the
fifth was Pundita Ramabai.

More urgent appeals came, showing the need of
prompt work, and Dr. Klopsch thereupon cabled

another $10,000. The money was sent direct to Bishop J. M. Thoburn, who had been chairman of the Interdenominational Committee in the famine of 1897. This Committee had special facilities for ascertaining which districts were in the greatest need.

It soon became evident that grain would have to be shipped in from other countries. Letters and cablegrams represented the need of relief as so urgent, and the condition of the sufferers as so appalling, that in order to save thousands who would otherwise perish it was decided to forward grain with all dispatch. The plan was to equip a flying relief ship to carry a load of American corn to Bombay. With this object in view Dr. Klopsch cabled the British Government announcing the readiness of Christian America to give of its abundant products to save lives in far-off India, and requested that transportation be provided for the projected cargo. To this message the British Government, after communicating with the Viceroy's Committee in India, replied that the Indian Government was deeply grateful for renewed American sympathy and would pay the transport provided the cargo was placed at the disposal of the Central Committee of famine relief.

It happened that during the closing months of the famine of 1897–98 the Navy Department had been authorized to send out a ship with a relief cargo, but happily the suffering had ended before this could be done. Dr. Klopsch at once moved to secure the ship from the Navy Department for the present emergency. This was done by the coöperation of Secretary of State Hay with Secretary of the Navy

Long. The *Quito* was obtained and appeals were at once sent out for contributions to her cargo. They came from every corner of the land, until 200,000 bushels of grain were loaded on the ship, which lay at the dock in Brooklyn. There was probably not a church organization or society in the land which failed to share in the life saving work. Little village communities and agricultural groups in the great corn growing states loaded up cars with corn and sent them on to swell the relief ship's cargo. In all 5,000 tons, or 200,000 bushels, were taken aboard. In addition to the corn there was a quantity of seeds suitable for sowing in India.

While the relief cargo of grain was being gathered, the work of collecting money and transmitting it directly continued. Lord Curzon, the Viceroy of India, transmitted to the Government of the United States a dispatch showing the extent of the calamity, and indicating that while the Indian Government was devoting its energies to fulfilling its duty to save 5,000,000 persons from starvation, contributions from American friends of India would be thankfully received and would be devoted to the material relief of the suffering. The dispatch was brought to the attention of Dr. Klopsch in the following letter from the Assistant Secretary of State:

DEPARTMENT OF STATE,
WASHINGTON, D. C., March 24, 1900.

DEAR MR. KLOPSCH: Recalling your interest in the business of Cuban relief in 1898 and your efforts to assuage suffering in Russia, India and Armenia, I take the liberty of sending you a copy of a press item which has just been given out

expressing the willingness of the Indian Government to receive
famine contributions from this country.

Very cordially yours,

ALVEY A. ADEE.

President McKinley, who had taken a personal
interest in seeing that the action of Congress in
providing for the charter of the *Quito* for the relief
in 1897–98 was made effective in the present
famine, showed his interest in *The Christian Herald*
relief movement by contributing $100. Secretary
Hay did the same.

Reports of the suffering and misery of the people
of India had become so appalling that in order to
save time and get the relief to them at the earliest
possible moment, early in April *The Christian Herald*
cabled an additional remittance of $25,000. It was
a most welcome gift and was the Easter offering
of the American people. Within a short time Dr.
Klopsch was able to announce that the whole nation
was helping India, its great heart having been
touched by the woes of that famine-stricken land.
But he knew the end was not yet. Therefore early
in April he announced that he himself would proceed to India to render what aid might be given by
his personal presence. He went first to London,
where he had an interview with Lord George Hamilton, the British Secretary of State for India, who
discussed with him the plans for the relief work.
Lord Hamilton expressed the warmest appreciation
of America's generous aid to India. He gave to
Dr. Klopsch letters of introduction to Lord Curzon,
the Viceroy, and to several other high officials.

In the meantime the arrangements were completed for the sailing of the *Quito*. The cargo was insured, and was valued at $100,000, which at the famine rates at which corn was then selling in India was equal to $300,000 worth of corn in Bombay. The ship's charter cost $40,000, which was paid by the generosity of the United States Government.

The *Quito* sailed from Brooklyn on May 10th. From topmast to deck the vessel was dressed with the flags of all nations, her commander, Captain Baird, having run up *The Christian Herald* flag and streamer on the foremast right below the Stars and Stripes. There was a programme of praise services, with remarks by the Rev. R. G. Hobbs, who had accompanied *The Christian Herald* famine ship *City of Everett* to India in 1897, Commander Booth Tucker of the Salvation Army, Rev. S. T. Willis, Rev. Richard Winsor, Rev. A. C. Dixon, and the Countess Schimmelmann. The prayer for blessing on the ship and cargo was by the Rev. Mr. Neeld.

Theodore Roosevelt, then Governor of New York, sent a note in which he conveyed "the heartiest acknowledgments on behalf of the people of this State on the splendid work you have done." A letter was read from President McKinley, regretting that the pressure of public duties prevented him from being present at the ceremonies. "It would have given me," he wrote, "peculiar pleasure to be with you on this occasion. The success of this work is eminently gratifying to me, as it must be not only to those immediately engaged but to the country at large."

Secretary Hay wrote, "I should be very glad if

it were possible to be present at the departure of the vessel which has been freighted by our philanthropic citizens through the agency of *The Christian Herald* to relieve the terrible calamity which is now devastating India, and to testify the interest I have taken in the work you have so nobly done; but I greatly regret that engagements from which I cannot free myself detain me here." Secretary Long also wrote expressing regrets at his inability to be present.

While the ship was on its way Dr. Klopsch was hastening to India. He left New York in April and arrived in Bombay Saturday, May 12th. He found the situation so appalling and the need for immediate help so urgent that he placed a large sum at the disposal of the Interdenominational Missionary Committee for the relief work, thus again considerably anticipating the contributions as he had done on other occasions. He cabled briefly telling of his meeting the Governor of Bombay and of addressing the members of the Interdenominational Missionary Committee. He then started for the interior.

A graphic story of the suffering as seen by Dr. Klopsch's sympathetic eyes, and a vivid picture of the conditions, was given by his own pen. Extracts from his account of his tour in India as published in *The Christian Herald* show how deeply the scenes of suffering moved him and how he sought to alleviate it. He wrote:

"Famine in India! How I dread to write about it! What pen can adequately portray the scenes which my eyes have witnessed? Scenes of desolation, of pain, of suffering, of hopeless despair, of heart anguish, of death! And what a death! Lingering, agonizing, torturous, terrible! An indescribable death, coming on gradually; slowly, but surely tightening its grip, until its victim, consciously helpless, the eyes abnormally distended and unnaturally lustrous, sinks down overcome with dread apprehension. Then a feeble but fruitless effort to rise again, a protracted, spasmodic gurgle, an occasional revivification; a final, prolonged, appealing, anxious, despairing look, the death rattle, and all is over. Then the funeral! If the undertaker be a jackal or a vulture, it may possibly be imagined, but it should never be described. Otherwise, the body is burned, and its ashes fertilize the sun-baked, kiln-dried, sterile ground.

"I had fully expected to witness great distress, intense suffering, yes, even death. I realized my own feebleness in the face of so great a calamity. I had nerved myself for the mission in hand; yet, I was in nowise prepared for the dreadful, shocking state of affairs I was called upon to encounter. On the Red Sea and the Indian Ocean, while sweltering in a range of temperature and a degree of humidity to which I was wholly unaccustomed, fellow-passengers had endeavored to convey to my mind some idea of the sad, heartrending scenes one is apt to meet with in the famine territory; but had I the power to intensify a thousand times all I heard, when face to face with the dreaded reality, I should have felt even then that 'the half had not been told.'

"On the day of our arrival, the streets of Bombay were literally alive with walking skeletons. Every step of the way we were beset and besieged by men, women and children in the last stages of destitution, piteously begging for a mite that they might eat and live. They prostrated themselves before us, calling upon us as the 'Protectors of the poor, our Father and Mother, our King and our God,' to save them from starvation.

"They lifted up their hands in earnest supplication, and uttered their petitions while vigorously slapping their naked, hollow stomachs to indicate that for a long time they had had nothing to eat. They held out their hands with a beseeching look, hoping that we might drop a coin that would purchase at least enough food to satisfy their hunger just for an hour. Gaunt men, emaciated women with parched bosoms, nursing shriveled, diminutive, hollow-eyed, sickly babies; children with legs and arms like clothes-pins, every rib plainly visible, all ran toward us and after us, completely surrounding the carriage and entreating us every step of the way.

"I was tempted to give them all I had, but Rev. Mr. Frease, who accompanied me, begged me not to do it, fearing if we gave to some that the rest would become frantic and endanger our safety. 'Where do these unfortunate people come from?' I asked. 'They come from the villages in families and groups to the larger cities, hoping there to be able to beg enough to keep them alive,' was the reply. 'How many of them are there in Bombay?' 'Tens of thousands,' responded my companion. 'The municipality sent seven thousand by rail to the Relief Camp at Thana, twenty-five miles away, the other day, but six thousand left in one night and returned to the city, walking the entire distance.'

"All along the drive of over two miles, between our hotel and the Marathi Mission, doorways, stoops and curbstones were occupied by these helpless unfortunates, many of them more than three-fourths naked and all of them miserably clad. The most persistent in their entreaties were the nursing mothers, and nearly every other woman belonged to that

class, and the saddest sight of all were the poor
child mothers, themselves in need of maternal
attention, hugging their emaciated, hollow-templed
and sunken-eyed babies with an intensity of affection that almost broke our hearts to witness — particularly in view of our own utter helplessness to
relieve their distress.

"Houseless and homeless, these unfortunates sleep
in the streets of Bombay at night. They lie down
just where they happen to find themselves when tired-
ness overtakes them, and it is no exaggeration to say
that I have seen as many as five hundred asleep on
the sidewalk of a single block, lying so closely that
it was almost impossible to thread one's way through
the maze. In the less frequented streets they sleep
also in the driveways, and in order to drive through
without accident it is necessary to send an advance
courier to wake up the sleepers. Of course, they
have neither bed nor covering, and to see the little
ones on the hard stones cuddle up to their mothers
was one of the most pathetic, touching sights that
I have ever witnessed.

"As in the city, so along the country roads of the
famine district, there are constant streams of grim,
gaunt, hungry, despairing people, bound from the
villages for the relief stations; for the Famine Code
requires the starving to break up their homes and
travel from fifteen to twenty miles, yes, sometimes
over thirty miles, in order to obtain relief. Hence,
no wonder that along the sun-baked, kiln-dried
roads of famine-stricken India, dead bodies have
strewn the way and sickened the hearts of our
missionaries, and that when certain death stares
these wanderers in the face they, as a last resort,
offer their children for sale at a few annas each, in
the hope that such a course will ensure the lives of
the little ones and enable their parents to journey

further on, with a prospect of getting to where relief awaits them!

· · · · · · · · ·

"We journeyed 150 miles south, and 200 miles north, of Bombay. Desolation and death were written all over the famine district. A more discouraging condition could not well be imagined. For miles and miles not a blade of grass! The sun relentlessly sent its destructive rays on man and beast. The hot soil, hard-baked, refracted the heat and rendered life a burden. Crowds of human beings, emaciated and debilitated, moved from place to place in vain search for food, mutely appealing for help that never came. Cattle, reduced to very skeletons, feebly crept about in quest of fodder, and in lieu of it licked the hot soil as though to propitiate its anger. Trees, stripped of all their bark to the very tips, stood out like white skeletons against the cruel, fiery sky. Vultures, perched on leafless branches, listlessly waited for victims. Not a breath was stirring. The silence of death had settled upon the country. I feel it now as I write, so much so that the scratching of the pen seems harsh and intrusive. There is something uncanny about this silence. It enters one's very being and benumbs one's senses. It kills ambition. The desire for life passes away and an absolute indifference to fate takes its place. We were in the great graveyard of India. It covered 350,000 square miles, equal to any eight States west of the Mississippi. Death and decay were round about us on every hand. Possibly we might never again get beyond its confines. Who could tell! Awful as it was, we did not realize it then, for that required thought, and this ominous, deathlike silence paralyzed thought.

"One experience which stands out from all the

others most distinctly in my mind, is our visit to
Ahmedabad. We got there about half-past five
in the evening, and without waiting to visit the
accommodations provided for our entertainment we
hastened to the poor-house.

"On the shadeless plaza before the gate were
nearly 250 reeking, filthy bundles of rags, containing
as many human beings in various stages of emaciation, some standing, some squatting in Oriental
fashion on the ground, others lying flat on their backs,
and still others lying with their faces to the ground,
in order to screen themselves from the burning rays
of the evening sun. The thermometer ranged at
about 110 deg. in the shade; not a breath of air was
blowing, and the heat and stench contributed to
make us physically as ill at ease as the sad scenes of
destitution, misery, pain and helplessness made us
so mentally. It seemed impossible that any part
of the great human family could reach such depth
of misery as was everywhere visible.

"On inquiring why these people were exposed to
the relentless rays of the sun without shelter or
shade, I was told that they had been brought in from
the neighboring villages on carts and were to remain
under observation for twenty-four hours in order to
determine whether symptoms of contagious disease
developed. They had come in during the afternoon,
they had lain there for three or four hours, they
were to remain there all night and to stay there
all the next forenoon. Possibly the evening of the
next day they would be admitted to the inhospitable
shelter of the Ahmedabad poor-house. Myriads of
flies were feasting on each individual bundle, and the
eyelids, mouths, nostrils and ears were all besieged
with battalions of flies gorging themselves on the
helpless victims of the India famine.

"The most distressing phase of all this indescribable misery was the dear little children who seemed to be in constant agony, internal and external. They did not cry aloud, because they lacked the vital inner force for such effort; though their faces were constantly crying no sound was heard, and as we looked at these innocent, helpless little things — so emaciated, hollow-templed, sunken-eyed, the nape of the neck so sharply indented under the skull that the head looked abnormally large and ill-supported — the burden of sympathetic grief became almost unbearable. Sometimes tears rolled down their cheeks, and the mother sitting next to the child would wipe the tears away with a part of her dirty, filthy garment, and something like a sigh would escape to indicate the depth of sorrow that was laying hold upon her heart. As we stood there watching this motley crowd, overawed, as it seemed, by dozens of tall, skeletonized men with long beards and large, abnormally lustrous eyes peering out of depressed sockets, half inquisitive, half reflective, our attention was directed to two groups of burden-bearers, each group bearing a cot; one set bound for the poor-house, the other set coming from it. On the cot bound for the poor-house was a man about twenty years of age, long and thin, sheltering with his hand his eyes from the sun. He was a fever patient, and was going in for treatment. On the other cot was a man who had received 'treatment,' and was now bound for the funeral pile, where fourteen were to be burned that evening.

"We went into the poor-house where over a thousand people in various stages of nudity and emaciation were seated on the ground, waiting to be served. It was time for the evening meal. We left them for the time being, and, taking a turn sidewise we entered the hospital section, which was the worst, with one or two exceptions, that I had occasion to visit.

THE CEREMONY OF "SAMPLING THE CARGO" OF THE RELIEF SHIP *QUITO* IN BOMBAY

We first went through the cholera wards, and there in every ward we found dead bodies on the cots or on the ground. Every fifth or sixth cot had a corpse on it. I asked why they were not removed, and an attendant replied that the victims had died after twelve o'clock noon, in which case there is no removal until the time for burning, which is eight in the evening. It was a gruesome sight to see these dead men and women, with expressions of intensest agony on their faces, lying there; and the only comforting thought was that they were beyond suffering, and that the famine in India, with its plague, its cholera, its smallpox and its fever, could no longer affect them.

"Down in a corner of one of the wards, in which we had found three dead bodies, lay a tall, broad-shouldered man, stone dead. He had died during the afternoon. Back of him was his little four-year-old girl, tenderly fondling him and vainly endeavoring to attract his attention. Her face seemed to indicate that she was beginning to realize that something was amiss; and yet there was her father, and what she apprehended vaguely could not very well be, so long as he was there. We stood looking on, our hearts almost breaking and the tears coursing down our cheeks, when a little commotion at the entrance to the ward claimed our attention. They were bringing in the patient whom we had seen on the cot outside, and who required medical treatment. The attendant lifted him up and raised him on his feet, then supporting him on one side, the feeble patient staggering as best he could with the aid of this support, he walked him to the corner and placed him down on the ground, face to face with the dead man whose little child was fondling him. The thing took but a few moments, but the horror of the situation so appalled us that, for the moment, we were stupefied. It seemed impossible that any one could commit so unnatural an act. We called the attention of the man to what he was doing. We asked him why he did not make room elsewhere for the patient. He replied that within an hour the dead man would be removed and the patient then could have the whole corner to himself.

"The worst that has ever been written about the suffering among the 60,000,000 of people affected by the famine in India fails even to approximate the actual condition of affairs. It is absolutely impossible to exaggerate the truth. The statement that millions are starving gives but a very general idea of what is actually taking place. To illustrate what fearful suffering prevails there, let me give you this instance from my own experience while visiting the famine districts:

"We arrived at Dohad, in Gujarat, the Garden of India, at ten minutes after one of the afternoon of May the 24th. Dr. J. H. McNeill, the Irish Presbyterian missionary located there, was at the station. Within five minutes I was seated in his cart and on the way to what until recently was one of the largest relief camps. As far as the eye could see there was not a blade of vegetation. The heat was intense; the thermometer indicated 108 degrees. A hot, blinding sandstorm filled our eyes and nostrils with microbe-laden dust, and the all-pervading stench from putrefying bodies impregnated clothes, hair and skin. Cholera had broken out a short time before and 2,400 famine sufferers had died within a few days and had been buried in shallow ground. Decomposition speedily set in and impregnated the ground with death-dealing malodor. Then the bodies were disinterred and burned. There were no disinfectants, hence the awful, sickening, disease-spreading, suffocating stench. At the outbreak of the

cholera the camp stampeded and 6,000 infected, half-
starved people spread contagion for miles around.
At the hospital I was appalled at the shocking condition of affairs with which at that moment I came
face to face, and that I ever got out of Dohad alive
is one of the greatest of the many incontrovertible
evidences of God's kind protecting care which my
life has experienced.

"We found 550 miserable human beings in the
worst stages of emaciation. In sixteen days 374
had been admitted, and of these all but twenty had
died. Others had been received since then, and now
men, women and children, some of them absolutely
nude, and all the others miserably clad, were lying
around suffering from relapsing fever, cholera and
dysentery, wallowing in the mire. Millions of flies
were permitted undisturbed to pester the unhappy
victims. One young woman who had lost every one
dear to her, and had turned stark mad, sat at the
door vacantly staring at the awful scenes around
her. In the entire hospital I did not see a single
decent garment. Rags, nothing but rags and dirt.
A native hospital attendant was standing at the cot
of a dying man. The death-rattle had already set
in, but the vitality of the patient held out a little
beyond the expected time, and the attendant seemed
provoked at the delay, and gave us impatiently to
understand that the man should have been dead
long ago."

Vivid descriptions were given of the visits to
Baroda, Godhra, as well as Dohad — all three in
one day — and the fearful scenes of death and suffering witnessed, but happily they are long past and the
harrowing story need not be repeated. Dr. Klopsch
continued his journey and everywhere was welcomed
by the missionaries, the officials of the Indian Gov-

ernment, and the suffering natives whose distress
he was doing so much to alleviate.

Dr. R. A. Hume, the famous missionary of Ahmednagar who received a decoration from the Indian
Government for his famine work, was a great friend
of Dr. Klopsch and warmly welcomed his coming
and seconded his efforts.

Dr. Klopsch was invited to visit the Taj Mahal
at Agra "the most beautiful tomb in the world," but
he declined. His account of his declination was
characteristic:

"'You surely will go to Agra and see the Taj
Mahal before you sail?' said my companion, when
I informed him that we were that day to begin the
last trip before our return home. 'Everybody that
comes to India visits at least that,' added he, by way
of encouragement, when I shook my head negatively.
We had come to see the famine fields and our time
was getting short and every moment of it was mort-
gaged in advance up to the hour of our departure.
Relief operations were of immediate and urgent importance, while sightseeing could be deferred."

The relief ship *Quito* reached Bombay on June 28th.
There was a wonderful reception. The Rev. Mr.
Winsor and his wife, who made the voyage on the
steamer, were the center of a very interesting demonstration. At the formal public reception there was
a large gathering, including the Viceroy's representative, many high state officials, influential natives,
and business men. In the addresses the speakers
with one accord warmly welcomed the arrival of
the relief ship, and expressed the deep gratitude of

India for the generous aid of the American people
conveyed through *The Christian Herald*. It was a
princely gift and came at a time of all others when
it would be of the greatest service in saving life.
Telegrams from the Viceroy, Lord Curzon, and the
Governor of Bombay were read to the audience
amid tremendous enthusiasm. These messages expressed the warmest congratulations upon the safe
arrival of the *Quito* and also upon the splendid life
saving work already accomplished in the relief
campaigns through the funds supplied by Christian
America.

The cargo was found in good condition. Unloading began at once and railway cars were soon filled
with the precious food. When all had been transferred to the cars they presented an imposing sight,
several great trains being filled with the 5,000 tons.
The cars were decorated, and soon the various trains
were speeding to their destinations in the interior.
But the food supplies from the United States still
had to be supplemented by cash contributions in
order to purchase grain and other necessities on the
ground. Therefore early in July another $100,000
was cabled by *The Christian Herald*.

Dr. Klopsch was not able to remain long in India,
but the time was long enough to satisfy himself that
every dollar collected by *The Christian Herald* and
every bushel of grain supplied was being properly
distributed. His presence in the stricken land was
an inspiration to the missionaries, to the relief committees, and to the people.

One missionary, writing from Chikulda Berer, said:

It was an inspiration to be daily in his company, so remarkable was his energy and so genuine and undemonstrative his sympathy in the starvation which he saw for the first time and all at once in its most awful form. I could scarcely have believed that a man with so lively a sense for the enjoyable side of life would depart without visiting one of the places which tourists love to see or giving a thought or an hour to the sight of the cities where duty took him. His mind was bent on seeing the famine, and he spared no effort to see as much of it as possible. He knew nothing of midday rest or afternoon siesta, but either wrote in the house or went about inspecting all day long. Although quite unused to the Indian sun, he thrice took a drive of from 6 to 14 miles in the heat of the day, and then spent one, two, or three hours on his feet inspecting a relief work or a poor house. I have known him to visit three places in a day and walk about in the blazing sun of May for several hours at a time till he had seen all he wanted.

Having completed the work he undertook in India, Dr. Klopsch returned to the United States after a most valuable and unique experience. His cordial reception by the people and press of India, the kind words he heard on every hand in appreciation of the benevolence of the American people deeply impressed him. In describing some of his experiences after his return Dr. Klopsch said:

"We arrived at the most advantageous time of the year. People were amazed — for at this season nothing is quicker in India than death and burial. It is by no means an uncommon thing for a man apparently healthy to be dead and buried within the brief space of five hours, and not infrequently the bare, ghastly skull of a man may be seen on the very field over which the day before he had walked in perfect health.

"There is a malignant type of dysentery that quickly perforates the bowels and drains the blood. Typhoid fever and plague, which everywhere abound, swell the list, and all these with death on every hand, contribute to make the white man feel that when he has done his duty he had better let it rest there and not tempt Providence. I am indeed very profoundly grateful that with the exception of a very brief attack of illness lasting one night I escaped every whit whole.

"Finally, the ever-present heat. I do not wonder that the people are indolent and apathetic. Day after day the same fierce burning sun beating down relentlessly, exhausting, depleting, devitalizing. Night after night the same muggy, close, humid heat to swelter in. The white man fumes and frets over his tantalizing inability to get even half his work done by the natives half-way decently in double the proper time. The native's grandfather never hurried, his father never hurried, why then should he do what his ancestors had never done?

"Apart from the famine, we practically saw nothing of India. Of those things usually considered sights worth seeing and of cities which every visitor must see, we saw nothing. But we saw what we went to see, and there was no mistaking the real object of our visit. Traveling twenty thousand miles just to ascertain the condition of a starving people on the other side of the world and to study how in the hour of their direst need we can prove most helpful to them, is not an every day occurrence and was not without its beneficent effect. It was a startling and impressive object lesson on the length to which a kind, sympathetic Christian people will go in order to give practical expression to noble and generous impulses. At the same time it helped to focus the attention of Moslem, Hindu, Parsee and

Christian on the world wide charity of the American nation."

The Christian Herald continued to receive contributions for the relief of the starving so long as there was need of them. Slowly the clouds lifted. Brighter news came from India. The rains fell, the lands were brought under cultivation, and the next season there was a good harvest, sufficient almost to provide for the people.

When the final account of the second India famine relief fund was rendered, in the spring of 1901, it showed that the income from all sources collected through the agency of *The Christian Herald* had amounted to $641,071.97. This sum represented 258,508 separate contributions, and these in turn represented a much larger number of individuals, as sometimes twenty or thirty contributions were included in one letter. During 1900 the net receipts directly through *The Christian Herald* exceeded $319,000. In the disbursements $290,000 was transmitted to the Interdenominational Committee at Bombay. When the actual famine relief work closed and orphan work began, the unexpended balance of $173,973.32 was transferred and applied to the support of over 5,000 famine orphans at some 60 missionary stations throughout India. As in all the relief funds, the balance sheet was published by *The Christian Herald*, showing in detail the sources of receipts and what the expenditures had been to the very dollar. This was certified to by a public accountant.

CHAPTER VI

SOLVING THE INDIA ORPHAN PROBLEM

HOW A PERMANENT FUND WAS ESTABLISHED — ANNUAL CONTRIBUTIONS — DR. KLOPSCH'S ELOQUENT TRIBUTE TO THE MISSIONARIES — HIS STORY OF HIS VISIT TO PUNDITA RAMABAI'S SCHOOL — PLEDGES OF SUPPORT — FIRST RE- SULTS OF THE WORK — A CHARACTERISTIC LETTER — INDIA'S CHILDREN HER HOPE — INDUSTRIAL TRAINING — AMBITIOUS BOYS — CARE FOR THE GIRLS — EVIDENCES OF APPRECIATION — DR. DEVIN'S REPORT — KING EDWARD CONFERS THE KAISER-I-HIND MEDAL ON DR. KLOPSCH.

ONE ever present, poignant problem was presented by the relief work during the two India famines. The food and money contributed, the medicines and clothing supplied, saved many thousands. But in spite of all that could be done many thousands also perished, and large numbers of these were parents who left helpless offsprings.

To save the children, to feed the orphans, was the thought that never left Dr. Klopsch. When a temporary respite was had from the famine of 1897–98, letters began to pour in from the missionaries showing the conditions and explaining the necessity of permanent provision for the orphans. The critical period, they explained, would continue for two or three years. Dr. Klopsch proceeded to solve the problem in his usual direct manner. He decided to establish an India Orphan Fund. This purpose was made known in the following letter, which was sent to twenty-two missionaries in India:

"DEAR FRIEND: We have heard with much pleasure of the great and good work which you were doing among the famine orphans of India. The report of it is as ointment poured forth, fragrant and full of sweetness, and we are glad on behalf of the readers of *The Christian Herald* to take an additional share in this labor of love. Acting on the advice of Bishop J. M. Thoburn, and other missionaries, we have combined the belated contributions to the Indian famine relief fund received at this office and the $13,000 recently received from several of the railroad companies of the United States who generously undertook to refund the whole or part of the freight monies paid to them for the transportation of grain donated last year for the relief of the starving people of India. And this combined fund we have now apportioned among those missionaries who have undertaken to shelter, care for and educate the thousands of homeless and helpless orphans who but for such assistance must have shared the terrible fate of their parents. We enclose a check for the first quarter in advance, and the same amount will be sent you regularly every three months during the next three years.

"We heartily appreciate the Christ-like work you are doing in caring for these helpless waifs, and pray that God will bless your efforts in their behalf to their temporal and eternal welfare.

Faithfully yours,
LOUIS KLOPSCH."

The Orphan Famine Fund was organized on a substantial business basis. Contributions were invited which were to be specifically set aside for the maintenance of orphans in India. The readers of *The Christian Herald* were asked to make an annual contribution which it was thought should be sufficient to support one orphan. As little as $15.00 a year in many cases served for this purpose. The contributions were numerous when Dr. Klopsch's appeals were understood. In acknowledging the quarterly remittances sent, the missionaries who were supporting and educating the orphans gave encouraging reports of the progress of the little waifs. Cheering accounts were received from all sources. They showed that the work was on a practical basis.

It was a providential dispensation that when the famine of 1900 came the means had already been taken for providing for the orphans. In that year the Rev. E. S. Hume, of the Interdenominational Missionary Committee, who was home on sick furlough, wrote:

The labors of the missionaries have just begun. No one will ever know how many have died as the result of the famine, but the number will probably be reckoned by millions, and several hundred thousand children will probably have been orphaned. Of these the missionaries have rescued probably not less than twenty or twenty-five thousand. For these helpless but promising children not only the missionaries but the Christians at home, who have helped save them, are responsible. There is no more urgent and encouraging form of missionary work than the training of this great company of children.

Many of the responses received to the appeal for orphan funds made through *The Christian Herald* came from children. Sometimes they combined their savings, often sending their penny collections. Contributions of this sort from the little ones always touched Dr. Klopsch deeply.

The problem of the orphans was described in *The Christian Herald* as follows: "The missionaries are looking ahead. They see in imagination some morning when there is not a cent in the treasury and there are a thousand eager faces looking for a breakfast. How would the missionary feel if he had nothing to give them? He would wish then that he had not undertaken the charge. Foreseeing such a contingency, he asks now how many children will the Christians of America authorize him to keep. It will cost $15.00 to $20.00 a year to support a child, and this sum will provide not only food and clothing but the cost of a Christian education. It is not much. Thirty cents a week more than covers it. How many men and women there are in this country who could spare the thirty cents a week easily! And how could they spend it in a way so delightful as that of obeying Christ's injunction, 'Feed my lambs!'

"And then think how far-reaching is this opportunity of Christian service that is placed within our reach. When these children grow up and go forth into the village homes of India to be the fathers and mothers of the next generation they will not go in heathenism as did their parents; they will know the blessedness of the Christian faith, and will be able to tell their children of the compassion which saved their lives and of the love which saved their souls. It really seems as if out of this appalling calamity may come the seed of the evangelization of India."

Dr. Klopsch in describing his visit to India in

1900 devoted one chapter of the account which he wrote of the trip to the school of Pundita Ramabai, near Poona, which had been aided after the famine of 1898. In describing the visit he took occasion to pay a fitting tribute to the self-sacrificing missionaries and he entitled his article "The Christian Missionary in India."

"The Christian missionary," wrote Dr. Klopsch, "is the bright and shining light that penetrates the gloom of India and inspires the heart with hope for the future. Wherever his abode may be, there the sick, the troubled and the hungry flock, and there they get comfort, help and food according to their necessities and the missionary's means. If a hundred thousand consecrated missionaries could be promptly sent to India, supplied with sufficient means, the three thousand souls who would constitute each missionary's parish would be brought into the marvelous light of the Gospel within a very few years. At the present time, there is but one missionary to every 200,000 souls, a ratio which would give Greater New York only seventeen pastors; Chicago, six; Boston, two; and San Francisco, one. But the time will come when, through the efforts of the heroic band of self-denying men and women now laboring for Christ in that benighted land, India will raise her own home missionaries, and by the very children to which she herself gave birth, be led to accept Jesus of Nazareth as Saviour and King. And the present famine is paving the way—for the children left without father or mother, home or friends, will be gathered into Christian orphanages, educated by Christian teachers, surrounded by Christian influences, become Christians themselves, and eventually go forth to tell the glad tidings of a free and a full salvation.

"It was my good fortune, during my brief sojourn, to be thrown into closest contact with a number of the godly men and women, who, full of faith, leaving the comforts of civilization behind them, answered the Divine call to uphold the standard of the Cross among an interesting but an exceedingly superstitious people, and who to-day, far away from their native land, are brightening and cheering countless lives and leading them out gradually, slowly but surely, step by step, into that blessed faith that shall yet bring peace to their troubled souls, and joy and happiness to their sad and now hopeless hearts. I congratulate myself on having for a while been permitted to mingle with them and to draw encouragement and inspiration from their presence and their lives.

"Pundita Ramabai had been seriously ill and confined to her bed for over two weeks, when she received my telegram from Bombay, inquiring whether it would be convenient for her to have me spend a day at Khedgaon on my way to Ahmednagar. Without regard for her own physical comfort, she immediately responded, cordially welcoming me to India and promising to meet me at Poona on the arrival of the seven o'clock train any morning I might designate. That same evening we started. The next morning, at the appointed hour, we glided noiselessly into Poona Station. On the platform, dressed in spotless white, stood the Pundita. She looked very pale and feeble, but she greeted us cordially with a pleasant smile. In her hand she held a diminutive bouquet of sweet-smelling flowers, which she gracefully presented and I gratefully accepted. Flowers in India are always used on every joyous or festive occasion. The train halted only ten minutes. There was no time for exchange of protracted courtesies.

"At a little after nine we reached Khedgaon. A multitude of men and women and children had gathered at the station. They had heard that the Pundita had recovered and was coming. She was their benefactress. Many of them but for her help would not have been alive. They owed everything to her. So they gathered to welcome her. They flocked around her. They embraced her. The young folks kissed her. Tears of joy were in their eyes. The Pundita was affected. She could hardly restrain her emotion. She almost wept. She returned the embraces and she looked happy. The scene was a very touching one and this spontaneous manifestation of gratitude very pathetic. It came from the heart, it went to the heart, and Ramabai found full compensation for a thousand cares and anxieties in that one welcome.

"Space will not permit me here to repeat the story of the happy day I spent with her and the 700 bright-eyed, lovely girls and young women under her care, but it was a red letter event which I shall never forget. The magnitude and superior quality of the work were a veritable revelation to me, and I am happy to know that the generous readers of *The Christian Herald* have enabled me to lift many a burden from the shoulders of this Divinely-called and heaven-ordained disciple."

The India orphan roll of honor was established by persons who undertook the support of one orphan. The pledge was given as follows:

I will endeavor to support (time) (number) India famine orphans, and will remit quarterly at the rate of $15.00 a year to *The Christian Herald* India orphan work for such support. It is my understanding the care thus provided for will include food, clothing, shelter, and instruction by proper teachers.

It is my wish that the orphan be a boy, girl, and located in an orphanage under the care of a missionary of (denomination).

In September, 1900, *The Christian Herald* cabled $25,000 to India to support 5,000 children for four months.

Dr. Klopsch in a letter dated July 25, 1900, proposed to endeavor to raise the support for 10,000 orphan children, and to pledge the support of at least 5,000 for at least one year. The Interdenominational Missionary Committee, which met at Bombay in September, 1900, accepted his offer, which it declared was unprecedented in the history of Christian charity, and accepted the conditions under which the work was to be carried on. In making his appeal Dr. Klopsch put the question in his usual incisive way. "Have you adopted an India famine orphan?" Then would follow an explanation of it as a work of Christian benevolence, and facts would be given of the good that was being accomplished. The full details of the plans for the orphan adoption would be set forth.

One of the missionaries in India sent a photograph of three little native famine orphans returning thanks after their simple meal. The Hindu "thanks hymn" translated was as follows:

> Love and thanks, O Lord,
> We little children give,
> That Thou our daily bread
> From a far country to us art sending.
> With the Holy Spirit all hearts fill;
> Grant a blessing upon all givers.

GOVERNMENT FAMINE RELIEF WORKS, GUJERAT, INDIA

FAMINE ORPHANS AT NELLORE, INDIA

Word continued to come in the following year from the missionaries of the results of the work. Dr. Harpster, the eminent minister at Gunter, wrote that he had taken special care that the stigma of charity should never attach to any of the famine orphans in his charge, and that other missionaries were doing likewise. They were treated on precisely the same footing as were the children of wealthy natives in the schools who were being educated at the expense of their parents. The orphans had the same food and the same attention as the other pupils. Miss Lillian Dietrich, who was in charge of the orphanage at Cawnpore, wrote that the 200 girls under her care were being trained to habits of industry and economy. Miss A. A. Brown, of the Kholapore mission, wrote: "It would do you good to see the bright happy faces of the waifs who have been saved from starvation by your readers. We have now over 500 of these children under our care. Some of them are child widows, whose lot would have been especially sad if we had not sheltered them. The girls are learning sewing and domestic work, and the boys are being taught better methods of farming, mason and carpentry work. They are all wonderfully bright and willing to learn."

Early in the spring of 1901 Dr. Klopsch announced that the suggestions of *The Christian Herald* for the support of the children orphaned in the India famine were taking definite shape. The response to the appeal had been so generous that he had sent a guarantee to the missionaries for the support of 5,000 orphans, and had promised to send a remittance of

$25,000 regularly at intervals of four months, making in all nine payments, $225,000, during three years. Such a guarantee was necessary, otherwise the missionaries would not have felt justified in keeping under their roofs children for whose maintenance no one was responsible.

In the selection the denominational preferences of the foster-parents of the children were respected. The selection was made by the Interdenominational Missionary Committee in India. A map was published in *The Christian Herald* showing the location of the orphanages and giving a classified list according to denominations of the group in each. The group included Baptist, Christian Alliance, Disciples, Lutheran, Congregational, Protestant Episcopal, Methodist Episcopal, Wesleyan Methodist, and Presbyterian. In all there were thirty-eight famine orphan stations.

Later a pamphlet was published on the India orphan work which gave the practical results as witnessed by the missionaries who were in charge. Dr. Klopsch prefaced this pamphlet by a personal letter, as he called it. The letter, which was thoroughly characteristic of the man, was as follows:

A PERSONAL LETTER FROM DR. KLOPSCH

AUGUST 10, 1903.

DEAR FRIEND:

The India Famine Orphan Work, in which you and I are jointly and deeply interested, is the most glorious and most promising missionary effort of the Twentieth Century. It is surely a divinely ordained work, destined to do more for the ingathering of India's three hundred millions than could possibly have been devised by mere human agency.

These 5,400 native dusky boys and girls, reared under Christian influences, and trained for Christian helpfulness, outrank two to one in point of numbers, all the Christian missionaries now operating in India. When they take their places, as soon they must, among the mighty agencies for good among their own people, they will influence countless thousands whose ears would remain forever closed to foreign preaching of the Word.

Let us unitedly bear the burden for another two years, and then, having sowed the seed the Lord put it in our hearts to sow, leave the rest to the God of the harvest, who will surely bring to glorious fruition the work we have constantly had in view.

May the Lord graciously incline your heart to a continuance of this beneficent work, and at last crown you for the share of the burden which, in His Name, you have so bravely borne.

Numbers 6: 24, 25, 26.

Wm. Mopsch

At the same time *The Christian Herald* published an article entitled, "India's Children Are Her Hope." This article stated that cheering and hopeful news continued to come from India of the results of the magnificent work being done there among the orphans. The missionaries were delighted with the opportunity afforded them of caring for the children and educating them in the Christian faith; and the children were showing wonderful intelligence, and not only availing themselves of the educational facilities placed within their reach, but were giving themselves to Christ with a true and sincere consecration. Many instances were given of the progress made by the children. The reports regarding the orphan girls were in particular encouraging. Miss S. S. Gardner, secretary of the India work of the Woman's Union Missionary Society, who visited the United States in 1903, reported excellent progress. Regarding the women she wrote:

There are 140 millions of women in India who can neither read nor write, so they cannot be approached with the written word. Forty millions of these are shut up in the zenanas. Twenty-seven millions of them are widows, and the only way to reach them is through the agency of their own sex. The few foreign missionaries cannot of course touch the fringe of this great mass of women; it can only be through their own Christian sisters, and India's Christian women must be trained and educated to meet this great responsibility.

The work of the women, since it does not include public preaching, is necessarily more in the line of teaching, and is largely made up of Bible teaching in the zenanas and in Hindu and Mohammedan day schools. In villages where they can gather large numbers of women together it is more nearly allied to preaching, — is purely evangelistic. They do much of the work in Christian boarding and day schools as teachers, matrons and general supervisors. We wish to train the children not only for teachers but for leaders. We must bring to the front those who will be able to take places of responsibility, and be able to organize and to carry out schemes for service among their fellow countrywomen. The writer has under her charge two schools, one for primary and one for the higher education of the Christian girls and women, and there have been notable results from both. Twelve hundred Hindu girls gathered in day schools in every part of the city of Calcutta are nearly all taught by teachers educated or trained in one or the other of these schools. The teachers in the schools thus are old pupils.

Industrial training formed an important work of the orphanages. An item of news a couple of years

later by Mrs. Aldrich, who with her husband, the
Rev. Floyd Aldrich, had charge of the Methodist
Episcopal mission at Narsinghpur, was the announcement of the marriage of seven young men who had
been trained and educated at the mission. Two of
them were expert shoemakers, one was a carpenter,
and another an overseer.

The Rev. H. Huizinga wrote especially of the
earnest desire on the part of the boys to learn trades.
There was a time when boys regarded mechanical
work as degrading. However, they were realizing
that a boy who knew how to make something or do
something was more independent than he who knew
nothing but the tilling of the land. When Mr.
Huizinga announced that he could take a few more
boys in the industrial department nearly thirty
offered themselves, and he already had fifty-two at
work. The practical spirit of the boys was shown
by the fact that the majority of them wanted to
learn to be shoemakers.

Miss Greene, at Phalera, gave an equally encouraging report of the girls. They were turning out beautiful laces and embroidery, which commanded a ready
sale, and were weaving cloth and blankets. Miss
Anderson, of Pasrur, gave similar testimony. She
wrote that girls who were utterly ignorant of the
commonest duties could sew, spin, and do other
kinds of work besides keeping their houses orderly
and neat. Miss Anderson added, "I have engaged in
the course of my life in many kinds of mission work,
but I have never done anything for the Master that
I have enjoyed so much, nor anything that has been

so fruitful of results, as this work among the famine
children."

This was the testimony also of other missionaries. They on their side faithfully fulfilled their
promises and patiently and tirelessly devoted themselves to the training and teaching of the famine
waifs. Dr. Klopsch made these and similar encouraging reports the basis for extending the work of
supporting orphans somewhat beyond the period
which was originally contemplated. The support which was originally pledged for one year, and
then for three years, was extended to seven years,
the understanding being that as the children grew
up and became self-supporting, or married, or died,
the demand on the fund should gradually diminish.
At the maximum of the movement there were fifty-
five hundred orphans under support. In all, over
$557,000 was sent to India for famine orphan sup-
port. At the time of Dr. Klopsch's death there
were on the lists about four hundred India orphans,
the annual allowance for whom was remitted at regular periods to the mission committee at Bombay.

Tributes to the orphan work came year after year
from the missionaries and from officials of the Indian
Government as well as from numerous travelers.

The Irish Presbyterian India Mission, which was
included in the sphere of Dr. Klopsch's orphanage
work, adopted a special resolution placing on record
its deep sense of the obligation to their warm-hearted
and noble friends in America, and submitted to them
through Dr. Klopsch and *The Christian Herald* the
expression of their sincere and heartfelt thanks.

"The love that has prompted the generous help accorded since the great famine," said the resolution, "serves as a link to bind in the bonds of Christian fellowship the three countries of America, India, and Ireland, and in thus overstepping all international distinctions it reflects the love divine."

The Rev. John Bancroft Devins, in his trip around the world in 1904, visited the orphanages wholly or partly supported by *The Christian Herald* Interdenominational Committee. He wrote very full descriptions of what he saw, and his accounts gave much satisfaction to the Christian people of the United States who were contributing to the support of the orphanages. The work was thus summed up by Dr. Devins:

The feature of *The Christian Herald's* many actions which has impressed itself most deeply upon the minds of all classes in India, English officials, Christian missionaries, Indian gentlemen, and the orphans themselves, is this — life has been saved and then maintained. Sentiment may be enlisted in saving lives, but principle is needed to enable the work to be effective. The conclusion which I have reached after nearly three months in India, in which time thousands of *Christian Herald* orphans were visited and reports received from many hundreds of those whom I could not visit, is:

Five thousand children have been saved from suffering and starvation; they are being maintained at slight expense, with sanitary surroundings, and they are being trained under influences which will inevitably lead most of them into Christian life and character; further a bond of sympathy, humane and divine, has been formed between patron and beneficiary, as helpful to the former as to the latter.

When Dr. Devins was having an audience in the Government House in Calcutta, the private secretary

to Lord Curzon, the Viceroy, remarked as he read
a letter of introduction from Dr. Klopsch:

"Well, you know what we think of Dr. Klopsch
and *The Christian Herald's* work for the famine
orphans of India. The Kaiser-i-Hind medal just
sent to him is the best evidence of our appreciation
that we can give."

This was true. In the various orders conferred
by King Edward to mark the New Year of 1904,
and to recognize distinguished services, the Kaiser-
i-Hind medal of the first-class was conferred upon
Dr. Klopsch in recognition of the work he had done
in behalf of the famine sufferers of India. This was
the official statement. It was a fitting acknowledgment of his work, and was appreciated not only
by Dr. Klopsch, but by the many thousands who
through his instrumentality had been enabled to extend the helping hand to India's suffering people,
and who felt that in the recognition extended him
they, too, were recognized.

CHAPTER VII

SUCCOR FOR STRICKEN CUBA

STRUGGLES TO FREE THE MOST BEAUTIFUL ISLAND — GOMEZ AND MACEO — BURNING CANE FIELDS — WEYLER'S RECONCENTRATION ORDER — AN EYE-WITNESS' ACCOUNT OF THE MISERY — WAR'S DESOLATION — VISITS TO THE PRISON CAMPS — SENTIMENT IN THE UNITED STATES — PRESIDENT MCKIN-LEY'S CHRISTMAS APPEAL — DR. KLOPSCH ON THE RELIEF COMMITTEE — HIS TRIP TO HAVANA — AN EXAMPLE OF HIS METHODS — SILENT SUFFERERS — GEN. FITZHUGH LEE — THE PRESIDENT'S APPRECIATION.

WHEN Columbus in his voyages of discovery first saw the shores of Cuba, he called it the most beautiful island that the eyes of man ever beheld. Such is Cuba as nature made it, a tropical paradise. But for centuries Cuba was the victim of misgovernment. Its people though bound by many ties of common blood to Spain were in almost constant revolt, either open or concealed, against the misrule of the mother country.

Free Cuba was the aspiration of nearly all native-born Cubans, whether they were of Spanish parentage or of African blood. A struggle was waged from 1868 to 1878, known as the "Ten Years War," whose avowed purpose was independence. Spain after finally quelling this insurrection made efforts to provide better government which would satisfy the Cubans, but these efforts were not successful.

In 1895 there was another uprising headed by the poet Marti. At first it was thought that this was confined only to the eastern part of the island, but within a year it had spread from one end to the other, that is from Santiago in the east to Pinar del Rio in the west. It had at its head two men of genuine military ability and leadership, who had been concerned in the "Ten Years War." They were Maximo Gomez, who was of Spanish blood, and Antonio Maceo, who was of the negro race, which comprises about one-third the entire population.

Both Gomez and Maceo knew that by war under ordinary conditions, Spain in the end would be the victor, for she had an army which was constantly recruited and had the means of regular military operations. The insurgents could and did organize an army of a certain kind, but in any circumstances it could never be made a fully organized military body. So guerrilla warfare was the natural mode of making what proved to be the final, and through the intervention of the United States, the successful struggle for independence.

Destruction of property was the chief means which Gomez and Maceo invoked. They proposed to make Cuba worthless to Spain. The central and eastern sections of the island are composed of vast sugar plantations. The western end is made up largely of tobacco farms. By destroying the plantations, many of which were owned by Spaniards, and some by Americans, Gomez and Maceo intended to prove that the only hope for the future was in Spain giving up her dominion. After a year or two one of the most common sights in the island was to see the red flames sweeping over the cane fields like a prairie fire.

So long as Spain claimed sovereignty, it was her duty to protect the property of her own subjects and of foreigners. The army, which was thrown into Cuba from time to time, was supposed to be employed as much for this purpose as in military operations against the insurgents, but after a while it was discovered that the troops themselves often engaged in the destruction of plantations, particularly if these were owned by Cubans who sympathized with the insurrection. It was not an unusual thing for the insurgents to be burning the cane fields on one side of a plantation, while the troops were setting fire to the other side.

Before the insurrection had progressed very far, Spain sent out General Valeriano Weyler as Captain-General. The Captain-General in Cuba was both the military commander and the head of civil administration. General Weyler took vigorous steps which he claimed were justifiable to end the insurrection.

It was apparent that the country people of Cuba, who were laborers on the sugar plantations, and who often had their own little farms, were for the most part in sympathy with the insurrection. They were not, however, filled with the military spirit, and from their quiet nature were usually described as *pacificos*. The majority of them were non-combatants.

General Weyler held that whether actually engaged in the insurrection or not, by their presence in the country they afforded aid to the insurgents. Therefore he issued an order, known as the "reconcentration order," bringing them into the towns and cities in what were military camps. As a military measure probably this order would not be questioned by military commanders anywhere engaged in war. But its effect, by herding the *pacificos* in camps, and really under guard, was to make them military prisoners. Everywhere that civilization prevails it is recognized that prisoners of war are entitled to be fed and clothed. This was what General Weyler did not do, either from indifference or through inability. The towns and cities were filled with these country people, who became known as the *reconcentrados*. They had no means of subsistence except such as was doled out to them by charity or by the local authorities.

In time this concentration, and the general destruction throughout the island, began to tell fearfully on the people. Hunger and fever took them off by the thousands. Indignation was felt in the United States at these conditions, yet not much was known about the actual facts. It was claimed that the accounts of suffering were very much exaggerated, and that the people as a whole were as well off as the people of any country in which war raged. At this time I went to Cuba in connection with my profession, as a newspaper correspondent. The impression made on me was described in letters to American newspapers. Some extracts will show the real conditions. A letter from Union in the Province of Matanzas among other things gave this description of rural Cuba:

Miseria is the disease that afflicts rural Cuba. The physicians who attend the dying *reconcentrados* in the towns coined the term. They had no word comprehensive enough to describe the loss of lives from hunger, exposure and lack of care; so they called it *miseria*. A majority of the burial certificates now give this as the cause of death. *Miseria* is simply misery. It is misery that has depopulated the concentration settlements, and it is misery that throws a shadow over the country districts. The country, like its people, is dying from lack of nourishment.

Union, in the old times, was one of the most attractive of Cuban villages. It might still be called attractive if there were inhabitants enough in it to give an appearance of life. The town has suffered destruction. It is desolate, but the desolation is not that of ruin. The buildings are not blackened walls or grass-grown ash heaps, as in other places. Nothing ails the place but lonesomeness. And it is not as bad here as elsewhere, for the fine sugar plantation *Conchita*, close by, has some cane fields which are not charred, and the mill is able to do a little grinding. The streets are clean, many of the cottages are pretty, and look as though the occupants were once prosperous. Even the *reconcentrados* are housed with something like comfort in a row of huts along the railroad track. They are few in numbers. To-day they hug their hearthstones closely if a bit of burning charcoal can be called a hearthstone. The children who come out to beg shiver in their rags, for a cold wind from the north has brought with it a sleety rain, and they are poorly fitted to stand such exposure. Old clothes would not go amiss here. But the *reconcentrados* in Union are not exhibiting their misery, and they remain in their huts. I noticed, as in concentration settlements, that the survivors are mostly blacks. They have withstood the policy of extermination better than the whites.

Union is like other towns. It had resources enough to live off itself for awhile. Those resources are nearing exhaustion. The country from which it should draw support has nothing to yield. On one side, toward Havana, are the burned cane lands. In the other direction, toward Matanzas and Cienfuegoes, barren fields, with neither cattle nor men, only the tall palm trees to break the solitude of nature. Coming in from the latter direction I have been impressed for the hundredth time with the absence of even the signs of life. The buzzards have almost ceased to circle over the fields. Nothing is left for them. Had a few hundred of the *reconcentrados* been put back in the field, allowed to rebuild their *bohios* or palm huts, been given seed and encouraged to exert what strength remained to them in cultivating the land, the aspect of the country would have been different. This was not done, and it is useless to speculate on what might have been the beneficial result on the economic conditions of the island. This phase of the subject has now to be studied with reference to the town communities. They are reaching the point where the sterilization of the country around them is having its natural effect. I have taken Union as an illustration because the conditions could be shown with less exhibition of visible and harassing distress than in most of the other towns visited.

Another letter told of the devastation of the beautiful country around Havana:

The country around Havana bears silent witness to the existence of war. Leaving the railroad station at Marianao a carriage was taken and the road followed, which gave a fine view of the handsome villas of wealthy citizens of Havana. Only a few minutes were required to reach the edge of the village. A couple of pickets were stationed there. *Paseo?* one of them asked. Yes, the American gentlemen were going for a pleasure drive, and they were allowed to pass without a military permit. Further on another picket insisted on having an umbrella handed out for his inspection. He was suspicious that it might be munitions of war.

Every phase of ruin was seen along that road, from the blackened ashes that yet smoldered to the roofless walls of once stately homes. Glancing down the avenues of royal palms and in the groves of mangoes and Indian laurels, we would see these ruined houses. In some the work of destruction was only half done. The doors and windows would be gaping wide open, without a sign of life about the places. Commonly, though, the houses would be unroofed, and the pillars and columns would be a crumbled mass. Sometimes a single wall would be standing. The palm-thatched huts along the wayside had been spared, and this made the route contrast with the desolation back from the highway, among the palms and mangoes, more striking. On some of the estates the trees and hedges had been cut.

A description of the prison camps in which the *reconcentrados* were herded was given in a letter from Matanzas:

We had the first sight of an extensive camp of *pacificos* at Campo Florido, which is an hour's distance from Havana. Hundreds of palm huts were spread out on either side of the railroad tracks. A barbed wire fence, eight feet high, was stretched along the outskirts of the settlement. Just outside the fence ran a deep ditch. On the knolls and hills were the *fortilinos*, or little forts, garrisoned and with sentinels on the lookout. Soldiers patrolled everywhere. Looking down among the huts, then at the barbed wire fence, the ditch, the soldiers occupying the commanding positions, it was no longer a mystery why the *pacificos* in the desperation of hunger did not break out into the open country. They would never get through that fence and across the ditch beyond the range of the guns. Those at Campo Florido were wandering aimlessly around within their pen like caged animals on exhibition.

At Juraco and other stations further glimpses were had of the *pacificos*. Smallpox has been very bad here, and no one cared to leave the train for a closer sight. The people were not the only things to be seen. I write of them as things, because under the present military policy they are not considered human beings. The other objects which excited attention along the route were the evidences of ruin — cane fields burned over, bare walls and chimneys of *ingenios* or sugar mills, heaps of ashes and blackened mortar, the absence of all signs of life except close to the stations and forts. Everywhere could be seen what seemed to be great bamboo bird cages. These were the houses of the people who tilled the soil. These houses had not been burned. Instead they were unroofed, the weather boarding, if it might be called that, taken off and the poles and rafters left. If peace ever comes they may be thatched with palm and again be habitable. But now they must shelter no one.

Matanzas is reached at last. We may not stop now to look out across the bay which has made it celebrated. There will be time enough later to hear of the lost trade and dead commerce of this Liverpool of the Antilles. We can easily understand that a splendid harbor cannot be filled with ships when the sugar they once carried away was this year only acres and acres of charred cane. But at present our course lays away from the harbor, through the narrow streets to Cascoro Hill. That is where most of the *pacificos* are located. It has been their home for months, and will be for those of them that survive for months to come. It is said to be the best settlement on the place for natural sanitary conditions, and also for supplies. Smallpox ran its course months ago, and having exhausted itself, is no longer to be feared. Some thousand of the *pacificos* have been sent into the country villages, which is worse for them, but better for those who remain. That is, they have a large town — Matanzas once had a population of 50,000 — in which to beg food, and there are fewer of them to be fed.

Hundreds of palm huts are on Cascoro Hill. They are built without order or regulation. All are alike inside. The gravel and dirt make the floor. Boards stretched along the sides serve for tables and for beds. A few have chairs, others simply rough benches. The household effects are usually a few old clothes in the corner. Two or three tin pans are the cooking utensils, which are seldom needed, because there is nothing to cook. The bedding is an old blanket or sheet spread over the boards. Sometimes a rude makeshift of a litter serves for a bed. Some of the huts have rough partitions, but many of them are single rooms. All show in their interior furnishings what would be called in the states abject poverty.

DR. AND MRS. KLOPSCH AT THE GRAVE OF THE *MAINE*
VICTIMS, HAVANA

RELIEF WORK AMONG THE CUBAN RECONCENTRADOS

A pause at the doorway of one of the huts was met with an invitation to come in. There was not room for all the visitors, but some crowded past the threshold. A young woman was rocking with a babe of six or seven months on her lap. She was intelligent and answered questions promptly. A boy, two or three years old, clad in nature's garb, stole up to her side. A girl of fifteen or sixteen drew a faded shawl across her shoulders, and, her modesty shielded, looked at the strangers. Through the opening of a partition we could see an aged woman raise herself from the litter on which she lay and peer out curiously. A man of thirty-five or forty sat on a stool and listened to what was asked. All he wanted, he said, was a chance to work in the fields and get something to eat.

The first question always asked of the *pacificos* was, "Have you had anything to eat to-day?" Sometimes they would say, "*Un poco*"—a little, but oftener the answer was, "*Nada, nada, nada*" — nothing, nothing, nothing.

And when asked about their houses in the country the invariable answer was: "*Los soldados la quemaron*" — the soldiers burned it.

Yet there were a few spots which escaped the ravages of war and were free from reconcentration camps. They were typical of the beauty of peaceful Cuba. One of these oases in the general desolation was thus described:

We had heard of the *ingenio* of Toledo. It is one of the sugar mills that has escaped destruction by either insurgents or Spanish troops. Looking across the miniature valleys and the verdured slopes of the hills, Toledo stood out to our view a picture of prosperity. Green cane fields formed a foreground for it, while groves of royal palms were grouped in the background. In the hollows were the *salvas*, or spreading elms, as these trees would be called in the states. There were also the mangoes, their branches drooping under the burden of the ripening fruit. More than all these was the sight of life, men at work in the fields, oxen ploughing, and cattle grazing, all reminders of what Cuba was before war made it a desert.

The movement in the United States for intervention in Cuba became very strong when the suffering there and the measures of General Weyler were fully known. Every effort was made by President McKinley's administration to have Spain ameliorate the situation and thus avoid American intervention. Spain heeded the suggestions and a complete change in her Cuban policy was made. General Weyler was recalled, and General Blanco, an able soldier and a most patriotic Spaniard, who had previously been in Cuba, was made Captain-General. The demand of the insurgents for independence was met by the offer of a compromise, which was known as autonomy, or home-rule. Spain endeavored in good faith to put this system into operation, but the time had passed when it could prevail. Spain also sought to relieve the distress caused by the reconcentration policy.

It was soon evident that with the best intentions, and with a sincere purpose to ameliorate the condition of the population, Spain was unable to do it. The suffering at the door of the United States was too great to be longer allowed to continue without succor. President McKinley, in the Christmas season of 1897, therefore issued an appeal to the American people for money and supplies to be used in behalf of the starving Cubans. The responses to this appeal were swift and generous. *The Christian Herald*, through Dr. Klopsch, telegraphed to

the Secretary of State, John Sherman, tendering the
coöperation of the paper in any relief work to be
undertaken, and at the same time contributing a
thousand dollars to aid the relief at the outset. A
day or two later the managers of the Red Cross
Society in Washington held a conference with the
State Department officials, and immediately thereafter Assistant Secretary Adee, in behalf of the Government, proposed the appointment of a Central
or Executive Committee of Relief, to consist of
three gentlemen, under whose direction the movement should be conducted throughout the whole
country.

President McKinley indicated his desire that Dr.
Klopsch should be a member of this committee. It
was constituted with Stephen E. Barton, of the
American Red Cross, as Chairman; Charles A.
Schieren, of the New York Chamber of Commerce,
as Secretary and Treasurer; and Dr. Klopsch. This
committee held its first session in the Bible House,
New York, on January 3, 1898, and organized for
practical service. It was determined to invite the
coöperation of the various Chambers of Commerce
and Boards of Trade throughout the country and to
take all necessary steps to enlist the sympathies of
the entire nation.

The vigorous measures that were initiated under
Dr. Klopsch's leadership at once brought results.
Contributions came pouring in to the relief fund.
Supplies were obtained, and the aid to the sick and
dying of Cuba was immediate. Dwight L. Moody
sent a stirring message and the great army of *Chris-*

tian Herald readers began swelling the list of contributions.

The Government of the United States designated the *Fern*, one of the naval vessels, to carry the cargo of food, and other supplies were sent by the regular vessels. General Fitzhugh Lee, the American Consul-General, who had been unremitting in his efforts to make the American people understand the extent of the suffering, sent appreciative words and gave further information of the distribution of the relief and of the pressing needs.

When the relief movement was at its height, came the destruction of the United States Cruiser *Maine* in the Havana Harbor. While it was felt that this event was sure to lead to war, those who were engaged in the relief work did not think that they should for that reason pause. Dr. Klopsch decided to go to Havana to see for himself the situation. He arrived in March and at once sent a cablegram giving the conditions as he found them, and showing what was necessary. He was accompanied by Mrs. Klopsch. They saw sights right in Havana that touched them as human hearts are rarely touched.

It was during this visit that I first met Dr. Klopsch. I had been in Cuba for a year or more and was pretty well acquainted with the conditions in all parts of the island. The evening of his arrival, Mr. E. R. Johnstone, the correspondent of the Associated Press, introduced me to him at the Inglaterra Hotel. He at once began asking incisive questions. I was somewhat out of patience with red-tape methods of relief, which I thought were too much in evidence.

STARVING CUBANS BEGGING FOOD OF A U. S. WARSHIP
IN HAVANA HARBOR

CONVALESCENT SOLDIERS AT THE CHILDREN'S HOME
MONT–LAWN

I told Dr. Klopsch that at Matanzas, fifty-five miles away, a little ready money at that time would be worth more than thousands of dollars later. I also gave him a description of the conditions at the town of Sagua-la-Grande, two hundred miles in the interior.

He asked me if I knew proper persons at those points who could be entrusted with a small sum. I replied that Mr. Brice, the Consul at Matanzas, and Captain Barker, the Consul at Sagua-la-Grande, would be the proper persons. Then Dr. Klopsch quietly asked how soon a check could be got to them. I explained that the train which left Havana at six o'clock the following morning reached Matanzas in two hours and arrived at Sagua between five and six in the evening. Then he inquired if I could find a trustworthy messenger. That was easily done. In response to further inquiries I mentioned a thousand dollars for each place as a sum which would do vast good, but said that a little more might be necessary at Sagua. Dr. Klopsch thereupon wrote a check for one thousand dollars for the Consul at Matanzas, and for two thousand dollars for the Consul at Sagua.

At ten o'clock the next morning came a telegram from the Consul at Matanzas sending thanks for the check. At seven the same evening came a telegram from the Consul at Sagua expressing his thanks. Later reports from them by mail showed how greatly the timely assistance had been to them in their relief work.

This incident gave me an insight into Dr. Klopsch's

methods. All he ever wanted was to know that the funds which were collected by him for charitable purposes were going into the right hands and would be used promptly. Once that was known he never hesitated to act.

Dr. Klopsch was in frequent conference with General Fitzhugh Lee and other Americans in Havana and also with some of the Spanish officials, who were coöperating in the relief work. No feature of the suffering seemed to escape him. One day I told him of "the silent sufferers." These were people who either had been rich or in moderate circumstances, but who, on account of the insurrection, had had all their means cut off. They had pledged and pawned about everything for which a dollar could be obtained. Their situation in life was such that a public confession of their poverty was impossible, yet they, like the starving *reconcentrados*, were in need of aid, and many of them were almost on the verge of starvation. The majority of these silent sufferers were Cuban families, but there were some Spaniards. Some bore names well known in Cuban history.

Dr. Klopsch inquired as to how they could be succored without wounding their sensibilities. I explained that a list had already been prepared, and that none of them would refuse relief if it came from the hands of those who understood the situation. Thereupon Dr. Klopsch wrote a check for a liberal amount which was placed in one of the Havana banks. A relief committee was formed, of which General Fitzhugh Lee, Mr. E. R. Johnstone, and

myself were members. A small weekly allowance was
made to the people on the list. Refugees in Florida
and in New York were also aided. This was continued until the war actually broke out, and at its
close, when there was still much suffering, the
balance which remained was distributed among the
most needy cases. Every dollar distributed in this
manner was receipted for, and one day in New
York when I showed Dr. Klopsch the names signed
to some of the receipts, he expressed his great satisfaction that persons of such prominence had been
willing to accept the aid in the spirit in which it
was given.

The orphans, of course, were among the objects of
his solicitude. General Fitzhugh Lee was specially
concerned about them. The relief contributions
therefore made provision for aiding several orphanages and this support was continued after the close
of the war and the establishment of the American
military authority.

Dr. Klopsch remained in Cuba long enough to
understand thoroughly the situation. He saw many
of the consuls and received from them personal
confirmation of the good purpose to which the
relief funds and supplies were put. He also learned
from them much of the political situation, and
received many evidences of the gratitude of the
people of the stricken island.

In April Dr. Klopsch returned to the United States.
He went to Washington and reported to Second
Assistant Secretary of State Adee and to Judge
Day, the Assistant Secretary. Then he was sum-

moned to the White House and introduced by
President McKinley to the members of the Cabinet
and several United States Senators who were there.
He gave the President a very full report of the conditions and of the necessity for continuing the
succor of the *reconcentrados* up to the last moment.
President McKinley expressed his appreciation of
the work Dr. Klopsch had done and thereafter gave
him many evidences of confidence.

When Dr. Klopsch returned to the United States
it was clear that war with Spain was inevitable.
On his suggestion, however, the shipments of supplies were continued up to the very last moment
until the Cuban ports were closed and all transportation stopped.

Then came the actual war, the American military
occupation, and the establishment of the Cuban
Republic.   In all the events from 1897 to the raising
of the flag of Free Cuba, there is no brighter page
than the record of Dr. Klopsch in relieving the
starving *reconcentrados* and alleviating the wide-
spread distress of Cubans of all classes.

CHAPTER VIII

FINLAND AND SWEDEN

FAMINE gripped the far frozen north of Europe in the winter of 1902–03. Both Finland and Sweden and a smaller section of Norway were affected.

There is no more interesting country in the world than Finland, bordering on the Baltic Sea and lying under the Arctic Circle. It covers an area equal to that of New England, New York, and Pennsylvania combined, and has a population of 2,500,000, including the Laplanders. The country is noted for the rocky islets on the coast and for the network of lakes, which are also dotted with islands. Much of the surface is of highlands, and also of marshes, while there are magnificent forests. It follows that farming, fishing, and forestry form the principal occupations of the large majority of the inhabitants.

The rigorous climate of Finland has produced a most vigorous people. The Finnish civilization is

a highly developed one, and the country's part in
history has been that of a sturdy race. It by some
may be considered evidence of progress that Finland is the first country in the world to permit
women to sit in the parliament or legislative body
and to provide for woman suffrage.

The cereal crops, rye, oats, and barley are the chief
dependence of the inhabitants of Finland for support. A little wheat is raised in the southwest part
and there is some corn. This is planted and matures
in the period of seven weeks in the very short and
hot summer. The chief crop is barley, which is raised
as far north as 69° north latitude on the shores of
Lake Inari.

Frost and flood are the worst enemies to the
Finnish farmers. Both are destructive to the crops,
on which they must depend. Sometimes also the
fisheries are a failure. All these unfortunate circumstances combined in the winter of 1902–03
to bring distress to large sections of the country.
At Christmas time, when the rest of the world was
rejoicing in plenty, 400,000 of the Finnish peasants
and farmers were suffering for food. Icy blasts
that meant death to the unprotected swept down
from the Arctic. Farms, forests, valleys, and rivers, all alike were sheeted in snow and ice and
there was not food for the people.

Finland is divided into eight provinces or governments, the most northerly of which, that of Uleaborg, comprises half the country, and it was in this
large territory and in a lesser degree in the provinces
immediately to the south of it, Vasa to the west with

a long coast-line on the Gulf of Bothnia, and Kuopio to the east bordering on Russia, that the ravages of the famine were mainly felt. Uleaborg was the worst sufferer, lacking as it did railway facilities to provide the means of distribution.

Dr. Klopsch soon knew of the suffering. A Finland Relief Committee in New York sought his coöperation. Count Andre Bobrinskoy, who had appreciated *The Christian Herald's* relief work for the Russian people in the famine of 1892, wrote to him from St. Petersburg that the distress was acute and wide-spread and that want was almost universal, the failure of the harvest having been more complete than that of 1867. Confirmatory information came from officials at Helsingfors and at Uleaborg.

There were 300,000 Finns in the United States, immigrants who had left their native land within a period of a few years. Most of them were quite poor, but they were industrious and were making good American citizens. They were sending the bulk of their scanty savings home to the still poorer ones in Finland.

"America can help," said Dr. Klopsch, and at once he proceeded to put the machinery of help in operation. Subscriptions were started by *The Christian Herald* and a remittance of $5,000 was cabled to the Finnish committee at Helsingfors. This was shortly followed by a second cable remittance. President Roosevelt was one of the first to subscribe to the Finnish fund. In a letter to Dr. Klopsch, Secretary George B. Cortelyou expressed the Presi-

dent's gratification at having the opportunity of contributing to the relief of the suffering, and enclosed
the President's contribution to *The Christian Herald*
Famine Fund, a check for $100. The fund by this
time exceeded $20,000. As usual the bulk of it was
made up of small subscriptions, — dimes, dollars and
upward to $10.

Dr. Klopsch, when the machinery of relief, so far
as the contributions were concerned, was in full operation, decided to make a trip himself to the heart of
the famine land, inspect the relief work and coöperate
with the Finnish Central Relief Committee and the
Lutheran pastors with whom he had been in communication. It was a midwinter mission of personal
service in pursuance of his fixed policy of personally
carrying out as far as possible the wishes of those
who had undertaken through *The Christian Herald*
the relief movement.

In the meantime reports continued to come of the
good the fund was doing and of the need for more
help. There was also much further information
about the sturdy Finnish people and their endurance
under suffering. At this period *The Christian Herald* republished the poem, "Peasant Paavo's Faith
in God," by the famous Finnish poet, Runeberg. It
is a wonderful picture which applies to the Finnish
peasant of all times, and is worthy of a permanent
place in the history of Finland's famines.

Another famous Finnish poet was Elias Lönnrot.
In the far remote regions, three quarters of a century
previously he had traveled around, dropping into
the huts of peasants, sitting by the fireside of the

2,000 SCHOOL-CHILDREN OF ULEABORG, FINLAND, SINGING TO WELCOME *THE CHRISTIAN HERALD RELIEF PARTY*

aged, rowing on the lakes with the fishermen, and following the flocks with the shepherds. He was collecting the poems circulating by word of mouth among the Finnish people. There were very few who then could sing them, and there was fear that they would be lost entirely. The poems thus collected by Lönnrot on these journeys he put together and in 1835 they were published by the Finnish Literary Society, under the name *Kalevala*. It contained the archæology of the Finnish people, the deepest wisdom and experience of life, the comprehension of the origin of things and of the mysteries of nature, the entire folk-lore of the nation, all described in most fascinating poetry.

A new morning dawned for the Finnish people and its literature. The civilized world soon recognized that living in the icy regions of Europe there was a nation which had contributed a precious pearl to the world's literature. Lönnrot continued his journeys, and his example was followed by others, and a revised edition of the *Kalevala* was published in the mature form of an epic. As a reward for his great accomplishment in the field of Finnish literature Lönnrot was elected professor of the Finnish language and literature at the University of Helsingfors in 1853; and he died in 1854 at the age of eighty-two. Such was the poetic source which Runeberg drew upon for his poem.

Dr. Klopsch in his journey went first to St. Petersburg. There he found that the Czar, moved by the benevolent attitude of the American people toward the suffering Finnish peasants, had personally interested himself in organizing relief work under the direction of the Imperial Government. It was a vast scheme, which was carried out later, but until after the melting of the snows and the subsidence of the spring floods work of this character could not be made effective. During the intervening weeks the great question was still to supply the people with the food necessary to sustain life.

Dr. Klopsch was accompanied by Mr. Gilson Willetts, a well-known newspaper writer. They proceeded by rail from St. Petersburg to Helsingfors. Thence the journey was made through Finland on sledges to the stricken districts. This was in March. At once cables began to come to *The Christian Herald* giving the leading incidents of the journey, the conditions found, and the need for more money. These statements were always met with prompt remittances by cable.

An incident, of many similar ones, was described by Mr. Willetts in one of the cables. Under date of March 14, 1903, he telegraphed from Uleaborg as follows:

"Five thousand persons, including two thousand school children, surrounded *The Christian Herald* party here today, bringing tributes of flowers and song as expression of gratitude for America's loving sympathy for Finland in her time of trouble. Everywhere we were received with demonstrations of welcome and gladness, and the joy of the Finnish people found expression in song. Our parting serenade at Helsingfors station when we left for the interior was particularly touching. The world's most famous male chorus sang, and five thousand Finlanders, men and women, joined in the ovation and tribute to Christian America. They literally covered our party with flowers."

Later on, March 17th, came a cable announcing the arrival of the party at the border of Sweden. The cable gave in brief terms a summary of the journey. It was as follows:

"Dr. Klopsch, with the *Christian Herald*-Finland relief expedition, today crossed the Swedish frontier from Tornea, Finland, to this place, having driven from Uleaborg by sledges.

"Throughout the entire journey of the expedition from Helsingfors to Tornea on the Finnish boundary line, its progress was marked by extraordinary demonstrations, the people welcoming the travelers with song, poetry, oratory and tributes of beautiful flowers to express their heart-felt appreciation of the generosity of the American people in helping Finland in her time of need.

"In three weeks the expedition has traversed the greater part of northern Finland by sledges, and practically every important center of distress north and east of Helsingfors, being the first party of Americans who have ever journeyed through northern and eastern Finland in winter. Finland's gratitude for American help is universal."

A most vivid and illuminating account of the story came later from the pen of Dr. Klopsch himself. Some extracts from it are necessary in order to show the incidents of the journey and the relief that was extended, but since the famine scenes are now long past, their harrowing details are as far as possible omitted.

Dr. Klopsch, telling of the arrival at Helsingfors and his interviews with the Central Relief Committee there, gave an explanation of the methods of the Committee, which after its interview with him adopted a vote of thanks to the American people. Dr. J. N. Reuter, a professor at the University, was designated to accompany the party on the tour of inspection. Two days were spent in making the necessary preparations. Dr. Klopsch thus describes the start for the frozen north:

"The snow was twenty inches deep and what the weather might be no one could foretell with any degree of accuracy. So we provided fur coats, mittens, storm caps, boots and rubbers, and laid in a stock of provisions sufficient to meet the requirements of four men for at least two weeks. Arrangements were made by wire for three sledges at Idensalmi, the last railway station. All our trunks were sent to Stockholm, and each of us started out with only one suit of clothing so as to reduce to a minimum the baggage to be carried.

"When we arrived at Helsingfors station a delightful surprise awaited us. The committee and a vast host of people had gathered to see us off. Fifty young ladies, each bearing a tiny bouquet with the stems held in a small colored glass receptacle with a wire collar, the end of which was shaped into a hook, were in the center of the station; and they advanced and fastened the hooks into my overcoat, literally covering my chest with flowers. They adorned me in accord with the custom of manifesting appreciation in vogue in Finland, and much to my personal embarrassment I was led to the platform. The moment I arrived the Helsingfors male chorus, said to be the finest in Europe, began to sing. After they

DR. KLOPSCH AND THE FINNISH RELIEF COMMITTEE IN SESSION IN HELSINGFORS

had sung three or four times I addressed the gathering, telling them that while I felt personally unworthy of this demonstration, I accepted it as intended for the American people, to whom I would faithfully report this manifestation of gratitude and appreciation. Then the male chorus sang the Finnish national air, and while they were yet singing and the people shouting 'God bless you,' the train drew out of the station and we were on our way to the famine fields in the interior."

At the various stops along the route to Idensalmi, they saw many evidences of suffering from hunger, and made arrangements for such relief as could be afforded.

"At Idensalmi," wrote Dr. Klopsch, "we experimented somewhat with snowshoes. If we could get accustomed to their use it would greatly facilitate our reaching homes which otherwise might prove inaccessible. We practiced half an hour and at the conclusion of our efforts all we could say was that we had not fallen nor had we made any progress. We must have been very awkward, for we completely failed in our attempts, although children as young as five glided by us with the swiftness of a bird. Darkness having set in we gave it up for once and for all.

"At six in the morning the world about us suddenly became musical. Some young farmers in the neighborhood had recently united and had formed a brass band. They wished to express their thanks to their American friends for what was being done for the poor of their country, and as they lacked eloquence they substituted a generous portion of the best music at their command.

"From Idensalmi we traveled twenty-two miles

by sledge to the post house at Hirvijarvi, stopping here and there on the way to visit the cottagers within sight from the road. Extreme poverty was everywhere prevalent. Most of the people visited belonged to the class known as tenant farmers. They lease the land on which their cottages are erected and pay the yearly rental in ten, twenty, or thirty, or more days' work on the farm of the owner. As a rule they ply a trade in addition to caring for their own garden, and thus in prosperous times eke out a comfortable existence. At a cobbler's home we found an old lady of seventy sick with fever, and four little children. The mother was out seeking work or food. Not a loaf of bread in the house and not a drop of milk or nourishment of any kind visible. The patient could not rise from her bed. The children looked swollen in body and face, distended as the result of eating innutritious and indigestible food. In this, as in every case, the visitors left bread and of their personal means enough money to tide the sufferers over their immediate requirements.

"The Finns are not a complaining people and are very reticent about their own affairs. It would never occur to them to tell an outsider that their stock of bread was exhausted or that they had last week killed their cow because there was no fodder to keep it alive, or that they had so long been without meat and vegetables as to have almost forgotten the taste of them. We discovered the best way of securing information from Finns concerning their own condition is never to ask them about themselves, but always about their neighbors. They will eloquently plead their neighbors' case, but they cannot beg for themselves, for with most of them it is harder to beg than to die.

"Early in the afternoon we reached Paisuva and

stopped to rest at a farmhouse. The farmer, a very pious man, gladly received us and made us feel quite at home. He was as hospitable as his means permitted. His house and his table were at our disposal. Lack of sleep and much traveling had made us tired. He took us into the parlor, which was also his bed-room. Lately it had pleased Providence to bereave him. A child of ten had been taken, and over the bed hung a photograph of the dead child on its bier with father and mother looking at the remains of their beloved dead. Ghastly as the picture appeared to us, dear it was to him; it reminded him of the beloved one waiting for him at the celestial gates. We stepped over to the bed and looked at it. His eyes were in the same direction. They were wet with tears. We said nothing, but we each felt that to him that picture was sacred. After serving us with delicious coffee and home-made cakes, he harnessed up his own horses in order to give ours a rest and took us to another village."

Continuing the story of the journey Dr. Klopsch wrote:

"After traveling all day in sledges we arrived at Kajani at 6.30 in the evening, wiping our feet carefully on the pine branches which took the place of rugs at the front door of every Finnish country home. We entered the hut, took off our rubbers — everybody wears rubbers here — hung up our furs, and found four rooms neatly furnished, all ready for our occupancy.

"A host of people had gathered to welcome us, according to Finland's custom, with song and flowers. The latter consisted of a tiny bouquet, but the former was very abundant and very touching. I addressed them in a few words, telling them of the generous hearted Christian people across the great deep, who, as descendants of Europe, gladly responded to every cry for help from the motherland, and cheerfully contributed to the needs of the old folks at home.   Professor Reuter, who acted as interpreter, translated my remarks into Finnish.

"A meal in Finland differs greatly from a meal in America. It is specially adapted to the climate, and while very acceptable in Finland, would be impossible in our own country. As one enters the dining room he finds a table set and on it there is caviare, smoked salmon, bologna, herring, sardines, ham, choice pickles, and ponderous quantities of unsalted butter and spiced Swedish bread, baked like pilot bread as to size and crispness. This all constitutes what is generally known as 'smörgåsbord,' or bread-and-butter table. A stranger not acquainted with Finnish custom would be apt to make a meal of these delicacies, in which case a surprise would await him, for very soon the dishes are removed and a regular course dinner, beginning with soup and ending with desert, is served in regulation style, the cold dishes having been intended only as an appetizer. All of the courses are exceedingly rich, pastry being eaten with the soup, and everything else swims in prodigious quantities of fat. But all this is necessary in a climate like that of Finland, where the thermometer frequently falls to 30° below zero and a fall of 50° in the temperature in a single day is by no means an exceptional occurrence. In large hotels smörgåsbord is served on a side table; each guest, taking a plate, knife and fork, helps himself to whatever best suits his fancy and then retires to eat, either standing or sitting at the table where the dinner proper is to be served. The piety of the Finlanders, and I use this word so as to include both native Finns and those of Swedish descent, is frequently manifest at this time, when standing erect with hands clasped and heart bowed many say grace before, and fre-

MARKET–PLACE AT HELSINGFORS, FINLAND

DR. KLOPSCH AND THE FINNISH RELIEF COMMITTEE

quently after, meals regardless of how many others may be present."

Kajani was the very center of the famine district. There Dr. Klopsch and party remained some time, gathering much information from Pastor Wayrynen, the head of the Lutheran Church for the district. He escorted them to the neighboring villages and told them about the people. The son of a peasant, he had made his way through college and now ministered to the very class among whom he had spent his early days. He told of their simple life, their firm unwavering faith in God, their unswerving honesty, their utter unselfishness, and their readiness to share the last morsel of bread with a suffering neighbor. He particularly dwelt upon their abstinence from intoxicants. In the entire district, embracing 49,000 souls, there was but one tavern.

Pastor Wayrynen said that the Finns were so intensely and consistently religious that many a time when throughout the entire week heavy rains interfered with the gathering of the slim crop that had survived here and there the untimely snows, and Sunday's sun shone brightly and the cool dry breezes would invite an effort to save what might still be saved, the Finns steadfastly and almost without exception refused to do manual labor on the Lord's day, preferring to lose what was left rather than do anything their conscience could not approve.

His account of the second day at Kajani Dr. Klopsch continued as follows:

"The first thing I learned was the greeting customary in Finland on meeting one another in the

morning. The first one to speak says, 'Hyvaa-
paivaa,' which means, 'Good day,' and the other
responds reverently, 'Jumala antakoon,' or, 'God
grant it.' Three sledges started out that morning
from Kajani on their errand of mercy. One contained all the bread the local bakery could supply.
It was hot and aromatic when we received it, but
the chilling breezes soon rendered it as cold as its
surroundings. Our first stop was Kirkoaho, and
here we visited all the different cottages within the
radius of time and opportunity. Everywhere the
same signs of utter destitution confronted us, and
we could not fail to notice a universal condition of
nervousness begotten of a continuous feeling of
uncertainty concerning the next meal of black bread
and water. And here for the first time we met one
of the most touching sights we were thereafter frequently called upon to encounter. I refer to infants
extracting nourishment from 'sugar plums' made
of hunger-bread tied up in the corner of a napkin
and dipped in salt water. Mothers will understand
why some of us shed tears when we saw it.

"Driving from one cottage to another we met a
funeral cortege of sledges coming from the opposite
direction. The path across the snow was too narrow
to admit of our passing each other. The first sledge
bore a white ribbon which indicated the presence of
the dead. In this instance it was the body of a child,
a girl of eleven. Over the coffin, a strange looking
arrangement, were strewn pine branches. Our driver
hailed the other, saying that we were the Americans,
and the cortege was about to be obligingly directed
into the depths of the snow at the side of the road
when we insisted that the right of way should be
granted to the mourners, but owing to the narrowness
of the road this could not be accomplished without
upsetting both parties; so we all got out, unhar-

nessed the horses, and lifted the sledges around each other. Inside of ten minutes the funeral procession continued one way and we the other.

"At Jorma, the next village, after visiting several cottages, tired, weary and heart-sick, we turned back and reached the hotel long after darkness had set in, but two hours earlier than we had considered possible, which we effected by urging our drivers on to the utmost speed by the use of a few Finnish words that seemed to potently appeal to them. They meant 'hurry,' but they were backed by a word which meant a gratuity of 40 cents each. They said nothing, but hurried on and brought us home as quickly as the horses would travel. The Finns generally are a people of but few words. A country like theirs, long winter nights and eight months of deep snow with nothing visible for miles at a time but spectral and silent pine groves, is not conducive to vivacity of spirits and great loquacity. Then again the leathern skies all through the winter are apt to depress the spirits and make the people deliberate of both speech and action.

"While sad and distressing scenes abounded everywhere, many cottages contained contented and happy families kept busy and cheerful by home employments devised by those who had laid it upon their hearts to relieve the fearful suffering and to stay the relentless hand of death. Looms were being operated by the women, fishing nets made by the children, woodwork manufactured by the men; and suspended poles containing bread, — always baked in Finland flat with a large hole in the center, — gave evidence that industry made practicable by the thoughtfulness of those entrusted with relief operations was providing the staff of life for multitudes who but for these measures must long ere this have filled an untimely grave.

"At midnight we arrived at Ransila. The post house had only one room to spare. There were two beds. Two of us occupied these and two slept on the floor. The windows, sealed as usual, kept out even a suspicion of fresh air and the atmosphere consequently was almost intolerable. The next day we visited Saraisniemi, and here we met the worst destitution in all Finland. But in order to reach Uleaborg I must hasten on. We left Helsingfors March 2d, and it was March 13th when to our great joy we again saw railroad tracks at Laminka. Here an ovation awaited us. The public evening school had arranged a reception. The scholars, young men and women, all peasants, sang for us, and the principal made a very eulogistic address in German. He almost exhausted his vocabulary in search for fitting terms to express his gratitude to each and every contributor to the fund that had saved his people from death. I responded in an address in German, at first directed to the school and then to the principal, congratulating him on the mission to which he had evidently been providentially called. At 7.30 we took the train. A great host had gathered at the depot and song followed song until the train drew out, landing us at 8 o'clock in the evening safe and sound without a mishap, providentially preserved, at Uleaborg, the most northerly city of the world.

"That night in Uleaborg was a restful one. For the first time in two weeks we slept in real beds. Throughout the country districts of Finland they use what I designate as telescope beds. These beds resemble an extension dining table. When not in use the bed-clothes are doubled up and the bed itself is telescoped to one-third its natural size. As the Finns are rather short of stature, the beds when extended to full length are under-sized. The headboard is always toward the center of the room so that the feet are toward the wall."

Describing the events of the party's stay at Uleaborg, Dr. Klopsch wrote:

"The morning after we arrived we were as usual besieged by a small army of mendicants who piteously pleaded with tears in their eyes for help. To some cash relief was given, while others were referred to the exceptionally efficient provincial relief committee. Before leaving the hotel we were waited on by the Lutheran clergy of the city, who came to pay their respects and to assure us that America had afforded a 'never to be forgotten assistance to a patient, long-suffering, and honest people who will ever hold in grateful remembrance the practical manifestation of true Christian love of which they had been the appreciative recipients when almost overwhelmed with affliction which they had tried hard to bear without complaint and without publicity.'

"At noon there was a great gathering in the public square in front of the hotel. Word was sent me that I should hold myself in readiness for a tremendous public demonstration. The Mayor of the city welcomed me. Before us were 2,000 school children who had been marshaled into position to sing to the American visitors, the first ever known to have traversed Finland during the winter season and who had come as friends on an errand of mercy at a time when traveling in that country required some greater incentive than the quest for mere pleasure and recreation. In addition to the children, about 3,000 adults had assembled, so that there were fully 5,000 people confronting us. The precentor led the children, and they sang as though it seemed direct from the hearts. Then the Mayor addressed us in English and I replied in the same language, which

Dr. Reuter kindly interpreted to the audience.
The utmost enthusiasm prevailed.   Cheer after cheer
went up and America and the Americans were
applauded vociferously.   Then a few flowers were
presented by little girls, each of whom made a brief
address, which we of course could not understand,
but the meaning of which we recognized from the
eyes of the tiny orators."

Some time was spent by Dr. Klopsch in attending
to the details of the relief and listening to the reports
which were made.   In the afternoon of the same day
the party took the train to Kemi, the most northerly
railway station in Finland and from which sledges
were again employed to take them to Tornea at the
northern point of the Gulf of Bothnia; thence to Ha-
paranda, the first stopping point across the Swedish
boundary, and from there to Majarvi, the first railway station in Sweden.   Describing various incidents of the day and trip, Dr. Klopsch said in his
letter:

"We were interrupted at every station by multitudes who had come to welcome and thank us in
song.   The majority of them must have traveled
many miles, for usually the villages are greatly scattered and consequently sparsely populated.   Invariably I appeared on the platform and addressed
them.   At Kemi 1,200 had gathered.   The winds
were icy, but for a full hour I stood bare-headed at
the station door.   Never had I seen greater discipline in the handling of a crowd.   Song after song
and speech after speech were delivered."

Recounting the farewell reception at Tornea, Dr.
Klopsch wrote:

"The public schools had been granted a holiday in order that all the children might help to honor the American visitors, and they were there in great numbers. On entering the municipal building we were escorted to a place in the assembly room. Two or three songs were sung by the people and then the Mayor made a very impressive address, in the course of which he paid the highest compliment to American philanthropy. Then came another song, followed by my reply, again interpreted by Professor Reuter. Then the superintendent of the schools made a long and very impassioned address extolling Finland and the Finns, their civilization, their simplicity of life, their virtues, and their institutions of learning. During his remarks the tears literally rolled down his cheeks. At the conclusion of his address he presented me with two volumes of the *Kalevala*. In reply I told him how near the sufferings of his people have brought them to the hearts of our own, and that since the first reports of famine the Americans had studied up carefully all about Finland and had learned of all their piety, their noble character and educational institutions, their high respect for womanhood, their art and their literature. Then, after the Finnish national song, followed a hand-shaking of unusual proportion, of which the children got the major share.

"Imagining that the reception closed then and there, I shook hands again with those in charge, and was surprised to learn that the demonstration thus ended was in reality but the commencement of things, and that now we would all meet in the ancient Lutheran Church, there to sing praises to our Heavenly Father for having influenced the heart of a great nation to come to the relief of the simple, pious people of unhappy Finland. So in a procession we all marched down the main thoroughfare to the venerable church with its ancient mural paintings, and there, crowded to its utmost capacity and led by the pastor, hymns of praise and thanksgiving were sung to Him who in the Heavens regulates the destinies of the nations of the earth. Then the entire assembly escorted us to the bridge between Sweden and Finland. On reaching the dividing line, Professor Reuter and Mr. Alopaens on behalf of Finland formally delivered us safe and sound in the presence of the great audience to Captain Samdbaum and Reverend Julivo, the representatives of Sweden. The people sang, and one of their number addressed us.

"To their farewell address I replied: 'Permit me to express to you and all the good people of Finland my heart-felt thanks for your generous hospitality to me while in your lovely land. Words cannot express how greatly I appreciate your simple life, which I have had exceptional opportunities to observe and which has been to me an object lesson that I shall ever remember. Your earnestness, sincerity and simplicity have greatly impressed me, and I leave you with unfeigned regret. Your custom of expressing your affection in song and flowers is indeed very touching, and has been to me a genuine inspiration. May God abundantly bless Finland and speedily drive from it the dark specter of famine that now enshrouds it. God bless America for what it has done for you to bring to your homes hope, comfort and sunshine.' Then followed the familiar cheer, 'Alakoon,' ('Long live Totori Klopsch!'), and while it was given we stepped across the line into Sweden."

Parts of Sweden and also a small section of Norway suffered from the same causes that caused the famine in Finland. The distress was mostly north

FINNISH CHILDREN IN A PEASANT SCHOOL

FARM LABORERS OF FINLAND

of the Arctic Circle, where the people had had snow and ice for months. It was estimated 200,000 Scandinavians were in want. Correspondents of American newspapers gave pitiful details of the famine in north Sweden. The Scandinavian people of the United States were prompt to come to the help of their countrymen in distress. Relief committees were organized and very substantial contributions were forwarded, which were distributed from the relief committee in Stockholm.

Dr. Klopsch could not be blind to this condition. *The Christian Herald* relief movements never knew geographical lines. Pastor Mauritz Stolpe, of the Swedish Lutheran Gustavus Adolphus Church in New York, wrote him briefly of the facts, saying that since the years of war in 1808–09 no one had witnessed anything like the condition in Sweden. He closed his letter: "Please hearken to the appeal of the stricken people."

Dr. Klopsch made personal observations and gathered the facts when he was in Finland. As soon as he reached Stockholm he made inquiry regarding the means of distributing relief funds. He thereupon transferred to the Central Relief Committee about $27,000 for Swedish relief, and more than $5,000 for the relief operations in Norway. He also took pains through the columns of *The Christian Herald* to bring the situation to the attention of the generous people of the United States.

The following special cable despatch from Stockholm, under date of March 23d, gave in very brief form the facts:

"The *Christian Herald* relief party, consisting of Dr. Louis Klopsch and Mr. Gilson Willetts, arrived in Stockholm from Finland yesterday. American flags were displayed on public buildings, the American Legation hoisting for the first time in its history the American flag for a private citizen.

"Today at noon the relief party lunched at the Legation. Minister Thomas in his address said this great charity had done more to bind Sweden and America closely together than anything that had been accomplished in 40 years.

"At 2 o'clock the unusual distinction was granted of a special audience of half an hour in the private chambers of the King and Queen, who were together.

"Their Majesties expressed their heart-felt thanks to the great-hearted American people for their kindness to the suffering people of Sweden. Both were moved to tears when told that there were many thousands of infant contributors to the relief work. The King said he was sure the Swedes made good American citizens, reflecting credit alike on themselves and on their adopted and mother countries. He hoped the visitors liked Sweden. He was proud, he said, to be King of such a country and such a people. At the Queen's invitation the relief party visited a hospital founded by Her Majesty."

The Central Relief Committee at Stockholm also sent a cable despatch to *The Christian Herald* saying that the Swedish sufferers desired to thank the American people for their magnificent relief.

Dr. Klopsch went from Stockholm to St. Petersburg, and then started back to the United States. The party stopped at Copenhagen, where an audience was given by the Danish Royal family. This was described by Dr. Klopsch in the following cablegram:

"COPENHAGEN, APRIL 11, 1903. — Today we were favored with an audience lasting an hour with King Christian of Denmark, Queen Alexandra of England, and the Dowager Empress of Russia. It took place at the Royal Palace.

"Queen Alexandra, who was the first to enter, expressed her profound appreciation of the good work done by Americans for India, during and since the famine. She had read and heard of its magnitude with ever increasing admiration. She begged that the generous people of America might be assured of England's sincerest gratitude.

"The Dowager Empress of Russia was moved to tears at the recital of our Finland famine experiences. Both Queen and Empress repeatedly expressed the deepest sympathy with the sufferers. The recital of incidents showing the self-denial practiced by many of the poor contributors to the relief fund evoked many times the expression, 'God bless and reward them.'

"King Christian, who spoke in German, was very cordial, and said at parting, 'Please convey my greetings to the Danes in America, from whom I have received many tokens of continued love and loyalty.'

"On Friday forenoon we had the pleasure of an audience with the Crown Prince, and in the evening we were entertained at dinner with his family, twenty sitting at a table."

After his return to New York, Dr. Klopsch was overwhelmed with evidences of the gratitude of the countrymen of the people to whose relief he had come in the hour of famine. The United States

Minister at Stockholm, Hon. W. W. Thomas, in July addressed to the Norwegian Cabinet Minister a letter enclosing from Dr. Klopsch a second check for the distressed people of northern Norway. "When we reflect," wrote the American Minister, "that these grand benefactions are not the gifts of millionaires, but the contributions of people of small means, that these sums all come from the little savings of the one million Americans who read *The Christian Herald* of New York, it seems to me that these noble gifts constitute an act of Christian benevolence which both in kind and amount are perhaps without a parallel in history.

"All honor to Dr. Klopsch, the little man with a great heart, who has organized and carried out this good and great work."

The Norwegian Minister, Sigurd Ibsen, replying to the American Minister's note and acknowledging the receipt of the second contribution, wrote further:

"I do not need to emphasize what an impression this renewed proof of grand benevolence will leave in this country.

"I beg you in the name of my colleagues and on my own behalf to present to Dr. Klopsch our deep-felt gratitude, and at the same time to accept for yourself the expression of our recognition of the part you have had in this matter."

In January, 1904, the Finlanders resident in the United States presented a special address to Dr. Klopsch in appreciation of his services. Parts of it are as follows:

DR. KLOPSCH.

Dear Friend: Although you received while in Finland many tokens of gratitude and esteem of the Finnish people in return for all you did in their time of dire distress, and while, since your return to America, there has not been wanting individual testimony as to the grateful sentiments of the thousands of Finlanders now resident in the United States for the aid extended to their suffering kinsfolk at home, it remains true that up to the present no formal recognition of your energetic generosity has been given by Finnish-Americans. If we have waited some time before acting on our inclinations, it has only been in consonance with the Finnish temperament, which does nothing in haste, but prefers to weigh its actions long beforehand. This has the effect, in the present instance, as we intend, of making the formal rendering of our thanks doubly significant, as the well-considered act of men who do not allow the memory of a good deed to fade, but cherish it enduringly.

So it comes that we, natives of the country whose sufferings you did so much to alleviate, and residents of the land whose ready and unstinted practical sympathy made you one of its foremost agents, have come together in our quality as representatives of the 300,000 Finlanders now on American soil, for the purpose of voicing our heart-felt appreciation, first: of the splendid spontaneous generosity of the American people, from the highest to the humblest, and whom we now address through you; and secondly: of the well-directed enterprise and sustained enthusiasm of *The Christian Herald* and its responsible staff that created for that characteristic generosity so prompt and efficacious an outlet. In the name, then, of our thousands of fellow-countrymen, from the Pacific sea-board to the Atlantic, most of them by far toilers in the humbler ranks of life, but many also representative of the professions, the press, and mercantile pursuits, we here tender you, Dr. Klopsch, this formal expression of our gratitude, our affection, and our esteem.

But we are not content simply to do this. We would further place on record our glad recognition of the fact that such acts of practical Christianity do more than aught else, not only to promote a helpful fellow-feeling, but also, and what is of more importance, to develop mutual understanding between nations, and so tend to weaken those manifestations of racial prejudice which form the most formidable barrier to the progress of civilization in the highest sense. That the conception of the "Citizen of the World" is so much more general and its value so greatly enhanced since the days of Oliver Goldsmith is due largely to just such beneficent acts as your exhausting journey to and through that distant land and your active prosecution of a great mission of charity, together with the wide dissemination, through your valued paper and other organs of the press, of a more intimate knowledge, gained through personal observation, of a foreign people, studied, in their hour of heaviest trial, with a practical eye and a deeply sympathetic heart.

We here in America, though far from our Finnish birthplace, still carry deep in our hearts those ideals of quiet, orderly progress and of high citizenship that our forefathers cherished, and we rejoice that your noble work of brotherly love has placed you in a position, not only to gain a just estimate of the qualities and aims of our beloved Finland, but also to help make these better known to the great nation among which we have found our second home, and with whose particular virtues you have contributed so powerfully to render us gratefully and lastingly familiar.

May the blessing of the Supreme Power, under whose beneficent sway it has been granted to do so much good to our stricken people, rest upon you and your undertakings, and upon the warm-hearted American people who have stretched out the hand of brotherly help to our kin, throughout the year that has just dawned!

New York, January 2, 1904.

In later years whenever there came word of further distress in Finland, he was again ready to help. Thus it was that in 1907, when the crops were not up to the usual, there was some distress and hunger. Dr. Klopsch immediately offered relief should it be needed. The reply came back, however, that the distress was only local and temporary and that relief from abroad would not be necessary.

CHAPTER IX

MODERN MACEDONIA

MACEDONIA, as a name, has no modern territorial significance. It is merely part of European Turkey and has been under Turkish dominion since the fifteenth century. There are a variety of races and nationalities, but authentically Macedonia cannot be claimed exclusively by any one of the neighboring countries. The people of the present day, who are Turkish subjects, include Bulgarians, Greeks, Servians, Turks, and other nationalities.

By far the largest part of the population is Bulgarian, and the Macedonian Bulgarians are by blood and by religious belief the same with the Bulgarians of Bulgaria. The difference is that after the war between Russia and Turkey, and the peace which was established by the Berlin Conference of 1878, Bulgaria became a semi-independent country, and in 1909 was able to secure its complete political independence, while Macedonia is still under Turkish dominion. Macedonia in fact in the past has been the vexing question in what is known in European politics as the "Balkan situation."

"Macedonia," wrote Henry Mann in *The Christian Herald* some years ago, "the land of Philip and of Alexander, the cradle of an empire whose victors sighed for more worlds to conquer, after many centuries of comparative obscurity once more attracts the anxious gaze of mankind. It is not the Macedonia of old, or even its shadow. But few crumbling remnants alone tell us of cities from which went forth the victors of Issus and Arbela. Their very race is extinct and its place has long been taken by descendants of those whom the ancient Greeks regarded as barbarians.

"Modern Macedonia is a part of European Turkey. It is not the name of any political division of the Ottoman Empire, but is applied indefinitely to the region included in the three provinces of Kossova, Monastir and Salonica, wedged in between Adrianople on the east, Albania on the west, the free or autonomous Balkan States and Bosnia on the north, and the Ægean Sea on the south. These three provinces have an area of a little more than thirty thousand square miles in extent, and a total population of about two and three-quarter millions, nearly all Christians of the Bulgarian or Greek churches, the former greatly in the majority.

"Macedonia is a rugged and also a fertile land, including broad masses of mountains and extensive sweeps of lowland, with a hardy peasantry which has learned through many years of misrule an unquenchable hatred of the Turk. The anarchy, insecurity and intolerance of all creeds calling themselves Christian, which prevail everywhere the Turk has full sway, sufficiently account for conditions in Macedonia. There is no foreign influence there to restrain Turkish crime, licentiousness and cruelty. The Albanian Moslems, who are brigands by nature and training, prey on the Christian Macedonians from the western boundary, while the Turkish levies from Asia, whose idea of soldiering is comprised in murder and plunder, inflict all sorts of outrages on the wretched inhabitants, whom they are supposed to protect.

"A simple and honest plain people, doing their best to live good lives so far as they are permitted by their masters, the Turks, the Macedonians well deserve the sympathy of nations more fortunately situated."

The same writer, telling of the conditions which produce insurrection, said that it was probable that European Turkey and the mountainous parts of Greece have never in modern times been free from brigandage. Many instances were given by him in which captives were held for ransom. A case which came close home to the American people was that of Miss Ellen M. Stone, the American missionary, and her companion, Mrs. Tsilka, the wife of an Albanian preacher. Early in September of 1901, Miss Stone, with a party of native Christians connected with the missions, was traveling from Bansko to Djumas, about a hundred miles east of Salonica, and in the mountain ranges of Macedonia near the

Bulgarian frontier, through a part of the country which was usually considered safe. While the party were passing through a defile in the mountains there suddenly appeared two groups of men, one in front, the other behind them, dressed as Turkish soldiers. All the party were made prisoners, and were subjected to a search for valuables. After taking their money, jewelry, and watches, the plunderers, who spoke the Bulgarian language, though dressed as Turks, liberated all except Miss Stone and Mrs. Tsilka. The main body of the party found their way to a place of safety, some of them carrying the news of the abduction to the American Board Mission at Samakov in European Turkey.

It quickly became apparent that the outlaws had a definite purpose in the capture of Miss Stone, for Mrs. Tsilka was liberated and sent to Bansko, to procure money for the prisoners' present needs. It was also announced that the bandits demanded a ransom of $110,000 for Miss Stone's liberation. This demand was made known in a letter from Miss Stone to Rev. Dr. Haskell, American Board missionary at Samakov, and a place was named where the brigands would receive the money, for which they pledged their word the prisoner would be restored to her friends. It soon became apparent that the capture of Miss Stone was not an act of mere brigandage, but was a political plot deliberately planned. It was the belief, which was subsequently confirmed, that the kidnapping was known to the leaders in the movement against Turkish rule.

The officials of the American Board of Foreign

Missions, when the first news came, believed that
the brigands, as soon as they realized that their
threats and demands were unavailing, and that no
ransom would be paid, would release their captive.
A different view of the case was taken by the State
Department at Washington. It was thought that
Miss Stone was in imminent peril, and that the captors would not likely be influenced by sentimental
motives or swayed from their purposes by pleas for
mercy. This opinion was shared by many people
in the United States, and it was decided by the
relatives of Miss Stone, and their pastors, to appeal
to the whole nation to subscribe the ransom. This
appeal was issued through the American Board.

At the last hour *The Christian Herald* was urgently
requested to assist in the movement for raising the
ransom. It did so gladly, and soon the telegraph
wires were flashing messages to liberal hearts in
many states, while the telephone was used for reaching persons in New York. Within five or six hours
subscriptions amounting to $2,000 were received.
One of these was from Wu Ting Fang, the Chinese
Minister to the United States. He took the opportunity of showing his gratitude for the generosity
with which America had helped China in the then
recent famine.

In an editorial, Dr. Klopsch discussed the situation. He did not stop to consider whether the
abduction of the American missionary was accomplished solely for the purpose of securing a ransom
or had ulterior political motives.

"The American Board," said the editorial, "has

declined to accede to the demand for a ransom on the ground that if the Board yields to such a demand, it would be placing a premium on brigandage, endangering missionaries everywhere, causing infinite pain and anxiety to friends at home, seriously embarrassing the missionary work, and jeopardizing the long years of consecrated toil. To pay the ransom, therefore, would be to establish a dangerous precedent. At the same time the natural solicitude of relatives and the sympathy of an interested public in Miss Stone's case have been so pronounced that the Board has sent out an appeal in her behalf."

Notwithstanding the well-founded suspicion that the capture of Miss Stone had been instigated by the Macedonian Revolutionary Committee, it became apparent that the Turkish Government was unable to secure her release, and that those who believed in raising the ransom to insure her safety should proceed with their efforts. So the work went forward and from all sources $65,000 was raised.

President Washburn, of Robert College, Constantinople, wrote that the chief difficulty in the case of Miss Stone was not to find money, but to find Miss Stone and the brigands. Ultimately this was done. Rumors came of release, and later on more positive news. More than five months after the capture, the release was effected. On February 18th a cable from Vienna stated that Miss Stone had been handed over to Dragoman Garguilo, of the American Legation. It appeared that the accounts were conflicting, but there was no question that she was free. Then came news that she was on her way home. When she reached New York, on the steamer *Deutschland* on April 10, 1902, Miss Stone told to the newspapers the story of her life among the brigands.

"When they captured us," she said, "they told us, 'We took you for money. We will release you when the ransom is paid.' We would have been treated badly if it had not been for the little baby, born to Mrs. Tsilka during our captivity, and whose presence seemed to spread a veil of safety over us. A few days before we were ransomed, the leader of the brigands said: 'There's a bullet for you and one for Mrs. Tsilka and the baby, if the ransom is not paid within a certain date.' But God delivered us out of the hands of the enemy. What was done with the ransom money I don't know. Whether it was used for political purposes in Macedonia, I can't state. All I know is that the brigands got it.

"Mrs. Tsilka and I often wondered if the outside world knew anything about us and what was being done to have us liberated. The brigands occasionally hinted of the rumors about us being dead, but further than that we knew nothing. We were kept in secret places and always traveled by night. When I wrote my letter seeking ransom, I wrote because they forced me to do so, threatening me with a loaded rifle.

"When the baby was born, the event caused a sensation in the brigand camp. The men would come and look at the baby. They would pat its fingers. When she was three days old, I carried her on a board over the mountains.

"On the last day of our captivity we started, as usual, to travel at night. We traveled about an hour, when there was commotion in the band. We stopped in the dark road, but in a few minutes we heard the command to proceed. I heard the order given to go back with the horses, but even then I did not realize that the brigands had turned us loose, until they were out of sight and beyond hearing. We looked around and found that there were only two men left with us. Then they led us to a little town, and we were told that our ransom had been paid and we were free. We lifted our hearts to God in faithful prayer.

"Some of the brigands wore Turkish costumes, some spoke Greek and others Albanian. Several of them dressed like Turks, looked like Turks, talked like Turks, and I have no doubt they were Turks."

Mr. William E. Curtis, the well-known newspaper correspondent, dispelled the mystery surrounding the negotiations with the bandits in a letter describing the affair. He explained that Mr. J. G. Leishman, the United States Minister at Constantinople, took charge of the negotiations after Consul-General Dickinson, who had been entrusted with the preliminaries, was recalled from Bulgaria. The minister opened communication directly with the brigands. He chose the Rev. W. W. Peet, Treasurer of the American Bible Society at Constantinople, the Rev. John H. House of Ohio, in charge of the American Missions in Macedonia, and Chief Dragoman Garguilo, interpreter of the American Legation at Constantinople as a committee, and dispatched them to

the scene of Miss Stone's capture. Dr. Peet carried
the ransom money, $65,000, and the brigands knew
it. Dr. House was soon in communication with Miss
Stone, who was then at a village called Razlag.
She wrote him advising him to pay the ransom.
Her captors, she said, insisted that it be paid before
they set her free. Minister Leishman knew from
the history of similar cases that such a demand was
customary, and he believed firmly that the brigands
would keep their pledged word. Dr. House, too,
advised compliance. The brigands themselves indicated how and where the money should be delivered, and their wishes were carried out. They
released the captives immediately.

The abduction of Miss Stone gave an insight into
the political conditions in Macedonia and on the
Bulgarian border. Later it was shown that an insurrection against Turkish misrule was being planned.
This movement came to a head in the summer of
1903. It must be remembered that the revolt was
against the Turk Abdul Hamid and his provincial
government, and that the Young Turks, who have
since sought to make the Turkish rule acceptable to
all nationalities within the Turkish dominions, were
themselves at the time engaged in their plans for
overthrowing Abdul Hamid.

At the beginning of September the insurrection-
aries had 20,000 well armed men in the field, chiefly
Bulgarians, who were fighting the Turks by guerrilla
methods. They overran a large part of Macedonia
and the Bulgarian frontier. But Turkey, always
prepared for insurrections by her oppressed subjects,

was ready for this emergency and at once threw a
large army into the field. Atrocities were committed
on both sides, but the disciplined outrages were on
the part of the Turkish troops. Macedonian towns
and villages were laid waste and swept bare of their
Christian population. In some districts there were
general slaughters in which women and children
were massacred. The war, if war it could be called,
was soon over, but the suffering grew. It became
known that 150,000 women and children were on
the verge of starvation, and that Christian inhabitants, terror-stricken, were fleeing hourly, fearing a
general massacre by the Mussulmans, whose fanatical hatred had been stirred to the highest point.
The Christian Herald, in an editorial, thus described
the Macedonian cry:

"It is a terrible story of the unspeakable horrors
of war that comes to us from Macedonia. From
those desolated valleys, with their homes a mass of
smoking embers, and their dead lying unburied; from
the forests in which the poor, miserable fugitives are
hiding from the fanatical hordes who pursue them;
from caves and holes in those wild and rugged mountains, there comes a cry to Christendom for aid.

"From those bleak mountains they can look down
upon their old homes, ruined by fire and pillage,
their little gardens, where only a few weeks ago all
was peace and happiness, with the children playing
at the mother's knee, but where all is now wasted
and blackened. War has swept over all, leaving a
track of blood and ashes, and a sorrow that none
save God can heal.

"Deaf indeed must be the ears that do not hear
the call of Macedonia for succor to-day; blind must

be the eyes that cannot see the vision of those exiles, as they lift up their voices in despairing appeal. Shall the call be answered? We leave the decision with the readers of *The Christian Herald.*"

Its readers answered the call. The missionaries in Macedonia wrote to Dr. Klopsch giving the conditions which demanded relief, and indicating the means that might be followed. Miss Ellen M. Stone herself sent forth an appeal. Putting aside all resentment and without even referring to her own perilous experience she appealed to the sympathy of the American people in behalf of the Macedonians in a letter which gave her personal knowledge of the conditions.

"The snows of winter," she wrote, "already cover those lofty mountain peaks, and have concealed the berries and leaves upon which the starving refugees were striving to subsist. Shelters must be provided for them somehow, and they be gathered where at least a small quantity of flour may be doled out to them, and a blanket to help them endure these winter nights, if their lives are to be preserved. No wonder that the pitying hearts of the relief distributors long for the great stores of army blankets, and for thousands and thousands of dollars to purchase supplies of food and clothing. Let us hasten with our gifts through the willing channel of *The Christian Herald*, that our Christmas song shall be made even more full of rejoicing than usual, because 'the blessing of Him that was ready to perish' has fallen upon us."

This was written at the Thanksgiving season, and later came stories of the black Christmas in store for the natives of Macedonia. Members of a committee of active Macedonian pastors in the United States also appealed to the American people through *The Christian Herald.* Dr. Klopsch decided that in view of the interest aroused, and in order that the readers of *The Christian Herald* be fully informed of the actual state of affairs in Macedonia and of the use made of their gifts, a special representative should be sent. For this purpose the Rev. Marco N. Popoff, a native evangelical pastor, was commissioned. He was thoroughly familiar with the centers of suffering and was personally acquainted with the missionaries and native Christian pastors and workers.

After a remarkably quick journey, Pastor Popoff reached Sofia, Bulgaria, on January 20, 1904. Five days later he cabled that a relief committee of twenty-three members had been organized, with the Rev. Edward B. Haskell as Chairman. At the same time acknowledgment was received from the Rev. W. W. Peet, Treasurer of the American Missions in Turkey, of the receipt at Constantinople of $10,000 for Macedonian relief. From Salonica, the Rev. E. B. Haskell, Chairman of *The Christian Herald* Relief Committee, wrote giving incidents of the distribution of the supplies. Many of them were very affecting. The funds were used chiefly in furnishing flour and blankets and in maintaining retreats for the sick and wounded.

Pastor Popoff wrote from Tarta Pazardjik, giving some characteristic incidents. Among other things he said:

"In a deserted coffee shop, I found forty refugees — men, women, children, marriageable girls and young men — all crowded together. At night they spread whatever they had on the floor and rested there. The women were spinning wool. I asked them who gave them wool. They said: 'It is not ours; we get it from the city women to spin for them. We prefer to have something to do rather than to be idle, although they pay us but very little.' For spinning three pounds of wool, which keeps a woman busy nearly a week, they get twenty-four cents."

In a letter dated at Lujene, February 8th, Pastor Popoff gave further interesting details of his journey among the fugitives who were scattered through the mountain villages on the Bulgarian border. He wrote:

"From Ichtiman, I started for Lujene. To reach this place I rode only one hour by rail, and nine hours by carriage over mountain roads. Lujene is the principal of three villages in the Rodope Mountains, about four hours' journey from the boundary line between Bulgaria and Macedonia. The three villages are nestled in a beautiful mountain dale, the three together having a population of 5,000, which derives subsistence from the forests mostly, by cutting and drawing fire-wood and lumber.

"Among the refugees at Lujene are about forty Protestants from Razlag. Rev. Sedloeff, their pastor, is himself a refugee. He is *The Christian Herald* representative there. I preached to them Sunday morning from the text, 'Though I walk through the

THE BULGARIAN ARMY GOING INTO WINTER QUARTERS

MACEDONIAN PASTORS AND OTHERS REPRESENTED IN
THE RELIEF WORK

valley of the shadow of death, I will fear no evil;
for Thou art with me.' In the afternoon about one
hundred and fifty people came to the hotel to hear
. from me what America is doing for them. After
my talk, an old man said to me: 'We are very
grateful for the aid given us, but we will be more
grateful if something will be done that will enable
us to go to our own places, although our homes are
destroyed.'"

The semblance of peace was slowly restored by
the Turkish Government, the danger from cold and
starvation passed, and the survivors of the insur-
rectionary movement and the refugees on the Bulgarian border went back to their homes. The need
of relief from abroad became less acute, and final
remittance of $7,000 was sent to the Rev. Mr. Peet,
of the American Board at Constantinople, and no
further appeals were made for contributions.

Summing up the work, *The Christian Herald* said:

"Benevolent hearts in the United States, Great
Britain, and Bulgaria have acted most harmoniously
and efficiently together in all this work of Macedonian relief. Catholic missionaries and Sisters of
Mercy worked side by side with evangelical missionaries, colporteurs, and preachers, and all received
funds through the hands of the American Missionary Committee at Monastir. Tenderly nurtured
women of rank, who knew the country and its various nationalities, as few others could know them,
have labored most self-denyingly, and with self-
abnegation, for the mitigation of the sufferings and
destitution in which the struggle between the Mus-
sulman rulers and Christian subjects had left the
country last autumn.

"*Christian Herald* readers have generously responded to this need. The winter is now over and gone, and the spring has appeared in that part of the world. The crocuses, violets, primroses, and dandelions have been found in sheltered nooks even on mountain sides, while on the hills and plains appear the almond trees, white with blossoms, and the fields of poppies and of winter wheat in their greenness. The latter is true in regions where the greatest terrors had not fallen, where there were still men left to plow and sow their fields last autumn, or women who might still brave the loneliness of their fields in sections where the dreaded Albanian and Turkish guards, or the regular troops of Abdul Hamid, or his irregular Bashi-Bazouks, were not terrifying and devastating the Christian population."

CHAPTER X

CHINA'S SORROW

MILLIONS WHO SUFFER FROM RIVER FLOODS — DISTRESS IN 1899 — FRESH CALAMITY IN 1901 — MINISTER WU'S STATEMENT — DR. KLOPSCH ON THE AMERICAN ATTITUDE TOWARD CHINA — LI HUNG CHANG'S MESSAGE — MINISTER CONGER'S CONTRIBUTION — DR. KLOPSCH'S RELIEF ORGANIZATION — PRESIDENT MC KINLEY AND SECRETARY HAY AID — AMERICAN MISSIONARY COMMITTEE — APPEAL FROM CHINESE CHURCHES — SPECIAL COMMISSIONER NICHOLS DISPATCHED — GRAPHIC DESCRIPTIONS OF THE REMOTE PROVINCES — IN THE HEART OF SHANSI — NATIVE CUSTOMS — HOW SHENSI WAS SUCCORED — WHAT THE "CHRISTIAN HERALD" ACCOMPLISHED.

CHINA came within the sphere of Dr. Klopsch's philanthropies. The ancient empire of Confucius always had a great attraction for him though he never was able to visit it. The four hundred million inhabitants he looked on, notwithstanding the difference in standards of civilization, as all coming within the common fold. When famine spread over any section of the vast country, Dr. Klopsch was ready to put forth his energies for its relief.

China's famines often have resulted from floods, rather than from droughts, and have spread disaster and death among millions of peasants. "China's Sorrow" is the name by which the great Hwang-Ho, or Yellow River, is known throughout the Empire. That the name is not misapplied is proved by the record of appalling disaster which is the history of the river for generations. In 1899 the tale of destruction and suffering was repeated with tenfold intensity, but the outside world was slow in learning of the disaster and of the suffering which followed. The first news came by way of San Francisco, brought by steamers from Hong Kong. It was supplemented by letters from American missionaries in the Shantung province, where the greatest distress existed.

American Consul Fowler, at Chefoo, sent out an appeal in behalf of the inundated population, in which he said: "Hundreds of villages are submerged, cities surrounded by water, homes, furniture, clothing, — in fact everything, — is under water or destroyed. The natives themselves are living in straw huts; many have absolutely no shelter from the winter's cold and snow, subsisting on bark, willow twigs, roots and so forth. The crops have been a failure, the seed for the next sowing is gone, and there is nothing for these starving millions to hope for in the future." The State Department published the substance of the dispatches from the consuls and urged that aid be sent from this country to the sufferers.

Dr. Klopsch at once telegraphed to Washington desiring to know the fullest details concerning the flood and famine, and offering in behalf of the readers of *The Christian Herald* to undertake the raising of a cargo of corn if the need were really of the exceedingly urgent character represented. He would supply the cargo if the Government would utilize one of the United States transports about to leave for the Philippines.

Secretary Hay replied that although the Government had on several occasions aided in alleviating the suffering in various parts of the world by transportation of supplies contributed by the people of the United States, the employment of United States vessels for such purpose had usually been done under some special authority of law, and in the absence of authorization of Congress the State Department could not direct the employment of any public funds for the purpose of chartering a vessel to convey the offered relief to China. Secretary Hay, however, referred to the War and Navy Departments the suggestion that the relief supplies be transported in a United States vessel. The War and Navy Departments took the subject up, but as the transports then in use for the Philippines were required for urgent national purposes it was found impossible to do anything. Dr. Klopsch later found ways for extending aid, but this famine in China was relieved earlier than had been anticipated, and the demand for help from the rest of the world did not become so pronounced.

Within two years China was in the grip of another famine, which continued to grow and spread distress till the appeal for succor became too urgent to be resisted.

In the spring of 1901 the newspapers began to receive intelligence of China's new calamity. A dispatch from Shanghai, under date of April 20th, gave the following succinct yet terrible picture of the conditions: "Shanghai, April 20: The famine in Shansi province is dreadful. Wheat is selling for $10.00 gold per 150 pounds."

The Rev. T. DeWitt Talmage called on Wu Ting Fang at Washington to make inquiries on behalf of *The Christian Herald.* "There is a dreadful famine," Minister Wu told Dr. Talmage, "and it spreads all over a great area. A vast multitude are suffering for food, so many thousands that we cannot number them. The population is very dense." "Are immediate measures of relief practicable?" Dr. Talmage asked. "Yes," the Minister replied, "there is much foodstuff in the nearby districts which could be purchased and sent to the famine district if the means were available. These regions are accessible through Shanghai and other ports. Rice is the principal food of the inhabitants, and probably it could be secured in large quantities for distribution. Flour and other provisions also could be bought and distributed."

The dispatches continued to give the world a glimpse of the new horror that had fallen on prostrate China. The provinces of Shansi and Shensi, with a population of 24 millions, were the centers of suffering, but the distress had spread to adjoining provinces.

Dr. Klopsch's view of China's need was a broad one. The memory of the Boxer outbreaks and of the anti-foreign movement was still fresh in the minds of people. In an editorial in *The Christian Herald* he took his position as follows:

"During all of the recent troubles in China our own nation has occupied a peculiar attitude toward that unhappy people. We alone have stood squarely upon the principle of international helpfulness, insisting that China should be succored and not despoiled. We wanted no territory. And we entered upon no campaign of conquest. We believed that the true way to impress upon China the advantages of a new and enlightened civilization was to heal her wounds, restore her self-respect, and set her securely in her own seat of judgment from which she could administer her own affairs. No nation save ours credited China's professions of a sincere purpose to put down the rebellion and to punish the offenders. The result has shown her absolute sincerity. China trusts the United States because we first trusted China. She regards us as her truest, if not her only, friend among the nations. It is not surprising, then, that in the presence of the awful visitation of famine China should turn to America for aid. Our benevolence in India and elsewhere has been an object lesson to the Asiatic races.

"There is another reason why China's appeal should not be allowed to pass unheeded, should further investigation show that she needs our help. At this time when our devoted missionaries are being so unjustly maligned and misrepresented it is well for Christian people to stand by them and give them the most cordial support and encouragement in their self-sacrificing labors. Deeds, not words, are the best answers to the maligners. Our missionaries in India, as every one knows, rendered in the late famine noble, humanitarian service which won them the applause of the whole world. Our missionaries in China, should the situation call for similar action, would doubtless demonstrate equally to friends and foes alike that they are true, self-denying followers of Him who went about doing good.

"China needs our prayers, if she should need our help also, she should have it — and quickly."

It was very soon evident that China did need our help, and needed it quickly. Li Hung Chang, the foremost official in China and the real head of affairs, who was known to people as one of the world's greatest statesmen, cabled through *The Christian Herald* a message to the American people. It was as follows:

GOVERNMENT, PEKING,
April 25, 1901.

EDITOR *Christian Herald*, NEW YORK.

Very serious famine spreads over whole province Shansi. Over eleven million population affected. Urgent relief necessary. Conditions warrant immediate appeal.

(Signed) LI HUNG CHANG.

(*Seal.*)

A touching appeal was circulated in China by the Shansi officials. Among other things, it said: "All our brothers in the world should be very sorry for us and should know how unfortunate we are. We wish our people to share some of your money, which you spend amusing yourselves and for traveling and for dressing and for all kinds of comforts, to rescue these poor people. It is much better to save the starving and dying men, women and children here than to build a pagoda or temple or even a church, because from ten to twelve million people are suffering to death."

Mr. E. H. Conger, the American Minister to China,

was at this time in the United States. He telegraphed a statement to *The Christian Herald* from
Des Moines, Iowa. He said: "Li Hung Chang and
Prince Ching both told me two or three days before
I left Peking that people were literally eating each
other. The Chinese people are able to live on almost
nothing for a long time. Li Hung Chang told me
that the Shansi people were eating the grass off the
ground and the leaves off the trees and even the
bark. They have eaten all there was to be had,
and are practically without anything to help now.
Probably ten million people are affected by the famine. Their condition is beyond description. They
have had no rain for two years." Minister Conger
accompanied his statement by a liberal contribution
to *The Christian Herald* fund.

Letters and telegrams came from American missionaries in China, and from some who were home temporarily, telling the same story, and pointing out the
necessity of immediate relief. They also explained
that the Shansi people always had been friendly to
the missionaries, and that Shansi was not a Boxer
province.

Dr. Klopsch within a short time had the complete
organization of relief in operation. He communicated with the State Department in Washington and
with Acting Minister Rockhill in Peking. His plan
was to purchase supplies and send them from Shanghai up the Yangtse to Wuhu, thence to Hankow,
and up the Han River to the head of navigation
in Shansi province. Mr. Rockhill replied by cable
that he would see to the purchase and distribution

of aid and that Li Hung Chang requested him to express to the organizer of the relief his sincere thanks and also the thanks of the Shansi famine-stricken for American benevolent action.

President McKinley was just starting on a long journey through the South and West. He was among the first to aid, not only by endorsing the relief movement of *The Christian Herald,* but by personal contribution. The following telegram was received:

President's Train, En Route, VIRGINIA.
April 29, 1901.

Dr. LOUIS KLOPSCH,
    The Christian Herald, New York.

The President is glad to hear you are endeavoring to raise a fund for the benefit of the sufferers in China. He hopes you may meet with the same success which you attained in similar good work for Cuba and India. He subscribed $100 for the fund. Please allow me to subscribe the same amount.

(Signed) JOHN HAY.

Dr. Klopsch cabled a request to Acting Minister Rockhill that he form an emergency relief committee in which American missionaries should predominate, and of which he should be chairman. This was done, and the committee was composed as follows: Rev. Arthur H. Smith, of the American Board, Tientsin, Chairman; Rev. Irenas J. Atwood, American Board; Rev. E. H. Edwards, China Inland Mission; Rev. H. H. Lowrie, Methodist, Peking; Rev. M. B. Duncan, English Baptist Mission. The first remittance of $20,000 was cabled to this committee, and several of the members started at once for Shansi.

The governor of Shansi sent an official escort to meet them. Word came that the news of *The Christian Herald* relief work had spread far and wide in the famine districts, and the expectation of the starving multitudes had been raised to the highest point. Li Hung Chang cabled from Peking to the Chinese Minister in Washington, expressing his gratitude to the benevolent people of America who through *The Christian Herald* were raising the relief fund.

From the native elders and deacons of the China Christian churches in Shanghai came a remarkable appeal. It was written in Chinese characters, and was translated by the Rev. F. C. H. Dryer, formerly missionary in that province. It was as follows:

The calamities that have befallen the Chinese Christians have been very great. Their steadfastness has been severely tested. Many of the brethren, however, through God's mighty preserving power, are much more zealous than they were before. From this it is manifest that nothing man can do can separate the love of God.

The suffering among all the Christians has been too great, for although they have escaped from within a step of death by the sword it has only been to meet with hunger and starvation. Not only are many in great want, but some have nothing to sustain life from day to day. Happily our Heavenly Father has bestowed mercy on us, for we have received letters from Shanghai and Peking informing us that an effort is being made to relieve our distress.

Alas for our Shansi Christians, who are left as a flock of sheep without a shepherd. We do not for the moment speak of their souls, even their bodies we do not know how to save. We have now appointed eight brethren to help in the important matter of the distribution of relief.

Please send quickly, that we may speedily deliver our brethren from their great and urgent distress. We hope that peace will soon be established and that the pastors will then be able to quickly return and organize the affairs of the church. We respectfully send our greetings of peace to all the missionaries.

From brethren of whom you have entertained anxious thought.

Written by lamplight, on the 15th of the 11th Chinese Moon.

Among other measures Dr. Klopsch decided to send a special commissioner on behalf of *The Christian Herald* contributors to China. He chose for this purpose Mr. Francis H. Nichols, a brilliant young American journalist who had been a newspaper correspondent in Cuba during the war with Spain. Mr. Nichols was courageous and adventurous. He proceeded at once to the scene of the famine and soon his vivid stories of the conditions there were received.

Before leaving Peking Commissioner Nichols had an interview with Prince Ching, the military governor, who, Li Hung Chang having in the meantime died, had become the leading factor in Chinese affairs.

Mr. E. T. Williams, of the American Legation, was present and acted as interpreter. Among other incidents of the interview, Mr. Nichols gave this account:

"Prince Ching motioned us to chairs at the white tablecloth, while a servant brought in little silver cups full of tea and a plate of cakes. With a manner which had not in it a trace of stiffness or formality he began asking questions about the famine relief fund. 'Is this money that the American people have raised,' he asked, 'the gift of a few men, or has it come from many sources?' I explained as best I could that the $60,000 forwarded to China's starving ones represented the Christian generosity and kindliness of thousands of Americans. I told him that the homes of the givers covered a territory as vast as the Chinese Empire. 'And all of these have remembered China,' he said meditatively. 'It is a splendid, generous act. On behalf of our people please convey to *The Christian Herald* my thanks. Words (and he pointed to his lips) can hardly express the gratitude I feel. This relief for the starving in China will go a long way toward binding us closer to the people of the United States. It is a friendship of many years,' he went on, 'between your country and mine. I really doubt if any other nation would have remembered us in our hour of need as the Americans have done.'"

Commissioner Nichols forwarded graphic descriptions of his journey to the provinces of Shansi and Shensi. At that period the famine was more severe in the latter province. He wrote: "The first hundred of the six hundred miles that lie between Peking and Singan are accomplished by rail to Pao-ting Fu. To American eyes railroads in China are strangely and wonderfully made. Tickets are sold in the European method as first, second, and third class. The latter comprises the major part of the train, and consists of ordinary open flat-cars which do not differ in the least from those used for freight. There is scarcely any system of way-bills or shipment. The company assumes little risk on anything or anybody that passes over its lines.

"After six hours jolting and bumping and the shouting of orders in Chinese, the train halted in front of a gray brick station. By means of three

carts and numerous questions of the interpreter I
finally succeeded in finding the residence of Rev.
J. Walter Low, of the Presbyterian Board of Missions,
to whom I had a letter of introduction from Dr.
Arthur Smith, head of the famine relief work. In
a little compound I found him; a superb illustration
of the sort of thing which a true missionary of the
Cross sometimes encounters in a heathen land. In
a town of 35,000 Mr. Low is at present the only
English-speaking person. A Princeton graduate and
an extremely cultivated and charming man, Mr. Low
is leading a life of lonely self-sacrifice amid the
scenes where former friends and co-laborers died
for the faith."

After describing his hospitable entertainment by
Mr. Low, Commissioner Nichols continued the account of his journey. A system of relay patrols
of Chinese soldiers had been established by agree-
ment with the foreign governments in Peking for
the sole purpose of escorting and protecting foreign
travelers. He resumed his story of the journey:

"Our patrol started from the door of the Tingchu
Yamen, and rode slightly in advance through the
gates in the city wall on the road towards the southwest. Each man carried a Mannlicher rifle, and wore
the red blouse of the Chinese Army. Big, strapping
fellows they were, on stocky, rugged ponies. Their
pigtails were curled up under black silk turbans,
and their faces were bronzed and reddened by the
sun, so that they looked far more like North American Indians than like Mongolians. Their manner,
too, was like that of Indians. They sat very erect

in the saddle and maintained a taciturn silence,
except when the leader would occasionally smile
and ask if the foreigners were comfortable. The
reply he received was always affirmative, although
compared with a Pullman sleeping car, traveling in
China is not of the happiest.

"In a literal sense all north China is covered with
the dust of ages. It gets in your eyes and ears and
nose and forms a thick coating on your hair and
clothes. A Chinese road is only the space between
the fields which is not under cultivation. The fields
are cared for and are reasonably smooth, but the
road is neither. Just before dark we came to
a massive brick archway that spanned the road.
Under it stood a bare-headed man in a black gown,
who violently gesticulated to the chief of our patrol.
The substance of what he had to say was that we had
reached Sinlo, and that quarters had been assigned
to us in the village inn, to which we were escorted
by a motley, chattering crowd.

"The inn is a one-story mud building. The floors
are of clay and the chairs are kept from falling
to pieces by bits of twine. The mandarin of Sinlo
called a few minutes after we had settled down to
the polyglot dinner, that included sharks' fins, lotus
seeds, and American canned sausages. The mandarin came in a sedan chair, and was preceded
by a score of servants carrying paper lanterns. He
was a stout, good-natured, rural Chinaman, who
asked all sorts of questions about the United States
as we sipped our tea together."

From Tai Yuen, the capital of the province of

Shansi, Commissioner Nichols wrote giving an accurate presentation of the conditions of a part of China rarely reached by white travelers, and told of the splendid results accomplished by the famine fund. He reached there late in October 1901. Part of his letter to *The Christian Herald* is as follows:

"Across the sun-baked plains of Chili, past terraces of budding millet and corn, past crumbling temples, across rivers and through mountain passes, we have traveled for the last ten days to this ancient capital of remote Shansi. Everywhere, as the representative of *The Christian Herald* famine fund, I have been received with the utmost courtesy and outspoken expressions of gratitude from the Chinese officials, and at times my progress has taken on almost the form of an ovation.

"Nothing could be more polite than the treatment accorded me by the mandarins. If I wanted an extra pony for the day's stage I always received it. If donkies had to be substituted for the heavy, lumbering cart over the mountain roads all I had to do was to ask for them and I found them waiting in the courtyard at daybreak next morning. The traveler across north China must inevitably become an adept at mandarin 'good form.' It is a complicated system of conduct, so absolutely the reverse of Occidental customs that one has to guard himself carefully in order not to make embarrassing mistakes. When the traveler calls on the mandarin he must send his servant ahead with his card, and then wait at the gates of the official residence until they are opened with slamming and shouting. The mandarin

MOBBING A FOOD DISTRIBUTOR IN CHINA

A TYPICAL FAMINE-STRICKEN FAMILY AT SUCHIEN, CHINA

stands at his doorway waiting to receive his guest, and escorts him to a chair at the left of a table. Two cups of tea are filled, being a little feast which must be eaten before the object of the visit can be discussed. When the call is returned the process is reversed. The stranger in the village goes no further than the doorway to meet the mandarin, but sends his servants to help him alight from his sedan chair. Once seated on opposite sides of the little table it is the height of rudeness for the foreign host to stand up or change his position for one moment until the mandarin rises to leave.

"There is a remarkable uniformity in Chili villages. At the entrance of almost every one is a corn mill. A flat stone, two or three feet in diameter, is supported on three posts. Through the center is an upright wooden spindle around which revolves the heavy stone roller. The mill is usually operated by a woman, who spreads the corn on the flat stone and then walks around it pushing the roller as she goes. Her cramped feet make her hobble painfully as she walks, and must add greatly to the difficulty of her task, but she looks perfectly contented and smiles at the passer-by.

"At the town of Shau-Yang *The Christian Herald* Commissioner was met by an old official and fifteen Chinese soldiers, each carrying the colors of the different regiments stationed in that prefecture. The procession was preceded by two heralds making an election night noise on two brass horns. They kept up a persistent tooting all the time I was eating my canned soup and ham at the inn, and then escorted

me on my way as far as the city gate, when the
official made a graceful little speech in which he
thanked the American people for not having hatred
towards China.

"The last fifty miles is over a sandy plateau dotted
with mud-walled towns and villages; then through
a gate in a massive wall and the traveler is in the
capital of Shansi. Tai Yuen was founded about
500 B.C. Its population is estimated at 40,000. Its
walls and gates are great wooden structures. They
are similar to those in Peking. As in all China's
cities, the streets are small, dusty lanes between
rows of one-story houses. Tai Yuen is one of the
most important places in north China. The roads
to Mongolia on the north and Kanshu on the west
radiate from it. It is the headquarters of the intricate Chinese banking system of Shansi, and is the
market for all the products of the province. On
many of the walls one sees today a proclamation
from the governor. It is a eulogy of the paper called
The Christian Herald and the generosity of Americans in sending money into starving north China."

In other letters Mr. Nichols gave further information about the people of remote Shansi and the vast
benefit that *The Christian Herald* relief had been to
the starving population when the famine was at
its height.

He also visited the province of Shensi. An advance relief expedition had gone to Shensi under
the personal charge of Dr. Moyer Duncan, who was
appointed by the Missionary Relief Committee in
Tientsin; and Dr. Duncan wrote from Hsi-An-Fu

in November, 1901, an account of his experiences.
A part of his letter is as follows:

Early in June it was doubtful whether it would be possible
to distribute any relief in this province, which suffered most
from the famine that swept the northwest provinces. The
committee that was formed by the Rev. Dr. Arthur Smith
allotted a portion of *The Christian Herald* fund to Shensi on
the understanding that its administration must be undertaken
only by foreigners. The ambassadors gave permission to
go into the interior if the Chinese were friendly and the way
opened out.

On the 26th of August Major Pereire, Dr. Jacob Smith and
myself reached the western capital. We were well received,
as we had been protected and cared for all along the route.
An imperial edict had been issued that we were going to distribute relief, and commanding all officials to treat us with
respect. Some twenty-six officials in all actively assisted us.
There were seventeen Christian leaders and teachers, and four
foreigners: Dr. J. A. C. Smith of the Baptist Missionary
Society; Mr. A. Trudinger of the China Inland Mission;
Mr. Tjader of the Swedish Mission to China; and myself.
The distributors were international and interdenominational,
and the Chinese recipients were Confucians, Buddhists, Taoists,
Mohammedans and Christians. It is satisfactory to know that
at least 90 to 95% of those assisted were the poorest and most
destitute. The relief was distributed personally by the foreigners to the parties relieved.

Mr. Nichols, writing from Sian, gave a very vivid
account of the way Shensi was succored. He wrote:
"Shensi is desolate. More than two and a half
millions of men, women and children, 30 per cent
of the entire population, have died of hunger or the
diseases which followed it. In the centers of distress
the survivors have sold everything from the roofs of

their houses to their children in order to buy food. Shensi is the oldest province in China. Ask any Chinaman when the history of Shensi began and he will reply, 'Soon after the world was made.'

"The province of Shensi is isolated. It has to depend for what it eats entirely upon its own fields. It is impossible to bring enough food from without to the people of the province to feed them. But Shensi is as a rule a productive province, and in ordinarily good seasons there is enough and to spare for every one. On the sides of the Shensi mountains it is hard to find a square foot from base to summit which is not covered with terraces under cultivation. The chief article of food is wheat, and by a system of fertilizing, the land is made to yield three crops of it a year. Millet and buckwheat are also products of the terraces, and in the bottom lands of the rivers some rice is raised.

"Soon after the hunger cloud had settled down over Shensi the Chinese officials organized measures for relief. Appeals for money were sent to all parts of the empire. In the middle of May came the longed-for rain. It was sufficient to insure an autumn harvest, but that was still five months away. The end of the famine was in sight, but horrors were not yet abated. By this time the enormous Chinese relief funds were exhausted. This was the state of affairs when Moyer B. Duncan, of *The Christian Herald* foreign relief committee, arrived in Sian.

"The last distribution of *The Christian Herald* relief fund to the destitute of Sian took place during my stay there. As one of the mandarins said to me when it was over, 'Few of these people ever heard of America before this famine relief began. They will always remember it as the land of *The Christian Herald.*'"

By the time that word was received of the results accomplished in Shansi and Shensi the collection of the funds in the United States had been closed because it was evident that the cloud was lifting. Dr. Klopsch had devoted the later contributions to the relief of Shensi. In due time he published his usual summary of the amounts received and distributed. For the first China famine a total of $128,280.68 had been expended. It had been a magnificent relief for the starving millions of the remote provinces of China made possible by the generosity of the American people.

CHAPTER XI

FURTHER FAMINES IN CHINA

SUCCORING THE DISTRESS IN 1903 — FOOD FLOTILLA — THE BLACK HUNGER
CLOUD IN 1906 — OVERFLOW OF THE GRAND CANAL — PRESIDENT ROOSE-
VELT'S CHRISTMAS APPEAL — THE "CHRISTIAN HERALD" CONTRIBUTIONS —
ACCOUNTS FROM SPECIAL CORRESPONDENT ELLIS OF MILLIONS STARVING —
THE PRESIDENT AND SECRETARY ROOT CONTRIBUTE — DR. KLOPSCH PROVIDES
CARGO FOR THE "BUFORD" — SECRETARY TAFT SPEAKS FOR THE RED CROSS
— RELIEF SHIP'S DEPARTURE FROM SAN FRANCISCO — SPECIAL COMMISSIONER
JOHNSTONE'S STORY OF THE DISTRIBUTION — OFFICIAL CEREMONIES — MIS-
SIONARIES' ACTIVITIES — FINANCIAL SUMMARY — PERMANENT EFFECTS —
PROVISION FOR THE ORPHANS — TRIBUTE FROM THE RED CROSS.

IN the vast domain of the Celestial Empire plenty may obtain in one section, while the crops may be a failure in another district and scarcity cause suffering to large numbers of people. This frequently happens, and sometimes it can hardly be said that from year to year the old Empire is free from hunger. In the spring of 1903, while the northern provinces had good crops and were able to take care of themselves, there was suffering in the south. The crops were a failure in Kwang Si province and more than a million natives were without food. The American Minister and the consular officers in China reported the conditions to the Department of State, and aid was asked for the Kwang Si sufferers. The missionaries sent similar reports and also appealed for aid.

The Department of State made the reports public, and supplied Dr. Klopsch with fuller information.

Without delay he cabled $5,000 to American Consul-
General McWade at Canton, and supplemented it
shortly by another remittance for $10,000. A reply
came, addressed to the State Department, as follows:

"CANTON, June 7, 1903.
SECRETARY OF STATE, Washington, D. C.:
"Viceroy Te Sou asked me to transmit through you
to *The Christian Herald* his profound and heart-felt
gratitude for the donation of $10,000 to starving
Kwang Si. It was urgently needed. He says it
is an added proof of America's friendship and
sympathy for China. I am vigorously preparing a
second American relief expedition."

Further contributions were made by *The Christian
Herald* readers and the funds forwarded so that
the relief expedition was carried out. The United
States naval vessels *Monterey* and *Callao*, which
were then in Chinese waters, assisted in the work.
The Rev. John E. Fee wrote from Kwaiping, which
was the center of distribution:

The distribution will be made in the usual systematic and
impartial manner, and will be under the supervision of American missionaries, and the literati, gentries and officials of the
stricken districts. The Rev. A. J. Fisher, of the American
Presbyterian Mission, will be on one of the relief boats, and will
be met at Wuchou by the Rev. H. K. Shumaker, of the United
Brothers in Christ Mission, and the Rev. J. E. Fee of the
American Presbyterian Mission. His Excellency the Viceroy
Te Sou will furnish a strong steam launch to tow the relief
boats up the West River. I will ask Lieut. Anderson of the
U. S. S. *Callao* to escort them up to Wu, where His Excellency
Wong Chih Chung, Governor of Kwang Si, will have boats and

small launches ready to convey the rice to the places where it is most needed. All of the relief boats will carry American flags and banners with inscriptions in the Chinese language stating that the rice has been bought for the relief of the starving natives with American donations raised by *The Christian Herald* of New York.

Later more complete details of the famine flotilla were published. Consul-General McWade wrote a full report to the Department of State. Among other things, he said: "I have the honor to suggest that copies of these dispatches be forwarded to *The Christian Herald* for publication. The contributions of the readers of that excellent journal for the relief of the famine-stricken sufferers have undoubtedly been the means of saving many thousands of human lives. I desire to join the poor sufferers in appreciative gratitude of *The Christian Herald's* abounding charity."

Commander Anderson of the U. S. S. *Callao* wrote to the Consul-General from Hong Kong enclosing a letter from Midshipman Sterling in regard to the conveying of the American relief expedition from Canton to Sam Shui. This letter also showed how practical the work of relief had been and how thoroughly it was appreciated by the starving people of the province.

The benevolence of *The Christian Herald* had permanent results, not all of which were restricted to famine. The Rev. Charles Beals, of Wuhu, early in 1904 wrote a description of a journey up the Chao River in the missionary house-boat which was bought by. the gifts of its readers. The boat reached the Huang-Lo-Ho district, which had been relieved by *The Christian Herald* during the flood two years previously. The evidences of gratitude were still made manifest in many ways.

In 1906 the black cloud of one of the great famines swept over central China. The floods in Kiangsu and Anhwei provinces were phenomenal. The whole plain west of the Grand Canal, in places 100 miles wide and more than 200 miles long, was flooded. The crops stood under water till they rotted. On some of the rice fields the waters did not abate for more than a month, the Grand Canal and the lakes running together.

A relief committee was organized in Shanghai, and an appeal was sent out to all the world. Official reports were received by the State Department at Washington from the American Minister and from the consular officers. These showed that the worst tales of suffering but feebly told the real story, and that immediate relief was imperative. The flooded area covered 40,000 square miles, which usually supported fifteen million persons.

President Roosevelt in Christmas week of 1906 issued a proclamation giving the facts and appealing to the American people. This proclamation stated that the crops had been destroyed by floods, that millions of people were on the verge of starvation, that thousands of dwellings had been destroyed and their inmates left without homes. "Our people," said President Roosevelt in the proclamation, "have often under similar conditions of distress in other countries generously responded to such appeals.

Amid our abounding prosperity and in this holiday season of good will to men assuredly we should do our part to aid the unfortunate and relieve the distress among the people of China to whom we have been allied for so many years in friendship and kindness."

Responding to the President's appeal, Dr. Klopsch in behalf of his readers immediately sent to the State Department at Washington a certified check for $5,000 to be applied to the work of relief. A contribution of $1,000 was also sent to the treasurer of a missionary committee at Chinkiang. "Let us hope," said an editorial in *The Christian Herald*, in telling of these contributions, "that the Chinese famine may not be of long duration and that conditions may so speedily improve that serious loss of life will be averted."

This hope was futile. News continued to come of the spread of the famine and of the people of China dying of hunger by the thousands. Dr. Klopsch therefore decided to respond to the appeal by organizing a complete relief movement. The news was that 15 millions of human beings in five provinces were affected. Of these, 8 millions had lost most of their property, including buildings and food supplies. All live stock had been either sold or eaten. Four million people were absolutely destitute. Nine cities were surrounded by famine camps containing an aggregate of 800,000 starving refugees who had been compelled to abandon their own wrecked and desolate homes.

William T. Ellis, a traveling correspondent of

The Christian Herald, happened to be in China, and he, after visiting the relief committee at Shanghai, wrote to Dr. Klopsch that he was there at the beginning of the most awful famine modern China had known. He proposed to go straight to the famine districts. This he did, and his letters presented a most vivid picture of the conditions that the American people were seeking to relieve. Writing from Chinkiang, Mr. Ellis said: "Millions starving. The reader cannot imagine it. Neither can I, though I write within earshot of an encampment of 30,000 refugees whose thin, pitiful wail for help has been in my ears all day, although even that has been less eloquent than the gaunt and haggard pairs of pale, yellow and thin, trembling, outstretched hands.

"Oh those hands! I shudder as I see them stretched out in vain, for one dare not give a dole of a penny lest he be literally mobbed by the shivering, famished creatures. For a single almoner to try to fill even a few of these hands is impossible; only the united charity of men and women throughout Christendom who love their brother men can avail in this awful crisis.

"What I have seen today suggests a vision of a line of beseeching hands — all the sufferers of this bitter famine ranged in a row, miles and tens of miles and scores of miles and hundreds of miles long. Such thin, trembling hands, many of them are! The old, old women, almost too feeble to stand, gazing at you hollow-eyed while their hands are extended in mute appeal — to think that the mothers of men and the mothers of mothers of men should anywhere come to this! Equally moving are the sick, stretched out on the bare ground, unable to rise, just feebly motioning for the succor that you cannot give.

"And the babies! How the cry of the children must go up before God! Wan little figures, some of them living skeletons, which mothers hold forth in tragic and mute appeal. Usually the poor little creatures are held close to the bare breasts of their mothers for the sake of a little warmth.

"Incidents could be piled upon incidents. Every one of these 30,000 refugees incarnates a story, a story of a home abandoned; of toilsome journey to this southern district in the hope of finding a pittance of food to allay that awful gnawing of hunger; of the eager hunt for shelter in a doorway; of being driven from spot to spot until at last a few feet of bare earth are secured out among the graves with the other refugees, — a space no bigger than a Chinese grave suffices for an entire family; of the daily and nightly huddling together in one mass for the sake of human warmth; of the search for dry grass with which to make a tiny fire; of the morning struggle for a portion of the government rice, and of that indescribable, terrible, primitive dole between life and starvation which the Chinese so often endure."

Correspondent Ellis wrote other vivid pictures of the famine camps and of how the relief from America was welcomed by the stricken millions.

Meantime *The Christian Herald* was cabling re-

mittance after remittance, until the total exceeded
$100,000. President Roosevelt and Secretary Root
gave the movement their hearty endorsement, and
added their personal contributions to *The Christian
Herald* fund. These were conveyed in the following letter:

DEPARTMENT OF STATE, WASHINGTON.
February 1, 1907.

DEAR DR. KLOPSCH: The President has asked me to say
to you that he is much interested in your work to raise funds
for the sufferers by the present dreadful famine in China.
He hopes that you will meet the same success that you have
had in similar appeals to the humanity and liberality of our
people.

As a contribution to the fund he has handed me his check for
$100, which I enclose, together with a similar check of my own.

With best wishes, I am

Very sincerely yours,
(Signed)   ELIHU ROOT.

While continuing to cable cash remittances, other
practical means of relief were also organized. *The
Christian Herald* through Dr. Klopsch made an offer
to the Government to furnish a cargo of 5,000 tons
of food stuffs for the Chinese, provided a relief ship
would be supplied by the Government to carry
the cargo. The offer was accepted and the army
transport *Buford* was assigned to this duty, it being
placed at the disposal of the National Red Cross
Society for the purpose of carrying *The Christian
Herald* cargo to China. An official announcement
was issued by the State Department saying that
the assignment of the transport for this purpose was
made at the request of Dr. Klopsch.

The *Buford* was at the wharf in San Francisco, and arrangements were rapidly carried forward to supply the cargo of 5,000 tons of American flour. Edward H. Harriman, of the Union Pacific system, and Marvin Hughitt, of the Chicago and Northwestern, donated to the famine fund free transportation over their lines from Minneapolis to San Francisco up to 1,000 tons of flour. The balance of the cargo was purchased in San Francisco through the Commissary-General of the War Department, and paid for by *The Christian Herald* fund.

In the meantime came evidences of appreciation of the life-saving work. The American National Red Cross made its acknowledgments through Secretary Taft of the War Department in the following letter:

"THE AMERICAN NATIONAL RED CROSS,
WAR DEPARTMENT,
WASHINGTON, D. C., April 23, 1907.

"MY DEAR DR. KLOPSCH: In the name of the American National Red Cross may I express to you, and through you to the contributors of *The Christian Herald* Chinese famine fund, the thanks and deep appreciation of the Society for the great work their most generous contributions made to that fund have accomplished in the relief of the starving multitudes in China. Without the great sum raised by *The Christian Herald*, and the bountiful cargo of the *Buford* provided by it, thousands of these poor people would have perished; but, saved by these merciful gifts, they can now live until their own fields provide the needed harvests.

Yours sincerely,
(Signed) WILLIAM H. TAFT,
President of the American Red Cross."

About the same time the State Department, through Acting Secretary Bacon, acknowledged the receipt of $50,000 to be cabled to the American Consul-General at Shanghai, so that $50,000 was available in China in a single day.

The *Buford* sailed from San Francisco on April 30. Special services were held at the dock in the morning, and were impressive and enthusiastic throughout. On the platform were many officials of prominence, including the governor of the state, and also many representative ministers. Mr. E. R. Johnstone, who was to accompany the vessel to China as the special representative of *The Christian Herald*, was also present. The Rev. Frank DeWitt Talmage presided, and made a brief address. He concluded, "May God bless the *Buford* in her mission of mercy. Standing here today in the presence of the governor of this commonwealth, and the president of our largest university, and the bishop of our largest Episcopal diocese, and the representatives of the Catholic and the Protestant churches, all of whom have contributed to this fund, we are here to ask a divine blessing upon the *Buford*, this new messenger of peace of America's international policies. May God bless the President of the United States and his great Secretary, and all who have contributed to this noble service of saving the physical lives of the dying men and women and children of poor, suffering, starving China."

Mr. E. R. Johnstone, on behalf of *The Christian Herald*, thanked the audience for its interest and sympathy in the relief work. He read a communication from Dr. Klopsch thanking the people of this Christian land of ours and our sympathetic Government for all the loving kindness, cordial coöperation, and generous sympathy that they had shown toward the starving people of China. The communication concluded: "I send my earnest prayers and best wishes for the *Buford,* her officers and crew (God bless them, one and all), and for a speedy and prosperous conclusion of her mission of mercy."

President Wheeler, of the University of California, Bishop William Ford Nichols, Governor Gillett and ex-Mayor Phelan, on behalf of the Red Cross, also spoke, all of them expressing gratitude for the great assistance rendered by *The Christian Herald* and its readers to the life-saving campaign in famine-stricken China.

"My Country, 'tis of Thee," was then sung by the audience, after which Dr. Frank DeWitt Talmage invoked the divine blessing upon the cargo. With the singing of the Doxology the exercises closed.

Half an hour after noon, amid the cheers of the spectators and the stirring music of the band, the *Buford* steamed away from her dock and out towards the Pacific, *The Christian Herald* relief flag streaming out as she moved down the bay. Among her passengers were twenty-five members of Congress and their wives, who were going to Honolulu, which was to be the first port of call.

"It was ten o'clock on the morning of Memorial Day," wrote Special Commissioner Johnstone, "that the United States army transport *Buford* dropped her anchor on the edge of the Yang-tse. We were

31 days out from San Francisco, and with stoppage for coal at Honolulu and Nagasaki had covered more than 2,000 leagues of ocean.

"First we were boarded by the brisk little gig bearing a customs officer, and then by Rev. T. F. McCrea, a missionary of the Southern Baptist church, and Mr. M. J. Walker, agent of the English Bible Society, representatives of the missionary committee. With them was an aide of Yung, Taotai or governor of Ching Kiang and the surrounding contiguous districts.

"In a few moments after the *Buford's* arrival the single-masted, lateen-sailed junks began to surround the steamer and to take up positions along her white sides. To foreign ears it was confusion worse confounded. The boatmen yelled, sang, wrangled, laughed, and ran to and fro in utter abandonment. But somehow out of confusion came a semblance of order and by three in the afternoon gangs of coolies, each under the supervision of a boss, and all under the eyes of the missionaries — Walker, McLane, Napier, and Lampton — had made a break in the cargo and were unloading from four ports, two on each side of the ship.

"Without announcement and only four hours after our arrival at Ching Kiang, Taotai Yung, accompanied by his chief magistrate and harbor master and a retinue of servants, came on board to make an official call upon the representative of *The Christian Herald.* Yung is a Manchu, and large and imposing, as I have found all northerners of rank to be. He wears a sparse moustache, has a dignified courtesy and a pleasant smile that are most fetching, and he was cordiality itself. Mr. Walker acted as interpreter, and the conversation ran about in this wise:

Myself: "Your Excellency, I come as representative of *The Christian Herald,* and those who through that paper have been instrumental in sending $450,000 in gold or its worth in supplies to your stricken and starving people, and to tell you that American hearts are full of sympathy for you and your people in their distress. They are glad to give of their substance to relieve your need. They are glad to show their feeling of brotherhood."

The Taotai: (Rising and bowing three times with hands clasped in an arch above his breast in Chinese salutation) "I am unworthy, unworthy. I am honored by what you say and by your representative presents. From mind and heart I tell you thanks. I charge you convey to *The Christian Herald* particularly, and to the Americans generally, my warmest gratitude and that of all my people. We will never forget what you have done. We will remember while life lasts this great ship, its cargo of food, and what it means to the starving. I am unworthy. I am honored."

"All this was said in sincerest fashion, and with a dignity that added great impressiveness."

Letters were written by Mr. Johnstone from various districts up the Grand Canal. From Huian he wrote: "Two hours ago I saw the first sack of *Buford* flour delivered to a starving applicant. It was a man, gray-haired, gaunt, grateful, if grave eyes filled with new light, joined palms lifted in salute, meant aught. The second sack went to a withered crone with half a dozen mouths to feed; the third to a girl not more than twelve and barely able to

shoulder and carry away the half hundredweight of
life-saving food.

"It was from the deck of one of the three junks
towed with infinite difficulty from Ching Kiang that
the delivery was made. It was supervised by Rev.
H. M. Woods, a missionary of twenty-five years'
service in China and whose house is in the center of
Huian, a prominent walled city of 150,000 people
situated on the Grand Canal, at the southern edge
of the famine district, and for months a principal
distributing point for American relief. Dr. Woods
was assisted by Messrs. Brown and Espey, young
missionary volunteers from Shanghai who for months
have undergone physical hardships, mental distress,
dangers from violence and disease in order that they
might save lives. The junk with 1,380 sacks of
Christian Herald flour was moored on the west bank
of the Grand Canal. To the left and on top of the
bank was a Buddhist temple, and through a narrow
stockade, built to keep away the importunate
crowds and leading into the temple court, passed
long lines of coolies bearing the cargo of sacks from
another junk. In the very storeroom in which the
pile of flour sacks rose was a glass-covered niche
from which beamed a placid Buddha.

"Very soon after breakfast the chief official of the
city and district, magistrate Sun, a handsome young
nobleman, paid me an official call. Sun and Yung
Chang, head of the district telegraph service, who
accompanied him, were profuse in their expressions
of gratitude to the donors of the flour; asked me to
send their message of thanks to America, and said

the kindness of our people would always bloom fresh in Chinese hearts as showing brotherhood of a practical sort.

"The deeper I get into the stricken region, the more I see and hear of the relief work, the prouder I am of my Americanism, the gladder over the generosity of *The Christian Herald* readers. I have said little or nothing of the horrors of the famine-stricken region. I shall not descant upon them. God knows they are real enough, affecting enough, terrible enough. Within the last few days I have seen more emaciation than you could find in the United States from one end to the other, I believe. It is impossible to conceive, much less describe, conditions in these densely populated centers."

From Tsing Kiang Pu, a city of 140,000 inhabitants, Mr. Johnstone wrote a further account. The name means "Bank of the clear river." It is a point where the Grand Canal is first broken by lakes and from which trends the great road to Peking, 500 miles or more away to the northward, that for tens of centuries has been the main traveled highway for the busy myriads of the great provinces along the sea.

"I rode out to see an old canal some three miles off," said Mr. Johnstone, "in redigging which the missionaries had given employment to some 4,700 refugees. The Rev. A. D. Rice, who had charge of the workers, accompanied me. Our way ran through thousands and thousands of the conical graves which take up so much available land in this country. Here and there were tombs of priests with impos-

THE U. S. TROOPSHIP *BUFORD*, WHICH CARRIED RELIEF
TO CHINA

UNLOADING THE *BUFORD'S* CARGO

ing headstones and circumscribing groves of stunted
pines. But earth was the usual weir of the dead,
each cone for all the world like the ant hills of
inner Africa, surmounted by a clay image of a hat,
sometimes fashioned like the bishop's mitre, again
like an hour glass, or rarely spherical with the
mortar board of the student over-topping all. Here
and there were fresh graves into which were thrust
bamboo splints wrapped with paper. If the paper
was smooth it was noted that the deceased has left
as many children as there were sticks. If rough,
grandchildren were indicated. I passed one with
five smooth paper sticks, and seven with rough.
'That will be an honored ancestry indeed,' said Mr.
Rice; 'she will have many to worship her now that
she is dead and throned in the Chinese heaven, or
so her descendants believe.' Everywhere were evidences of careful husbandry. Most of the small
farms were in wheat, and the yield was wretched.
Bugs and worms and drought had cut the crop
into half or less of the usual output. In scores of
places a small ox was dragging a corrugated cylinder
of stone across a threshing floor that might have
been left bodily from the Palestine of the days of
Solomon."

Commissioner Johnstone continued to visit the
various relief stations and send accounts of the
good work that was done in the distribution of
the *Buford's* cargo. He also forwarded a very
interesting description of his interview with Tuan
Fang, the lord of 80 millions, the great Chinese
Viceroy.

Tuan Fang's kingdom stretches for more than a thousand miles north and south and is full five hundred broad at its narrowest. It embraces the great province of Kiang Su, which borders the eastern sea, and is probably the richest, as it certainly has the most learned men of the Empire.

"Tuan Fang," wrote Mr. Johnstone, "is a Manchu. He turned to where I was seated on his right and said, 'I greet you with deep respect and gratitude, in that you have come so many thousands of miles to bring flour to my hungry people. I feel, Sir, (placing his hand on his heart) to my deepest being how kind *The Christian Herald* and Dr. Klopsch, its editor, have been. They have won the gratitude not only of the Chinese people, but of China's officials, and their thoughtfulness will never be forgotten. It is wonderful what they have done.'

"I replied that Americans in general, and *The Christian Herald* in particular, were glad to give tangible evidence of their high regard and sympathy for the Chinese. Again the Viceroy expressed deep gratitude. Ere we finally made our adieus, the Viceroy said: 'I much regret that my illness will prevent my giving you a feast as I had intended, nor can I return the visit with which you have honored and pleased me. I wish for you all and for Dr. Klopsch, your families and to all who gave toward the flour, health and prosperity. May you have a safe voyage home and be able to tell your people of our gratitude and praise.'"

When it became clear that all which was possible for the relief of the famine-stricken people of China in the way of collecting funds and sending food had been done, and that the new harvest would be sufficient to sustain the population, the collection of money and supplies was discontinued. In due time the usual certified, audited statement was rendered by Dr. Klopsch. It showed a total of receipt of the second Chinese famine fund, under the auspices of *The Christian Herald*, of $427,323.91. Of the cash remittances $175,000 was made through the State Department, and $75,000 direct through the American National Red Cross. The cost of the flour purchased for the *Buford* was $110,000, and the railway freight for transporting it to San Francisco, which was donated, was $40,000. The detailed statement showed that there had been 149,000 separate contributions to the fund. Balance, aggregating $112,-833.52, was transferred to the support of orphans of the famine in the care of numerous missionaries.

In presenting the audited statement of receipts and expenditures Dr. Klopsch, in an editorial in *The Christian Herald*, described it as the "glorious work in China." Appreciation came from the Shanghai relief committee. Edward S. Little, the chairman of the executive committee, wrote:

SHANGHAI, July 6, 1907.

DEAR DR. KLOPSCH: The great famine which has devastated several prefectures of this province is now over. The people and officials very highly appreciate all that has been done to save them from a terrible death at the hands of the hunger fiend.

A great part of the success of our work has been due to your noble efforts, and I wish in the most positive and hearty way possible to express to you from our committee our very sincere thanks for the wonderful work you and your widely-circulated paper have accomplished. . . . The total amount of contributions realized through our committee and the Ching Kiang committee and other sources reached a total of $1,600,000 Mexican ($800,000 gold). Of this sum, about $1,000,000 ($500,000 gold) was realized from America, and largely through your good self. We have relieved over a million persons with these funds by direct assistance, and very many more by the indirect results which have accrued through our efforts by compelling officials and gentry who held stocks of food stuff to realize at reasonable rates. Great numbers of people in the famine area have thanked our sub-committees for this very reason. A number of them had sufficient money to buy food stuffs to see them through, even at enhanced prices, but not at the terribly inflated rates that were ruling. The vast importation of food stuffs from our committee compelled holders of grain to reduce prices and thus enable the above class of people to hold out till the harvest.

A very great amount of relief works have been put in, which tend to ameliorate conditions of life in the country and in some measure to prevent a recurrence of famine by flood. We shall do our best to persuade the Government to carry on to completion the works so begun.

A further great benefit that will result from this famine work will be the bettering of the relations existing between the Chinese and foreigners. Both sides have come to understand each other better, and have seen another phase of each others' character. I have no doubt whatever that a further result has been the breaking down of anti-foreign barriers, so that missionaries from this time on have an access to the people's attention and hearts such as has never been known before.

The work has involved of course an enormous strain upon us, physically and mentally, and entailed an immense amount of labor; but all have worked well and a very great success has crowned our united efforts.

The orphan work in China naturally followed the famine relief work. At the close of the fearful visitations, the missionaries found themselves burdened with a new responsibility. In a number of provinces where the suffering had been most severe, hundreds of poor families were completely wiped out by death, while others were reduced to two or three members, mostly children. These helpless little creatures were taken by relatives or strangers to the missionaries, and many of the latter soon found themselves in the difficult position of having to support a large family of orphan waifs for whom they had no provision beyond the regular mission stipend.

At this time the appeal was made to *The Christian Herald*, and Dr. Klopsch after investigation undertook in behalf of its readers to aid in the orphan work. Remittances were forwarded to the missionaries who were in most urgent need. A permanent provision was arranged for various orphanages. The unexpended balance of the famine fund was devoted to the support of some three thousand orphans, under the personal direction of the missionary committee, of which the Rev. W. C. Longden was Chairman. This fund is still in operation. There are now about two thousand orphans on the roll. Remittances are sent regularly every quarter in advance.

CHAPTER XII

SYMPATHY WITH THE NEW JAPAN

CLOSE BOND WITH THE AMERICAN PEOPLE — FAILURE OF THE RICE CROP IN 1906 — DISTRESS OF THE POPULATION — THE "CHRISTIAN HERALD" STARTS THE FUNDS — COÖPERATION IN RELIEF MOVEMENTS — SKETCH OF THE JAPANESE RED CROSS — MISSIONARY COMMITTEE — PRESIDENT ROOSEVELT THANKS DR. KLOPSCH — HOPE DAWNS — STATE DEPARTMENT REPORTS — PERMANENT AID FOR THE ORPHANS — GRATEFUL LETTER FROM GOVERNORS OF THE SUCCORED PROVINCES — JAPANESE GOVERNMENT'S RECOGNITION — BARON OZAWA'S SPECIAL MISSION — ORDER OF THE RISING SUN CONFERRED ON DR. KLOPSCH — FURTHER ACKNOWLEDGMENTS.

IN the awakening of the Orient, Japan has been the first of the old nations to shake off the sleep of centuries. From the time when Commodore Perry opened the doors to Western civilization the history and the customs of the Japanese have had a fascinating interest for the American people. But they have also been interested in the marvelous progress since the Japanese have prided themselves that they were the pupils of America. There has been a spirit of mutual friendliness.

After the conclusion of the war with Russia, Japan began to experience the industrial and financial depression which is not unusual with the victors in war. Reactions of this sort are, however, overcome and the advance of a nation is not halted. But there are some events which cannot be anticipated. One of these is the failure of crops.

In the summer of 1906 reports were received that

the northern provinces were in the grip of famine. The American missionaries at Sendai made known the situation. The Government had established relief stations and was making heroic efforts to mitigate the suffering, but there was the cruel fact that the rice crop in what was usually one of the finest granaries of the country was a failure, and that a large number of people, estimated at one million, were without food.

The Rev. H. Loomis, of the American Bible Society at Yokohama, wrote *The Christian Herald:*

"The Japanese officials are doing all in their power. They will be most grateful for any voluntary contributions, but are too self-respecting to appear before the world as beggars. Knowing the readiness of your people to assist in every good work, I take this opportunity to request help to relieve this great distress. Such action will demonstrate to the Japanese the spirit of Christianity and your sincere interest in their welfare."

The Rev. J. H. De Forest, of the Sendai Missionary Committee, wrote:

"The national pride of the Japanese prevents him from making any public appeal for aid. But to ask for aid is a very different thing from receiving aid proffered by sympathetic friends. It was solely in this support that foreigners ventured with hesitancy to place an appeal before the foreign communities. It is our privilege to help soften the sorrow of thousands of homes and if this be done as friends the act will win the gratitude of all classes."

It became known that many of the people in the

famine-stricken provinces were living on roots and bark. Though every effort was made at least to supply enough subsistence to save the suffering peasants from starvation, many did die from lack of nourishment. In some cases they sought to live upon what was known as "hunger-bread," which was a composition of earth mixed with powdered rice, straw, and acorns. Some of the poor people had nothing but crushed acorns and earth.

As letter after letter came from the missionaries, intelligence was received from other foreigners in Japan, and as the Government officials reluctantly told of their efforts to relieve the distress and confessed their fears that these would be unavailing without aid from abroad, a sustenance relief movement was started in the United States.

Dr. Klopsch began forwarding money even before *The Christian Herald* readers had time to send in their contributions. In *The Christian Herald*, he wrote:

"'Give us bread, give us bread, or we perish,' is the pitiful cry which comes from the northern provinces of far-away Japan to Christian America. Mothers frantically pressing the emaciated little forms of infant children to their parched breasts, as if by embrace to keep the feeble spark of life from becoming wholly extinct; wives whose hearts are breaking as they see the bread-winner of the family growing weaker and weaker day after day, without prospect of relief; and husbands whose looks of hopeless agony speak louder than words of the terrible dread and apprehension that fill their hearts, are straining their

EMPEROR MUTSUHITO AND THE EMPRESS OF JAPAN

THE DECORATION OF THE "RISING SUN"
Presented to Dr. Klopsch by the Emperor of Japan

eyes in the direction of this country whence hail the
missionaries who have told them of the beautiful
story of one Jesus, who went about doing good,
who fed the multitudes, and whose followers in this
blessed country are working in the foot-steps of their
Master."

President Roosevelt, voicing the feelings of the
American people, addressed an appeal in behalf of
the suffering nation.   In this he said:

"The famine situation in northern Japan is proving
much more serious than at first supposed, and thousands of persons are on the verge of starvation.   It
is a calamity such as may occasionally befall any
nation.   Nations, like men, should stand ever ready
to aid each other in distress, and I appeal to the
American people to help from their abundance their
suffering fellow-men of the great and friendly nation
of Japan."

The diplomatic and consular officers of the United
States in the meantime had forwarded official reports
confirming all that had previously been received from
private sources.   The reports stated that a large part
of the population in the famine provinces was
reduced to subsistence on roots of trees, leaves, barks
and acorns.

In the consular advices, some of the recipes for the
preparation of what was designated as "emergency
food" were given, and they revealed with startling
emphasis the desperate straits to which the sufferers
had been reduced.   One illustration shows the
character of this "emergency food." It describes
the straw-cakes, which were seven parts water, one

and one-half parts cheap flour, with three-quarters of a pound of lime and a half pound of potassium bicarbonate. The straw was cut fine and boiled an hour and a half in sixteen quarts of water. The roots and chaff were skimmed off and thrown away. The straw water was strained through the lime, after which the potassium bicarbonate was added, and then more straw put in. This boiled straw was washed with fresh water and strained, and the residue thoroughly mixed with cheap flour, forming the consistency of tough dough. This was made into cakes and allowed to dry, after which it was pounded and beaten, then it was mixed with water and boiled into soup. This recipe made about eight quarts of food.

Various committees were formed in the United States, the American National Red Cross Society exerted itself, and the Japanese National Red Cross was selected as the chief source for distributing the relief. Japan was fortunate in having its National Red Cross Society, which labored in harmonious conjunction with the missionary and other foreign relief workers. The Society had its origin with *Haku-ai-sha*, or "Society of Extended Benevolence," founded by a number of philanthropic Japanese noblemen when the Satsuma rebellion broke out in 1877. After the rebellion was suppressed, the promoters of the *Haku-ai-sha* effected a permanent organization and made preparations for future emergencies, training surgeons and nurses for active field service. They established at Tokio the *Haku-ai-sha* Hospital, where poor patients were treated gratuitously, and where surgeons and nurses were trained. Later it placed itself in connection with the International Committee of the Red Cross at Geneva, and entered into fraternal relations with similar societies in other countries. It also changed its name to the "Red Cross Society of Japan."

By 1905 the Society had nearly a million members, each of whom was pledged to contribute not less than three yen ($1.50) annually for a period of ten years. The Society has a Central Board or Headquarters in Tokio, and branch offices in all the prefectures, called "local stations." A General Assembly of all the members, held in Tokio once a year, is honored by the presence of the Emperor in person. At this Assembly the election of thirty members of a standing committee for the term of three years takes place. The membership of this committee is honorary. The officers do not receive salaries.

The Emperor has endowed the Society with a fixed capital, which produces $2,500 a year, and the Empress has granted an annual endowment of a similar amount to the Hospital of the Society. On the twenty-fifth anniversary of the foundation of the International Committee of the Red Cross in Geneva, the Empress made a gift of $50,000 to the Society, as a hospital fund, and granted the free use of an immense tract of land situated in the suburbs of Tokio as hospital grounds.

In the statutes of the Japanese Red Cross Society, the expression often recurs "relief in case of political disaster or national calamity." When in 1888 the eruption of Mount Bandi occurred, and several hundred persons were killed, the Society sent to the scene of disaster physicians equipped with all that was necessary for succor. It also did efficient service on many other occasions, notably with the wreck of the Turkish warship *Ertogul* in 1890, and after the great earthquake in 1891, it succored many hundreds of injured.

In connection with the Society there is a large and influential body called "The Lady Volunteer Nursing Association." It was founded in Tokio by princesses and the wives and daughters of nobles and prominent persons.

At the period of the famine in the northern provinces, the Japanese Red Cross was very thoroughly organized and equipped in all its branches and in a position to render the very best service to the suffering people. Its President was Count Matsakata, one of the elder statesmen, who had twice been Prime Minister and several times Minister of Finance. The Vice-Presidents were Baron Hanabusa and Baron Ozawa.

With such an efficient body coöperating with the missionaries and other agencies, the American people rightly felt that the relief which they contributed would be well and speedily applied. Dr. Klopsch had the same feeling. Early in March, he had cabled $20,000 to the Japanese Red Cross for the famine and received immediate thanks from Count Matsakata. This money was spent in the purchase of food, which was immediately forwarded to the field for the relief of the neediest cases.

More aid was rushed for emergency purposes, both to the Japanese Red Cross and direct to the Missionary Relief Committee at Sendai.

IN A JAPANESE PEASANT HOME

THE POOR QUARTERS OF A JAPANESE PEASANT FAMILY

In one week *The Christian Herald* cabled through the State Department $50,000. Mr. Eki Hioki, the *Chargé d'Affaires* at the Japanese Legation in Washington, received official dispatches from the Government at Tokio saying that the money sent from America had been received and sent to the different centers in the famine district and there expended for food.

So spontaneous and liberal were the contributions through *The Christian Herald* that President Roosevelt sent a special telegram of commendation to Dr. Klopsch as follows:

"THE WHITE HOUSE,
WASHINGTON, March 21, 1906.
"MR. LOUIS KLOPSCH,
The Christian Herald, New York, N. Y.
"Let me heartily thank you, and through you *The Christian Herald*, for the admirable work done in connection with the famine sufferers in Japan. You have raised $100,000, and you have rendered a very real service to humanity and to the cause of international good-will.
"(Signed) THEODORE ROOSEVELT."

Dr. Klopsch sent the following reply:

"NEW YORK, March 21, 1906.
"To HIS EXCELLENCY, THE PRESIDENT.
"*Dear Mr. President:* It was a very gracious act to wire me your personal appreciation of *The Christian Herald* work for the Japan famine sufferers; and for our readers, our staff, and myself I thank you most sincerely, and beg to assure you that your very generous message will stimulate us all to greater achievement.
"(Signed) LOUIS KLOPSCH."

Slowly hope dawned over the suffering provinces. The Japanese Government, besides doing all it could for the relief of those actually suffering, had shown proper foresight for the future, and had distributed seed for planting the next season's rice crop. In April a cablegram came to Dr. Klopsch, from Rev. C. S. Davison, the Secretary of the Missionary Committee at Sendai, saying that while half a million were still receiving aid, the prospects were better owing to public works and warmer weather. The Missionary Committee had made four distributions of relief, one being exclusively with contributions received through *The Christian Herald*. It planned to close the work by the end of May.

The State Department in Washington received from Hon. Huntington Wilson, the American *Chargé d'Affaires* at Tokio, an official report that the crisis was over. In his letter he said:

"The Government estimated the number of people in need on March 8 to be 700,000. A gentleman who had been investigating the situation on the spot estimated at the same date that some 900,000 were in more or less distress, and that of these about 500,000 were really suffering, and some 250,000 in vital need and now receiving assistance. The famine had now reached, and probably passed, its worst stage. The means of relief are improved. The severe winter is now breaking up, which will, with the melting of the snow, improve the means of communication and make more out-of-door work possible. As the spring and summer advance, there will be work in planting for land-owners, tending silk worms, picking mulberry leaves, etc.   For these reasons the suffering should now steadily decrease. A measure of relief will be needed, however, until the autumn, when the local rice crop is harvested. Perhaps by the middle of June the number of those who must be given food will be reduced by about one-half, and so gradually fall off.

"Americans may well feel pride in the splendid work done by the Foreign Committee at Sendai, of which the great majority, Dr. De Forest, Mr. W. E. Lampe, The Rev. C. S. Davison, Mr. M. B. Madden, and William Axling, are citizens of the United States. The work of these men, and the donations from the United States, collected by *The Christian Herald*, and through the Red Cross Society, are like the President's humanitarian appeal, highly appreciated in Japan."

An official report of the Interior Department of the Japanese Government gave in detail the relief work in operation, which showed that the Government had made sufficient provision for all emergencies during the coming summer, the object in view being to carry over the sufferers until the next harvest.

When the violence of the famine abated, the usual orphan problem, which seems to be inseparable from such calamities, presented itself.   One of the missionaries, the Rev. J. H. Pettee, sent Dr. Klopsch a vivid description of the care that was taken to properly provide for the waifs.   Some of them were brought six hundred miles.

The Missionary Committee, of which Dr. W. E.

Lampe was Chairman, gathered the orphans together and placed them in two large orphanages at Sendai and Okayama, some twelve hundred in all. The last contribution from the United States to the famine-stricken people was divided, according to the decision of the official committee, among the orphan asylums which were especially caring for the orphans from the famine districts.

Dr. Klopsch, in dealing with the Japanese orphanages, decided to operate on the same principles that he had found so successful in India, that is, finding American patrons for individual orphans. At the time of his death there were 386 orphans in the care of two orphanages, for which individual support is sent regularly every three months in advance, the patrons making their remittances through *The Christian Herald*. It was a remarkable instance of the interest taken that in connection with this Japanese relief work there had been more volunteer offers of individual support than there had been orphans to be maintained. Dr. Klopsch's experience with the India and China orphanages gave assurance that the patron's pledges for Japan orphans' support would be faithfully kept.

In July Dr. Klopsch presented the audited statement of the Japanese famine fund under the auspices of *The Christian Herald*. The total disbursements amounted to $241,822.80.

The gratitude of the Japanese people, and of the Japanese Government, was shown in many ways. Late in July, Viscount Aoki, Japanese Ambassador in Washington, sent the following letter:

JAPANESE EMBASSY,
WASHINGTON, July 26, 1906.

SIR: Upon the request of the three Governors of Mizagi, Iwate and Fukushima, Japan, I beg to transmit to you the enclosed letter, in which they jointly express their sincere thanks for the collection you have made for the relief of the famine-stricken people of those three provinces.

In thus carrying out the request of the three Governors, I have the honor to express my own appreciation of your humane and fraternal action and to ask that you will be good enough to make a public announcement of the grateful thanks of my countrymen and of myself for the material aid which was so generously and so cheerfully given by the high-minded people of the United States for the relief of the unfortunate sufferers of northern Japan. I am, sir,

Very respectfully yours,

To DR. LOUIS KLOPSCH,   (Signed) VISCOUNT S. AOKI.
Editor of *The Christian Herald*, New York.

A facsimile of the letter from the three governors, with the translation in English, is reproduced below.

以書翰致啓上候陳者昨三十八年歳々帝國東北地方ニ
城岩手福島三縣下ニ亘ケル飢饉ニ際シテハ貴社ハ卒先義
國民ニ同情好意ヲ表セシメ被害民救恤ノ目的ヲ以テ之ヲ
貴國慈善家ニ訴ヘ義捐金ノ醵集ヲ盡瘁セラレ鉅額ノ
金圓ヲ寄贈セラレクルハ本大臣ノ深ク感謝スル處ニ有之候
己ニ御寄贈相成候義捐金ハ其都度正領収真ニ當該
官憲ヲ經テ夫々窮民救助ノ資ニ充テラレタリ當時飢渇
ニ頻セシ幾多ノ窮民ハ茲ニ貴國民同情ノ下ニ大ニ其心意
ヲ慰セルルコトヲ得候就テ貴國慈善家ノ同情ニ對シテハ

外務省

内務大臣ヨリモ感謝意ヲ傳致スヘキ旨本官ニ依頼
モ有之候間右御了知相成度此段御通知旁々本大臣
ハ茲ニ貴下ニ向テ敬意ヲ表シ候敬具

明治三十九年十一月廿六日

外務大臣子爵林董

クリスチャン、ヘラルド新聞社長
ドクトル、ルイス、クロツプシユ貴下

(TRANSLATION)

June 8th, 1906.

To the Editor and Proprietor of " *The Christian Herald.*"

SIR : We beg to gratefully acknowledge the receipt of your earlier contribution of 170,854.27 yen,[1] from the first to the third remittance, inclusive, and of your three later remittances made through the American Red Cross, amounting to 110,552.77 yen, which two sums were duly transmitted to us by our central government, through the medium of the Red Cross Society of Japan, to be expended for the relief of the famine sufferers of our three provinces.

We join in expressing to you, and, through you, to those sympathizers who responded to your philanthropic appeal, our profound appreciation, and that of the people of our provinces, for the deep sympathy and cordial good-will so generously manifested for our unfortunate sufferers from natural calamity. We beg to assure you that we will unite our best efforts in making prompt distribution of your donations among the needy sufferers and in seeing the noble purpose you have in view carried out satisfactorily.

Respectfully,

(Seal)   Y. KAEMI, Governor of the Province of Miyagi.

(Seal)   N. OSHIKAWA, Governor of the Province of Iwate.

(Seal)   Y. ARITA, Governor of the Province of Fukushima.

The Director of the Japanese Red Cross, in a letter to Dr. Klopsch, also expressed the appreciation of that Society for the relief that had been extended, and gave details regarding their distribution. He said that the sufferers expressed their appreciation and gratitude with tears in their eyes for all the kindness shown them by the contributors to the fund.

How deep the sentiment of gratitude was, appeared months after the famine was over. In February,

---

[1] A yen is 49 cents.

1907, Minister Aoki wrote Dr. Klopsch from Washington recalling the pleasure he had had in July, 1906, in enclosing a letter in which the three governors jointly expressed their sincere thanks. He added that he was now requested by His Majesty's Minister of State to transmit a letter in which Viscount Hayashi, speaking in behalf of himself and of his colleagues of home affairs, expressed to Dr. Klopsch their sincere thanks for the generous contribution of the people of the United States who so willingly responded to the call for relief of the distress caused by the famine.

The letter from Viscount Hayashi, after reciting the contributions and the action taken with regard to the remittances, closed by saying:

I have much pleasure in assuring you that the sympathy thus shown by the American people was a source of great consolation, no less than of material help and comfort to the inhabitants of the stricken districts, who were at the time in great distress.

The Japanese Government did not stop with these acknowledgments. A little later Baron Takew Ozawa, one of the Vice-Presidents of the Japanese Red Cross Society, came to the United States on a special mission. It was to decorate Dr. Klopsch, who had been created a special member of the Society, with the Order of the Rising Sun. Baron Ozawa was an honored guest of the Periodical Publishers Association at their banquet in Albany. On that occasion, in addressing the guests, he said among other things, speaking of himself and his associates:

"Our mission is, briefly, first, to decorate Dr. Louis Klopsch with the Order of the Rising Sun, for his kindness and sympathy."

The presentation of the Order was made in the office of *The Christian Herald* in New York. The date was May 15, 1907. There were present on the occasion, besides Baron Ozawa, his secretary and interpreter, Mr. Masatake S. Togo, and the editors and heads of the various departments of *The Christian Herald.* Thus spoke Baron Ozawa:

"In the name of my Imperial Sovereign, the Emperor of Japan, and of Her Imperial Majesty, the Empress, I am commissioned to convey to Dr. Louis Klopsch their royal acknowledgments for all the kindness and generous aid which you and *The Christian Herald,* its editors and its readers, have extended to the people of our country during the late famine. Furthermore, as a token of His Imperial Majesty's regard, he has personally directed me to invest you with this decoration of the Order of the Rising Sun, a duty which I take pleasure in performing in obedience to His Majesty's command."

Dr. Klopsch, after receiving the decoration, said, in substance, that the honor, which had come so unexpectedly, was one which he accepted in the name of the hundreds of thousands of contributors whose Christian generosity had made the relief work in Japan so successful. He desired Baron Ozawa to convey to their Majesties, the Emperor and Empress, his sincere acknowledgment. He referred to the universal sympathy which had prevailed in this country for the unfortunate Japanese peasants during the

period of famine, and to the fact that then, as on
various other occasions of a similar character, the
generous-hearted people had chosen his journal as
a channel for their benevolence.   "Our nation, as a
whole," he said, "entertains feelings of the warmest
admiration and friendship for the people of Japan."

The Order of the Rising Sun has an interesting
origin.   There are four orders of distinction in Japan,
the two most important being the Order of the Rising
Sun and the Order of the Chrysanthemum.   The
orders were all founded at about the same time, at
the beginning of the reign of the present Emperor.
The Rising Sun was first conferred in 1875.   The
decoration has engraved, in Japanese characters on
the back, the words, "for merit."

The Order is given to Japanese or foreigners who
have rendered great service to the Emperor or the
Empire.   It is much coveted.   It holds the same
place in Japan that the various orders of knighthood
hold in European countries.   The badge is made to
represent the Rising Sun of Japan.   There is a center
disk of crimson, and from this radiates the golden
rising of the sun.   The spaces between are in white
enamel.   The decoration is suspended from a white
ribbon, edged with crimson.   It is worn on the left
breast on occasions of ceremony.   At other times a
little button of crimson silk is worn in the button-
hole of the lapel of the coat, serving as a recognition button.

Previous to this decoration Count Matsuyata,
President of the Japanese Red Cross, had forwarded
Dr. Klopsch, "as a token of our high appreciation

for the kindness and sympathy you have shown to
our country in many different ways and in com-
memoration of the Red Cross work of the Society
as well," a medal struck with copper articles actually
employed by both belligerents in the severe battles
of Port Arthur and Mukden.

A further effort of the Japanese Government and
people to show their appreciation was made in 1908,
when Mr. T. J. O'Brien, the American Ambassador
at Tokio, communicated the request of the Government that it be furnished with the names of the
individual contributors to the famine fund so that
it might send to each one its individual acknowledgments. Since there were more than 85,000 of
these contributors, it was impracticable to carry out
this graceful idea, and a general acknowledgment was
again made through *The Christian Herald* to the
contributors as a body.

CHAPTER XIII

FAIR ITALY'S APPALLING CALAMITY

HISTORIC VOLCANIC ERUPTIONS — THE TERRIFYING CHRISTMAS WEEK OF 1908 — BEAUTIFUL MESSINA'S DESTRUCTION BY EARTHQUAKE — THE TIDAL WAVE — NEIGHBORING TOWNS WIPED OUT — THE "CHRISTIAN HERALD" CABLES AID FOR THE SURVIVORS — REV. DR. CARTER COMMISSIONED TO VISIT THE SCENES OF SORROW — THRILLING STORY OF WHAT HE SAW — REGGIO AND THE SICILIAN COAST — "MOTHER AND CHILD CHARITY" PROPOSED BY DR. KLOPSCH — HEROIC QUEEN HELENA'S AID — ASSISTANCE GIVEN THE WALDENSIAN CHRISTIANS — VISIT TO ITALY BY ROYAL INVITATION — AMBASSADOR GRISCOM'S COURTESY — AUDIENCE WITH KING VICTOR EMMANUEL — DR. KLOPSCH'S ACCOUNT — APPRECIATIVE COMMENT.

ITALY, the land of story, has been known in history for the destructive disasters it has suffered. Vesuvius and Etna time and again have poured forth their fiery streams and overwhelmed towns and cities. Buried Pompeii and Herculaneum are the record of the fury of Vesuvius nineteen hundred years ago. But all the disasters have not been due to the volcanic eruptions. The greatest of the modern ones, the calamity of centuries, was due to an earthquake.

After Christmas in 1908 the world was startled by the news that a frightful earthquake had visited southern Italy on the morning of December 28, changing the geographical outline of a large part of the country, destroying cities, towns, and villages almost in an instant, and carrying down to a sudden and shocking death a great multitude of human beings.

Italy is shaped much like a boot, with its toe placed against a rock. Calabria, the toe of the boot, and the rock, the picturesque island of Sicily, were the districts in which the most appalling loss of life occurred. The rest of the region, however, was shaken with lighter tremors, which were felt as far north as the Italian Alps. The death-dealing disturbance had for its center the Straits of Messina, lying between Calabria on the mainland and Sicily. Three great volcanoes, Etna, Vesuvius, and Stromboli,were within the area of the shock. Many times in previous years severe earthquakes had visited this ill-fated region, but all of these experiences were utterly eclipsed by the mighty spasm which blotted the beautiful Calabrian city Reggio out of existence and laid in ruins various smaller towns on the mainland, as well as the cities of Messina, Catania, and other towns in Sicily.

The earthquake shocks began about half past five on the morning of December 28, while the people were asleep, and lasted about thirty seconds. Subsequent shocks, which came in rapid succession, were a few seconds longer in duration. The whole of the Straits of Messina were convulsed. The sea became greatly agitated. Suddenly a huge tidal wave swept through the Straits, carrying everything before it, tossing ships as though they were of paper, tearing big vessels from their anchorage, and filling the water with wreckage. This monster wave, accompanied by a roaring and terrifying sound, swept inland doing tremendous damage and adding heavily to the list of mortalities inflicted by the earthquake.

LITTLE JAPANESE ORPHANS AT OKAYAMA, SUPPORTED BY *THE CHRISTIAN HERALD*

Soon the ruins of the crumbling towns caught fire and columns of smoke arose in all directions.

The first accounts which reached the outside world came from the terror-stricken refugees who fled from Messina. They told how in their beautiful city when the first shock came the earth seemed to rise for a moment and then to fall away. The fronts of the houses along entire streets fell forward to the roadway, as if dashed down by unseen hands, and the people were precipitated to the lower floors, and in some instances clear to the streets. In an instant the city was in an uproar, falling walls, the rending of timbers, the shrieks of the people, mingled in an indescribable pandemonium. All who could, made their way into the open. Some who retained their self-possession tried to rescue their families, but before anything could be done, other shocks followed, and the weakened walls that were still standing fell in on the people below, the grinding of brick and stone, as it rushed downward to earth, making a deafening roar, which drowned out for a moment the cries and shrieks of the people. The crowds, barefooted and in their night clothes, ran hither and thither, as cries of warning and of appeal echoed, first from one quarter and then another. The sky seemed black as ink, and rain and sleet beat down upon the ruined city, but while it added to the distress of the hapless people, it was insufficient to extinguish the flames which began to burst out of many ruins and soon laid a large area in ashes.

Amid the horror of it all, many went stark mad and ran shrieking from street to street until they fell exhausted among the heaps of dead, or escaped to the country, where they were found. Searching parties described them wandering about unable to tell who they were or where they had lived.

In the lower part of Messina the tidal wave rose soon after the quake and caused the loss of thousands. In the straits the water rose like a wall to the height of eight and nine feet, and then swept shoreward to fill in the depression caused by the subsistence of the coast land. The fishing boats disappeared in the wild waters. The large ships in the harbor were hurled against one another, the smaller going to the bottom in the twinkling of an eye. Others were dashed against the quays, and both ships and docks were reduced to unrecognizable beams of twisted iron and timber. And on went the wave, apparently gaining strength as it rushed up into the town for a thousand feet. At no point was it lower than a man's arm-pits, and hundreds were drowned.

The receding waters carried out to sea masts, broken hulls, boats turned bottom up, and the lighter parts of houses which it had gathered in its sweep into the city. One survivor said he saw the water strike the cathedral and pass over its roof. The ferry-boat from Messina was half-way across to Reggio when the waters opened and the boat went down until the officers were sure it touched bottom, then it seemed lifted mountain high, to be again dashed downward. It escaped being wrecked and at last reached the spot where Reggio had stood, but where now was only a heap of rubbish, in which lay the bodies of thousands of victims.

Such were the first accounts received. Then came estimates that 25,000 people had lost their lives. Soon the figures were placed at 50,000, then at 100,000, and finally it was known that 200,000 human beings had perished on that awful morning. The mind could not grasp the horror of this instant destruction of life. It was too stupendous.

Yet there were survivors, many thousands of them, and these must have instant relief. The day after the news came, Dr. Klopsch sent this cable message to the American Ambassador at Rome:

"GRISCOM, MINISTER, ROME.

"*Christian Herald* advances by cable through State Department $20,000 for relief with deepest sympathy for King and stricken people. More to follow.

"(Signed)   LOUIS KLOPSCH."

Announcements of this gift were also telegraphed to King Victor Emmanuel, to the Italian Ambassador in Washington, and to Hon. William H. Taft, as President of the American Red Cross. In the following issue of *The Christian Herald* was an editorial, which said:

"Sicily, where Garibaldi celebrated his greatest triumphs that ultimately resulted in the present United Kingdom of Italy; Sicily, the land of bright sunshine, lovely flowers and luscious fruit, the land of perennial summer, has been stricken and laid low. Several of her chief cities and many of her populous and prosperous towns and villages have been wiped from off the face of the earth. Two hundred thousand of her people have perished, and 2,000,000 have been utterly impoverished. They are in fearful straits. They don't speak English, hence they cannot plead understandingly with us for themselves. But I can, and will plead for them, and I know I shall not plead in vain."

Generously the American people responded to the call for help. Dr. Klopsch, knowing from past experience what could be expected from the generosity of his readers, telegraphed in their behalf $30,000 to the State Department additional to the original $20,000 which was sent within twenty-four hours after the disaster occurred. This made a total of $50,000 advanced personally by Dr. Klopsch in anticipation of contributions. Assistant Secretary of State Bacon at once cabled the money to Italy. That brilliant woman, Miss Mabel Boardman, of the Red Cross, who had coöperated with Dr. Klopsch in many of his efforts, aided most effectively in the Italian relief.

Ambassador Griscom, who was doing everything possible to advance the relief work and fitting out a ship with supplies at Naples, was greatly hampered by the lack of funds; but *The Christian Herald* check, together with the money collected and forwarded by the Red Cross, made the charter of a vessel possible. The steamer *Bayern*, lying at Genoa, was secured, and a cargo of food was at once rushed on board. Doctors and volunteer nurses offered their services, which were gladly accepted. The ship cruised along the Sicilian and Calabrian coasts, and Ambassador Griscom went with the steamer and remained several days, while Mrs. Griscom worked unceasingly as chairman of a committee of

RESCUING A VICTIM OF THE ITALIAN EARTHQUAKE

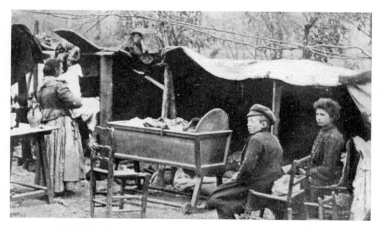

HOUSEKEEPING IN THE STREETS AND PARKS

American women in Rome to provide supplies of clothing for the victims of the catastrophe.

The Christian Herald arranged to have its special correspondent in the devastated district in the person of the Rev. William Carter, of the Madison Avenue Reformed Church in New York City. He was in Switzerland when the earthquake occurred, but on receiving his commission to go to the earthquake zone as its representative, he started at once for Messina. Graphic accounts of the scenes of suffering were received from Mr. Carter. From Messina he wrote:

"Never in the world's history has there been a greater calamity than this, never indeed one so great. Pompeii, Herculaneum, Lisbon, Martinique and San Francisco, with all their horrors, seem puny beside this tremendous devastation and its awful slaughter. Lisbon, the largest of the earth's catastrophes until now, with its 50,000 victims, is just about one-fourth as appalling as this cataclysm with over 200,000 victims in more than a hundred cities, towns and villages. From Palmi, on the north, to Melito on the south of the Calabrian coast, and from Messina on the north, to Nizza on the south of the Sicilian border, the earth was shaken to its very center, and the work of centuries overthrown in a moment of time.

"That a city of 150,000 people, like Messina, could be wiped out in a single quake of the earth's crust seemed impossible, unless the earth should open as a gigantic mouth and swallow it completely. I therefore came to Messina with the feeling that I should not find things as bad as chronicled, and that my work in writing about it would be rather corrective than otherwise.

"My first view of the city, however, dispelled all such thoughts. From the deck of the steamer in which I entered the harbor, I found pile after pile of awful ruins, and as far as I could see there appeared no end. Nowhere, and I say it carefully, nowhere in Messina did I see a habitable dwelling. Every house, every store, every building of every kind was either lying in a heap of dust and debris, or, if the outer walls were still standing, the roof and inner walls had fallen in on their helpless inmates.

"We only get an appreciation of facts by some unitive measure, some standard or gauge well known to all. To hear that a coast town in Sicily has been overwhelmed only gives to the average man in America the idea that an insignificant town of mean huts and dwellings has been destroyed. Here, however, was a city larger than Denver, Columbus or Toledo, with municipal buildings, palaces, mansions and public improvements as great, if not greater, than any of those mentioned. It is no mean city, therefore, on which this scourge has fallen, but one of such pretentions as rightly rank her among the world's commercial centers. In 1904, the last exact statistics available, 7,703 vessels, carrying 486,000 tons of merchandise, cleared from her harbor, and with her famous oranges named after her, Messina supplied the world.

"Alas, what a change is there now! In a moment of time 108,000 of her citizens were carried down to death, all of her commercial houses were overthrown, her magnificent docks destroyed, and the homes of her people made into dust heaps and charnel-houses."

In another letter, Dr. Carter described the work of relief, and especially of the *Bayern*. For Ambassador Griscom, Capt. Belknap, the American Naval Attaché, and Major Landis, the Military Attaché, everybody had words of praise. He also wrote of the brave efforts of the King and Queen Helena.

Dr. Carter was at the ruins of the American Consulate when the remains of the Consul, Mr. Cheney, and his wife were recovered after nineteen days search under the direction of Vice-Consul Lupton. There was no struggle manifest, no contortion. The only thing that indicated any consciousness was the sheet convulsively grasped in the Consul's hand. It was apparently a first convulsive horror, and then a merciful death that must have followed instantaneously. Tenderly the bodies of the dead Consul and his wife were lifted out and placed on stretchers near at hand, and then carried down a heap of ruins to the ground below, where two caskets were awaiting them, and there the soldiers gently placed them and sealed the inner leaden casket and screwed down the cover of the outer one, and bore them to the boat that was to take them to their last resting place.

Describing other incidents of his work for *The Christian Herald*, Dr. Carter wrote:

"It was night as I left Messina. I was anxious to see Reggio, Palmi, Melito and the rest of the coast, and so I had to go. The captain of our vessel told

me that so violent was the upheaval in the straits
themselves that places which before were 2,400 feet
and more in depth are now 300 feet or less. Certain it is that the coast line has been materially
changed, and from the soundings, the conformation
of the ocean bed also.

"As we near Palmi, we see three Italian war vessels lying at anchor in the harbor distributing supplies, as well as rescuing the sufferers. The ruins
don't look as bad here as at Messina, but what a
sight it is after all! Of a little over 10,000 inhabitants, 4,500 lie under those piled up heaps of ruins.
In that little town 3,700 victims were carried down
to death in a moment. It was here and at Scylla
and Messina that the tidal wave did its worst.

"As we draw near to Reggio, we see a sight
even more appalling to the eye than Messina at
first glance. Out of 35,000, 31,000 were lost. Yet
strange to say, Reggio is today more habitable than
Messina. We see some shops open and doing business still; in Messina, not a single shop is open save
those opened in the streets, on rough boards, for
the distribution of supplies. Here some people can
still live in parts of their homes.

"Just a little south lies Palerro on the coast.
Palerro was small, just a distant suburb indeed of
Reggio, seven miles away. But notwithstanding its
smallness, 3,300 dead lie in the ruins of that once
thriving place. So it is all down the coast as far
as Melito. Seismographic waves are not stopped
by curves or angles. Like an express train rounding
a turn at lightning speed, the earthquake wave

rounded the southern extremity of Italy, struck
Melito a deadly blow and left 2,300 dead lying in
its wake.

"But why follow it further! The sights and
scenes witnessed are enough for a life-time. Calabria for eighty-six miles, or from Palmi on the west
coast to Messina, to Gerace on the east coast, is one
long line of ruins, with fifty towns or more overthrown, while innumerable villages and hamlets in
the mountains in between them have been partially
or totally destroyed. On the east coast of Sicily,
from Messina to Nizza, a distance of seventeen
miles, a score of towns lie in dust heaps, while off
the coast and in the mountains dozens of others are
gradually sending in their lists of dead.

"Yes it is truly awful, it is horrible; but God is
good, and Christian sympathy is not wanting; and
soon we shall see smiling fields amid these scenes of
desolation, and thriving cities plying again their
thousand wheels of trade; for Messina, Reggio, Palmi
and all the rest of these coast towns will build again,
as they did after the earthquake of 1783, and work
out their lives even in the shadow of impending
death."

Meanwhile, having done their part in the general relief work, where their gifts were the means
of saving thousands of famishing and destitute, the
readers of *The Christian Herald* found providentially allotted to them the special task of providing
shelter, food, clothing, and medicines for the poor
Italian widowed mothers and their helpless babies.
Dr. Klopsch, in a cable message to the Italian Pre-

mier, obtained the approval of Queen Helena to establish a Mothers' and Babies' Fund, under the Queen's own supervision. Her Majesty personally conducted the organization of this work, and it was quickly under way.

Queen Helena, who made this beautiful "mother and child" charity her own, had attracted the attention of the whole civilized world by her splendid conduct during the events immediately following the catastrophe. She was by the King's side when he hastened in a special train to the scene of the disaster. Queen Helena was an angel of mercy. It seemed as if she were everywhere at the call of want. No sister of charity ever worked more wisely or with greater tenderness. The peasants of Calabria were very loyal to their King and Queen, whose pictures adorned many humble cottage walls, but thenceforth Queen Helena was for them a patron saint of mercy.

It is interesting to study the steps by which this queenly woman developed into a character so fair and gracious. Born a princess of the little Balkan principality of Montenegro, she was one of six daughters and two sons who composed the family of her father, Nicholas. Since Montenegro is not a rich country, the children of Nicholas were trained in the Spartan virtues of fearlessness and economy. Helena from childhood was accustomed to the free out-door life of a mountain girl, riding and hunting with her brothers, and climbing with them the steep hill-paths as safely and swiftly as any village maiden might. She and her sisters were educated in St.

Petersburg under the direction, and at the expense, of the Czar, Alexander III, a near kinsman of the royal house of Montenegro. Helena was married October 4, 1896, to Victor Emmanuel, Prince of Naples and heir-apparent to the throne of Italy. After the assassination of King Humbert, Victor Emmanuel succeeded to the throne, and Helena took her place among the royal women of Europe. She is a devoted wife and mother. Her children, three girls and a boy, are the objects of her personal care.

Through the funds raised by Dr. Klopsch, the sum of $1,000 per day was supplied to this special benevolence during the emergency, and was faithfully expended in a way that met with the Queen's approval. This was one of the most effective agencies in the Italian work, and relieved much distress.

A special message from the Italian Ambassador conveyed Queen Helena's thanks to Dr. Klopsch. It was as follows:

ROYAL ITALIAN EMBASSY,
WASHINGTON, D. C., February 11, 1909.
DR. LOUIS KLOPSCH,
  Christian Herald, New York.
On behalf of her gracious Majesty, Queen Helena, I have the pleasure of expressing to you, and through you to *The Christian Herald* and its readers, her Majesty's warmest thanks for the conspicuous and generous contribution to her fund for mothers and children of the earthquake-stricken regions.
(Signed) MAYOR DES PLANCHES.

Early in the relief campaign, an appeal was made to *The Christian Herald* in behalf of the Waldenses, whose churches and people in both Sicily and Calabria had suffered greatly from the earthquake. The Waldenses are the descendants of the famous band of Christians who were bitterly persecuted for their faith in the sixteenth and seventeenth centuries, and who gave hundreds of noble martyrs to the cause of Christ. Their original home was in the valley of Piedmont, but thriving despite persecution, they became, though small, one of the most energetic and devoted Protestant missionary churches the world has known.

In the section of southern Italy devastated, the Waldensians had forty-five churches, some in seacoast towns and others in remote villages in the interior. Hundreds of their members were killed in the great cataclysm, and the injured reached a much larger number. Most of the churches were in ruins. To assist the injured and homeless Waldensians, *The Christian Herald*, in answer to their appeal, sent $5,000 to Rev. Arturo Murton, President of the Waldensian Missionary Board in Rome. Pastor Murton, in a letter to Dr. Klopsch, acknowledged the great benefit received from the sum. In this letter he said:

The language of suffering is understood by every human being, but it moves those who have never known each other before to such sympathy that only intimate acquaintances and long intercourse could secure. The appalling disaster of Messina and Reggio will mark a special date in the triumphs of Christian charity. We are particularly indebted to your kind-hearted and generous-hearted countrymen for their prompt and conspicuous help, and I beg you to convey our expression of deep gratitude to the readers of *The Christian*

Herald for the valuable contribution of $5,000 you have kindly remitted to our committee.

As the Lord has provided for the bread that perishes, on behalf of the sufferers, He will certainly also enable us to dispense to them the bread of life and help us to find the means necessary to rear again His house out of the ruins.

The Waldensian Evangelical Church, through the Rev. F. Albert Costabel, Delegate to the Evangelical Churches of North America, also wrote Dr. Klopsch, as the representative in America of the Waldensian Church of Italy, to tell him in its name, and in his own, how deeply grateful they were to him, and to the subscribers of *The Christian Herald*, for the most generous and welcome gift. His letter concluded:

It is a cause of great comfort and joy to me to have the privilege of sending you their thanks for the new hope such Christian sympathy and magnificent liberality have caused to shine upon their blighted lives.

Subscriptions to the earthquake relief fund were closed early in March. The audited financial statement showed receipts of contributions from all sources of $71,805.90, and disbursements of the total amount, except $5.92.

Some weeks after the relief work was concluded, Dr. Klopsch decided to make a brief trip to Europe for the sake of recreation and the rest which the ocean voyage would afford him. He allowed himself just a month for the round trip to Hamburg and back to New York. When it was known in Washington that he was going to Europe, the Italian Embassy at once communicated the news to Rome and arrangements were made to have the King receive Dr. Klopsch.

He had not himself planned a visit to Italy, fearing that his time was far too limited. But when he reached Hamburg, the messages which came were so imperative that he felt bound to make the journey. This he did and was received with marks of the greatest gratitude on the part of the Italian people, and of high honor on the part of the Italian Government.

Dr. Klopsch's story of his visit to Rome and his audiences were penciled by him in hurried intervals on loose sheets of paper. It is written in his direct, nervous style. His own account of the interview and of his visit to Rome is so much more graphic than could be written by any one else that the story is given complete as he wrote it, and as it was published in *The Christian Herald:*

An Audience with King Victor Emmanuel III

I had determined to take a month's vacation to put myself in good trim for the summer's work at Mont-Lawn, and together with my wife took passage on the Hamburg American Liner *Amerika* on April 10. My program was very short. Nine days over, ten days on shore and nine back. We were three days out when I received a wireless cablegram informing me that when Baron Mayor des Planches, the Italian Ambassador at Washington, heard that I had started for Europe, he expressed the hope that I would visit Rome in order that I might see the King. To facilitate matters, he immediately forwarded, by the *Kronprinz Wilhelm*, letters of introduction, which I would find on my arrival at Berlin.

As this was in twenty years my first protracted outing with my wife, and our plans had all been arranged in advance, I hesitated to make the trip to Rome, as it would cut out five of the ten days we had planned to spend together in Europe.

But when I reached Berlin, the letters forwarded by the Italian Ambassador determined my course. There was an introduction to His Excellency Prime Minister Tittoni, another to customs and railway officials requesting them to show the traveler every courtesy in their power consistent with their duty, and another one addressed to me personally urging me to go to Rome where the Government had already been advised of my prospective visit. The last letter was so cordial and insistent that I concluded it to be my bounden duty to go.

Monday morning at a quarter past one I took the train at Leipzig and traveled forty hours, reaching the Eternal City Tuesday afternoon. I at once communicated with Hon. Lloyd C. Griscom, the American Ambassador, and received from him a letter stating that the King was at his country palace and regretted much that he could not receive me the following day as he and the Queen were scheduled to leave in the morning direct for Naples where they were to meet the King and Queen of England and the Dowager Empress of Russia. Now I had promised my wife that I would sail home with her on the *Amerika;* she to sail from Hamburg, Germany, on Thursday, and I on the following day from Cherbourg, France. Hence I could not await the King's convenience without disappointing her. I therefore

telephoned Ambassador Griscom that I must leave
Rome the following day, and also telegraphed my
wife to that effect. That was nine o'clock in the
evening.

Two hours later a large envelope addressed to me
and marked *urgentissimo* (very urgent) was left at
the Hotel Quirinal, where I stopped. It was immediately brought to my room, and on opening it I was
informed by Ambassador Griscom that he had read
over the 'phone to Prime Minister Tittoni the Italian Ambassador's letter and acquainted him with
my inability to stay longer than the next afternoon.
Shortly after he had received a letter stating that
His Majesty the King had decided to come to Rome
in the morning and would receive Dr. Klopsch in
private audience at 10.30. Would Ambassador
Griscom kindly inform Dr. Klopsch of the King's
determination?

Then next morning a coach was ordered, and in
accordance with the program a visit was paid to
the Ambassador's residence, where the driver was
supplemented by a tall footman wearing a red, white
and blue cockade at the side of his high black silk
hat. Then I was driven to the Royal Palace, while
the pedestrians on the streets peered in through the
open windows to get a glimpse of the lonely occu-
pant of the impressive equipage. We arrived a few
minutes after ten and I alighted, and, flanked by
the footman, walked through a very long courtyard
on either side of which there were numerous soldiers
dressed in gorgeous uniforms who saluted in military
fashion as we passed them. Then down another

courtyard at right angles with the former until we reached the entrance to the palace, before which there were still more soldiers. Here the footman left me, and ascending the steps I was escorted by two uniformed men up two flights, at the head of which a door opened and I was ushered into an ante-room where two gentlemen in waiting received me, mentioning my name and introducing themselves. One of them then went back to guard the door leading to the royal reception room, while the other engaged me in conversation.

We discussed many subjects, including the pace of different European countries in the construction of *Dreadnoughts*. "Think of it," said he, "$15,000,000 for a single *Dreadnought*—75,000,000 lire. How very, very much money! Our country is too poor. We cannot do it." Then he talked of the great things America had done for Italy to relieve the suffering incident to the fearful calamity that had befallen his country. Just then the door opened and he immediately left me and went inside. A minute after he returned and announced "His Majesty will now receive Dr. Klopsch."

I may say here that as when I left New York I had no idea of a royal audience, I lacked the regulation clothes, but Ambassador Griscom had set me at rest by saying that His Majesty was a very common-sense man, and that a dark suit would answer the requirements. I therefore entered the royal reception room in a plain dark cut-away suit.

Almost at the very door the King received me, taking my hand and shaking it, remarking at the same time, "What a beautiful work you are doing! Come sit down." And down we sat, but not before I had thanked His Majesty for inconveniencing himself to grant me this interview. When we were seated, I had abundant opportunity to notice the quiet, unassuming King and to enjoy his excellent English. He spoke freely and without any hesitation, as though English were his mother-tongue.

He said that the princely generosity of America had deeply touched his heart, and he was glad of the opportunity to give expression to his sincerest gratitude for the very practical sympathy of the American people, and in behalf of the Queen he wished to thank me personally for what she, through the liberality of the readers of *The Christian Herald*, had been enabled to do for the relief of widowed mothers and fatherless babes. "America," he continued, "is a rich country; indeed very, very wealthy, and its people know how to use the bounties of a Kind Providence in a way that must be pleasing to the giver of every good gift."

Then he asked me, "How do you raise such vast sums? Do the millionaires of your country give you large amounts?"

I replied that the money comes chiefly from people in moderate circumstances who give as God has given them and in His name. "Then they must be very good people. Do they give large sums?"

"No," I answered; "the average contribution is $2.75."

"Oh, that is very large; 14 lire is a great deal of money in Italy."

Then I cited some specimen cases of real sacrifice, and the King was deeply affected at the incidents brought to his attention. He told me that he knew a good deal about the charitable work of *The Christian Herald*, but when I told him that in fifteen years it has received and disbursed over $3,000,000, it seemed to the King almost incredible.

"Fifteen million lire," he said, as though in Italian money he could better realize the enormous proportion of this labor of love.

He changed the subject for a while, saying that he was very sorry that Ambassador Griscom was to leave. "He is a fine man and very popular here. Too bad he must go."

I ventured to remark that he would probably continue to stay for some time, as owing to the crisis in Turkey it was unlikely that Ambassador Leishman, who had been transferred from Constantinople to Rome, could leave his present post for a while.

"Only a few days perhaps," he replied, thus implying that this new order of things in Turkey was practically an accomplished fact.

"Is it not marvelous that the Sultan could so long retain the throne while all Europe was making tremendous strides, and Turkey alone remained stagnant?" I inquired.

"Thirty-seven years," the King replied, and then continued, "The Sultan was a very hard-working man. He worked eighteen hours a day and knew minutely all that was going on. I am surprised that the Young Turk movement could have so suddenly overwhelmed him. He must lately have been very poorly and incorrectly informed."

Changing the subject again, the king said:

"I was very much pleased at meeting ex-President Roosevelt the other day at Messina. He is a fine man. He must be shooting wild animals by this time."

I expressed regret at the injury which the Queen was reported to have met with while ministering to the suffering at Messina.

"It is said that she fractured a rib," said I.

He replied, "Oh no, she stumbled and fell, striking against a bottle, bruising herself, but now she is fully restored."

"You have met many crowned heads?" queried he. In reply I mentioned a number, among them the Queen of England and the Dowager Empress of Russia.

"I am to meet them both to-morrow at Naples," was his response, with a smile that indicated that he anticipated a pleasant time.

"You have also met the Emperor of Russia?"

"I have," I answered; "I fear that he is not very happy, the papers say he is not."

"There you are mistaken; the Emperor of Russia is very happy and contented, and one must not believe half the papers say," he said with a pleasant smile.

"How many copies does *The Christian Herald* circulate?" the King inquired.

"Two hundred and forty-six thousand a week."

"Two hundred and forty-six thousand," repeated

he.   "That is a large number.   You must reach over
two million people a week."   He figured here in Italy
that every paper is read by ten people on the average.
"How long do you own the paper?"

"About twenty years."

"What was its circulation then?"

"Thirty-one thousand."

"You must be very proud," was his comment on
this bit of information.   "I have also heard of your
great work in India," he added.

We talked over several of the more important
charitable enterprises which our subscribers had
enabled us to engage in, and particularly of our
Children's Home at Mont-Lawn, at which over five
hundred Italian boys and girls and twenty-five hundred others are entertained every summer.   The
King requested me to send him a descriptive circular
of the Home, as "that charity is so beautiful."

We had conversed over an hour, when the King,
looking at his watch, said, "I will now have to take
my train to Naples."   We arose, he shook me by the
hand and wished me a pleasant voyage home, led me
to the door, and with another hand-shake we parted
and the audience was over.

The next day the daily papers of Rome printed
a very complimentary account of the great work of
The Christian Herald, making especial appreciative
mention of the generous share it took in Messina
relief work, particularly among mothers and children
under the direction of gracious Queen Helena.

CHAPTER XIV

OUR OWN AND NEARBY LANDS

HOME RELIEF WORK — NEW YORK IN THE WINTER OF 1893–94 — REV. STEPHEN MERRITT'S TRAVELERS' CLUB — DR. KLOPSCH ESTABLISHES FOOD AND FUEL STATIONS — END OF THE DISTRESS — SUFFERING CAUSED BY CROP FAILURES IN 1894 — SUCCOR FOR THE WESTERN STATES — INCIDENTS OF A PERSONAL VISIT — AID IN THE GALVESTON TIDAL WAVE OF 1900 — HELP FOR THE KANSAS FLOOD SUFFERERS IN 1903 — CONTRIBUTION TO THE SAN FRANCISCO EARTHQUAKE SUFFERERS IN 1906 — HURRICANE AND FLOOD IN PORTO RICO IN 1899 — "CHRISTIAN HERALD" CONTRIBUTIONS — DESTRUCTIVE WATERS AT MONTEREY, MEXICO, IN 1909 — DR. KLOPSCH SENDS MONEY AND BLANKETS — APPRECIATION.

THE American people are blessed with a happy freedom from frequent and long-continued suffering. Yet calamities sometimes come. Occasionally there is need of temporary help in some section of the country, while at the same time in other sections there is an abundance, and those who have it are ready to give. In the winter of 1893–94 there was much suffering among the poor in New York City. It was a time of industrial and financial depression. The season was unusually severe, and there was a great dearth of employment among both skilled and unskilled workers. Thousands of families were in temporary, yet deep poverty.

At a time when there were multitudes of hungry men thronging the streets of New York, thousands of them absolutely homeless and destitute, the problem of the poor appealed to the sympathizing hearts of Christian people everywhere. Among the agencies actively engaged in relieving the most urgent form of suffering, the pangs of hunger and cold, that of the Eighth Avenue Mission, established by Stephen Merritt, the preacher-philanthropist, was unique. Mr. Merritt was the father-in-law of Dr. Klopsch. He had established a year previously the "Travelers' Club" for all comers, which was an outgrowth of his Eighth Avenue Mission. The Travelers' Club at the outset was composed of the poorest, lowest, and most wretched unfortunates, who assembled in the large hall of the Eighth Avenue Mission between five and seven o'clock every morning and were refreshed with a wholesome and abundant meal of meat, bread, and fragrant coffee. All were welcome regardless of nationality, color, or creed. It sufficed that the wanderer was hungry.

During the distress of this hard winter, two thousand persons a day were fed at the Eighth Avenue Mission. The readers of *The Christian Herald* helped to contribute the funds which made this possible.

Relief on a more extended scale became necessary. Some of the pastors and missionary workers in the tenement districts appealed to Dr. Klopsch to do something for the poor at home, and he responded by establishing a "food-fund" and opening more than a dozen relief stations in different sections of the city, most of them on the East Side. Coal, wood, and oil stations were also established, from which was distributed fuel. Medical aid was also provided.

Dr. Klopsch rented a building in Stuyvesant

Street, as a "food-fund headquarters," and organized a committee of eighteen city pastors, each of whom arranged for a local headquarters, either in his church basement, or some suitable apartment near at hand. Thousands of destitute homes were gladdened. Not only money and food, but quantities of garments, hats, shoes and rolls of cloth were sent in response to the calls for help. The Stuyvesant Street place took on the appearance of a general country store on a large scale, and the branch relief stations were kept busy distributing food, fuel and clothing to some twelve hundred families, averaging five persons each, according to a regular system which included an investigation of each case before relief was granted. Contributions came from all over the country, especially of food and clothing. In the town of Moundridge, Kansas, the generous people loaded up a freight car with a quantity of flour, which was equivalent to the whole week's bread supply for the fund, and shipped it to New York. It was known as the "Pioneer Car," and when it reached New York the flour was baked into loaves and distributed. Then contributions came from other sources.

A feature of the relief work was the mission band which undertook the labor of distribution. From a modest beginning with a few missionaries as district visitors, the band gradually extended its operations as the means multiplied, until twenty-seven missionaries and assistants were engaged in house to house visitation among the destitute poor. Throughout the entire work Mrs. Klopsch bore an active part, coöperating with the missionaries in their duties and personally visiting many distressed homes where hunger and despair had shut out hope until her husband's relief measures through the "food-fund" turned the gloom to sunshine.

Toward spring the distress lightened in the tenement districts, and with the advent of milder weather and improved industrial conditions, many of the idle were able to obtain work. Consequently the relief was closed. The pastors of the city churches, who had coöperated in the relief, united in a testimonial as to the remarkable efficiency of the "food-fund," and praising it as a timely Christ-like service to humanity. The signers included: Rev. R. S. MacArthur, D.D.; Rev. C. W. Millard; Rev. J. C. Thomas; Rev. H. Faust; Rev. J. A. B. Wilson; Rev. C. Wright; Rev. J. B. Stansberry; Rev. E. L. Fox, and Rev. Wm. Hamilton.

In the late fall and early winter of 1894 stories came of suffering in Nebraska and Kansas. A drought during the previous summer had made the crops a failure. It was a bad year everywhere for the western farmers. In a score or more of counties of Nebraska and Kansas, and in some sections of Texas, Colorado, and Oklahoma, many families were in actual want. There was really a famine in one of the richest agricultural regions of the United States. The suffering people, however, were slow to make known their distress. They hoped to get through the winter without succor from outside. But it became apparent that unless aid came from beyond their own states, many would not get through the winter at all. Letters received in *The Christian*

Herald office from more than a hundred different localities in Kansas and Nebraska told the same story of privation, — fine farms destroyed by the two years' drought; empty barns, and still emptier larders; stock dying for want of feed, and men, women, and children weakened from long hunger and freezing for lack of clothing and fuel.

Dr. Klopsch, when the facts were known, established a relief fund for the western sufferers. This he supplemented by a central relief depot in upper Broadway to which boxes, barrels, and packages of clothing and supplies could be sent for free transportation to Kansas and Nebraska. All seemed eager to help the West, and both supplies and money poured in. The nation's great heart was touched. A corps of volunteer distributors was established in the West to distribute the supplies that were forwarded. Thanks came from the Governor of Nebraska, and from officials, which showed that the gifts were not only needed, but that they were being properly handled. Dr. Klopsch decided to go West himself in order to see how the work of distribution was going on, and report to the readers of *The Christian Herald* the use made of their contributions.

"No one can travel over the plains," he telegraphed, "and see the present condition of these people, without being convinced that their story of destitution and helplessness has not been told."

He first went to Nebraska, then to Colorado, and from there to Kansas. The tour took three weeks. Public officials, local committees, and the people everywhere welcomed Dr. Klopsch, and profited by his advice as to the best method of distributing the relief. He had two points in view. These were to reach and relieve as expeditiously as possible those sections where the suffering was the sharpest, and to create new centers of Christian work at advantageous points.

Dr. Klopsch made a special contribution from *The Christian Herald* fund of $1,000 for the relief of the Nebraska Grand Army of the Republic veterans, since many of the old soldiers were in great need. "In the carrying out of this work," he wrote, "I have traveled more than half-way through Nebraska, throughout the entire length of Kansas, and through Colorado as far as Denver."

Not only immediate needs, but the future also had to be looked to, since the next year's crop must be provided for. The Chicago Board of Trade, appreciating the situation, appointed a committee to raise a seed-fund. Various leading seedsmen sent to *The Christian Herald* vegetable seed in generous quantities. One philanthropic seedsman, J. J. H. Gregory, of Marblehead, Mass., provided vegetable seed to plant about a fifth of an acre to a thousand families. Others made similar contributions.

In the meantime, with the advent of spring, the conditions improved, the people were able to provide for the next season's crops, and it became possible to close the relief work. In addition to the contributions of food, clothing, and other supplies, *The Christian Herald* had raised $26,825.40.

The gratitude of the western people was made manifest in many ways. Numerous resolutions

, and thanks were expressed to the
he Christian Herald. At the Annual
of the Grand Army of the Republic of
pecial resolution was adopted thanking
ind his readers for their contributions
need.

On the night of September 8, 1900, the southern
and central counties of Texas were swept by a West
Indian hurricane of wide-spread extent and unprecedented violence. For thirty hours it raged
unabated, and it was accompanied by great tidal
waves which swept the entire coast line of the state,
submerging many of the cities and towns along the
Gulf, and carrying death and devastation far inland.
Nearly a hundred towns and villages suffered from
the onrush of the great wall of water from the Gulf.

The city of Galveston was the greatest sufferer,
being in the center of the storm track. Galveston
is built on an island. The storm began Saturday
morning, and by noon the whole city was alarmed,
and the people were abandoning their houses. The
wind and rain were violent beyond description. By
three in the afternoon the Gulf waters were rushing
into the Bay. At dark the whole city was under
water, and 40,000 souls were facing death. Nearly
all the buildings were destroyed. The big sea-going
steamers *Alamo, Launton, Red Cross,* and *Kendall
Gylla* and others were wrecked in the harbor, and
over one hundred other craft of all sorts suffered a
like fate. The mainland was strewn with wreckage
and corpses. Seven hundred bodies were washed
ashore at Virginia Point. A relief train, which

started from Houston, found the territory covered with lumber, debris, pianos, trunks, bedding, furniture, and dead bodies. The whole country was strewn with wrecked property. In all between six and seven thousand persons lost their lives in the Galveston disaster.

But there were the survivors to think of and to care for. As the tales of heroism shown amid the awful scenes became known, there were also accounts of the relief that would be necessary temporarily. Great quantities of food and medicines were needed in order to confront the danger of temporary famine. The state of Texas, and what was left of the city of Galveston, made noble efforts to provide for their own, but the rest of the country was also called on.

"This is not a cry from a foreign land," said *The Christian Herald*, "but from our own Christian brothers and sisters at home."

Immediately on receiving the first intelligence of the disaster, Dr. Klopsch had telegraphed to Governor Sayers to draw at sight for $1,000 for the relief work, and asking how help could be most speedily and effectively rendered. Governor Sayers replied accepting the gift with thanks. Offers of help were also telegraphed by Dr. Klopsch to the Galveston and Houston authorities. *The Christian Herald* further opened a relief headquarters in Galveston under the charge of special commissioners. The contributions which were received were promptly and, effectively applied, and the contributors knew that they were sharing in the great work of relief.

A period of distress came to the people of the

Southwest in the summer of 1903, when the worst flood that had been known in thirty years visited Kansas and Missouri. It became evident during the last days of May that the Kansas and Missouri rivers were swelling to the danger mark, the spring freshets having been late and extremely heavy. On the last day of May the flood came with terrific violence, accompanied by heavy rains, and soon the lowlands along the river front at Kansas City were a vast sea. At Kansas City, Topeka, and other points extending for many miles either way, the raging rivers swept over embankments and covered the bottom-lands with from eight to thirty feet of water, carrying havoc and death with the inrushing flood. Sixteen bridges over the Kansas River went down under the force of the torrent.

The scenes of suffering and anxiety during the three or four days when the flood was at its maximum were never seen equalled by the people of that part of the country. In Kansas City 20,000 persons were homeless. In Topeka 7,000 flood refugees had to be cared for. The streets were like canals, and the country for miles around was flooded. In North Topeka, hundreds were imprisoned in their houses by the swift rise of the waters. Men and women could be seen in the upper parts of the houses waving clothes as signals of distress, or shouting for aid. The darkness of the nights was made appalling by the frequent cries for help. In the daytime, bodies could be seen floating down the rivers. Many daring rescues were reported. One man drew from the river a cradle with a baby in it, the little one unhurt and having escaped death almost miraculously.

In response to appeals for aid on behalf of the homeless refugees, Dr. Klopsch telegraphed to Mayor Craddock of Kansas City, Kansas, and the Rev. Charles M. Sheldon, of Topeka, authorizing them to draw on him for $1,000 each for relief work, which was done. Further contributions were received and were promptly forwarded until the emergency was passed.

Writing from Topeka to *The Christian Herald*, Pastor C. M. Sheldon said: "Topeka is divided into two parts by the Kansas River. The south side was not affected by the flood, but the north side, containing about 10,000 people, was completely submerged. Many people were drowned, and the entire number of inhabitants rendered homeless for the time being. Many houses have been completely swept away, and the damage to property is beyond computation. It is safe to say that thousands of people in Topeka will lose everything, and the churches on the north side are in very great need.

"A large part of the money that I receive from outside sources, I shall try to use in the reëstablishment of the religious and educational work of the city where it has been affected. Topeka would not have turned to the outside world for help, if it had not felt unable to cope with the situation. Whatever *The Christian Herald* can do will be gratefully received, and if we have more than can be well used here, we will simply pass it on to the thousands of suffering farmers and citizens in other parts of the state."

It was on an April day in 1906, the 18th, that the
nation was stunned by the news that San Francisco
had been smitten by an earthquake, and that the
entire business section of the beautiful Californian
city lay in ruins. After the first brief message, no
word came for some time. Wires were down in all
directions, and communication was entirely cut off.
But later came confirmation of the great disaster.
Survivors, who told the story of that terrible morning's experience, said that crowds of people ran together in the streets, many of them half-clad. As
the earth swung and rocked beneath them, and as
buildings toppled, the frantic people cried out to
each other amid their sobs that it was the end of the
world. They talked in shrill voices half hysterically.
The oscillations from north to south seemed to twist
the ground to its center. Many felt the straining
and indescribable nausea which accompany earthquakes.

Spectators described their sensations when the
earthquake struck. They were awakened from
peaceful sleep by the crash of breaking glass, the
straining of timbers, and the rocking of floors. The
blow seemed to come from the north, and it caused
the earth to heave violently. People who sprang
from their beds grasped anything within reach to
steady themselves. The walls of the rooms seemed
to be moved out, and the furniture and other articles
were shaken and roughly thrown to one side. Shrill
screams of terror rose above the noise of grinding
timbers and falling masonry. The earth shocks
were sharp and definite, and the oscillations were

like those of a vessel in a choppy sea. Then when the terror was at its highest tension, there was a plausible relaxation, and final tremor of the ground, and the earthquake was over. But what a transformation had been wrought in a few moments!

All that eventful day the fires spread and the city was like a furnace. Dynamite was employed, and whole blocks of buildings were blown up and leveled in the hope that the fiery destruction might be stayed at the open spaces, but it was a vain hope. By far the greater part of the ruin of San Francisco was wrought by fire which literally seemed to spring up out of the ground after the shocks had ceased.

Some idea of the vastness of the ruin was gathered when it was known that 30,000 buildings were destroyed, and fully 300,000 persons made homeless, while more than 1,000 persons lost their lives.

Refugees poured from the city by tens of thousands.

When the report of the disaster reached the other parts of the country, relief committees were organized at once. General Funston, who was in command of the United States troops in San Francisco, appealed for tents, clothing, and food, and soon considerable quantities of provisions began to reach the city from nearby towns. These were quickly swollen by food and clothing from towns further away.

The relief work in San Francisco was in charge of the American Red Cross. Dr. Klopsch, on behalf of *The Christian Herald*, immediately addressed W. C. Langdon, the Secretary of the Society, enclosing a contribution of $5,000, and promising more.

Further contributions were made, and *The Christian Herald* readers knew that they were helping in this relief work, as in so many other calamities when succor was called for.

The beautiful tropical island of Porto Rico was swept by a hurricane in the autumn of 1899. It had been ceded by Spain to the United States as the result of the war for the liberation of Cuba, and was therefore an American possession. The Government was then carried on by the military authority.

Flood followed the hurricane, and from all over the island came reports of its tremendous extent and terrible destructive power. The great rivers were swollen to the proportions of mighty torrents, and swept everything before them. Towns, villages, and plantations disappeared. Whole houses were afloat, their occupants vainly hoping to find some secure lodgment, only to be tossed and assailed until the structure parted and the helpless ones were engulfed in the torrents of water.

The hurricane and flood not only destroyed life, but they destroyed the means of life. Porto Rico is a densely populated little country having more than a million inhabitants. Coffee is its chief product, and the coffee plantations were almost entirely destroyed.

The first measures to be taken were for immediate relief, and after that for restoring the coffee crop. General George W. Davis, who was the military commander, at once undertook to afford systematical relief, and to take charge of the supplies and contributions that were received from the United States.

Mrs. Guy V. Henry, wife of General Henry, and then President of the Women's Aid Society of Porto Rico, issued an appeal through *The Christian Herald* to the Christian mothers and daughters of America in behalf of the suffering women and children of Porto Rico. Among other things she said:

"A country devastated by flood and famine cries out to us for aid at once. Not like India, or Armenia, or Russia, calling from a foreign land, and under a foreign flag, but with our own flag waving over its municipal buildings and carried through the streets by its little children singing 'America'; the land they all love and look to for aid now that flood and destruction have laid waste that delightful island. Shall the cry of the homeless, starving people who welcomed us but a few months ago with gentle voices and open arms fall on deaf ears and plead in vain to unsympathizing hearts? Hear the call, oh great American people, and rise with grand response with one hand stretched out and send help."

This and other appeals were not unheeded. It was believed that fully half the population of the island were in need, and at least a quarter of a million were on the verge of starvation. Food, clothing, and money were provided for them through the recognized agencies. And great as was the need, it was relieved. Thousands of tons of food were supplied, great quantities of clothing, and in some cases ready money. *The Christian Herald* continued its contributions until the Government agencies were sufficiently established to insure the people of Porto Rico against further suffering.

A near neighbor of the United States was visited by disaster in the late summer of 1909. An awful flood overwhelmed the thriving city of Monterey in northern Mexico, carrying down to death more than 2,000 human beings, and destroying $3,000,000 in property. Only an earthquake could have been more sudden and troubling than the swift rush of waters which engulfed the Mexican city on the night of August 27. Monterey generally has difficulty in getting enough water for its ordinary needs. The bed of the Santa Catalina River, which winds down from the mountains, in summer is as dry as a bone, and the gaunt arches of the bridges span no water except at certain periods of the year. The district had been suffering from a drought, running more than fourteen months, and above all things rain was most desired by the people. When a rain storm came in July there was much rejoicing. A dry period followed, but on the evening of August 27, the rain began to fall, gently at first and then increasing to a down-pour. When the people went to sleep in their adobe houses, a good stream of water was rushing along the river bed beneath the arches of the bridges, and some of the flimsy huts had begun to leak, but no alarm was felt. Those who were awakened later by the thunder of the torrents of water, which seemed to fall in one great sheet, began to get uneasy. The blackness of the night was terrible, and the water was pouring down the streets as if they were soon to become a part of the Catalina River itself.

From the direction of the river came the alternate boom and roar of the flood. The water swayed

HAVOC WROUGHT BY THE FLOOD IN MONTEREY STREETS

THE RIVER FRONT IN MONTEREY DURING THE GREAT FLOOD

against the structures on the river bank, shaking them as if they were of paste and cardboard. Great sections of earth were carried away, walls toppled, and the houses were crushed like egg-shells, the wreckage bearing down stream in a tangled and ever increasing mass. Engulfed in the angry waves were hundreds of hapless people who were unable to make their escape to upper parts of the city.

Morning came, but the rain never ceased; at times it seemed to increase in violence. The people made their way to the river banks, or rather to the edge of the lake, which was boiling through the city. For several blocks inward from the former bed of the river nearly every house had disappeared. For nearly four miles this was the situation.

The storm continued for two days and a half. Then it began to slacken, and relief efforts were at once begun by the Mexicans and foreign residents. Philip C. Hanna, the American Consul-General, was one of the most active in relieving the distress. Knowing that aid from other sections would be necessary, he telegraphed to Dr. Klopsch saying that thousands were homeless, and that the suffering must continue for months to come, and that assistance would be appreciated.

Dr. Klopsch's reply was promptly sent, as follows:

NEW YORK, August 31, 1909.

HANNA, CONSUL-GENERAL,
Monterey, Mexico.

Will honor your sight draft for $1,000 as our first contribution toward relief of stricken people of Monterey.

(Signed) LOUIS KLOPSCH.

The Consul-General at once telegraphed his grateful acknowledgment of the money, which he at once employed in buying food and clothing for the destitute.

The relief efforts of *The Christian Herald* continued in conjunction with the Consul-General and with the American Red Cross Society. One great need, as explained by Consul-General Hanna, was for clothing as the fall weather came on. This was met by Dr. Klopsch shipping blankets. First there were a thousand or so, then a larger number, until *The Christian Herald* readers had contributed twenty thousand blankets. They also sent a hundred sewing machines, which were wanted.

Consul-General Hanna acknowledged the benefit in a telegram to Dr. Klopsch, and also in his official report to the State Department. This was made evident by the following telegram:

MONTEREY, MEXICO, October 24, 1909.
SECRETARY OF STATE,
WASHINGTON, D. C.

The thousands of blankets from the American Red Cross, *The Christian Herald*, merchants and private citizens are arriving and being distributed in Monterey, and sent to outlying towns affording relief to thousands of delicate women and children in the stricken districts. Scores of bags, bales and boxes of second-hand clothing are arriving from all parts of the United States. Demand very great, and much more will be needed. Corn, beans and rice come from different parts. Mexicans more fully than ever convinced that Americans are their friends. I have the hearty coöperation of clergy of all denominations and Mexican Red Cross.

Dr. Klopsch also telegraphed direct to President Porfirio Diaz the desire *The Christian Herald* to aid the suffering and received an immediate message of appreciation from Mexico's great executive. The Mexican relief work was the last which it was permitted Dr. Klopsch to help, and it was a gratification to him that the aid extended through *The Christian Herald* should have been to a neighbor so friendly and so closely allied to the United States as Mexico.

CHAPTER XV

THE BOWERY MISSION

HUMAN DRIFTWOOD OF A GREAT CITY — ROMANTIC WAY IN WHICH DR. KLOPSCH BECAME INTERESTED IN THE MISSION — FINANCIAL RESPONSIBILITY ASSUMED — LIFE BOAT FOR MORAL SHIPWRECKS — MRS. BIRD'S NOBLE LABORS — SUPERINTENDENT HALLIMOND — TWENTIETH ANNIVERSARY — A WOMAN'S STORY OF THE THANKSGIVING DINNER — THE BREAD LINE — PATHOS OF A FUNERAL — CELEBRATED VISITORS — PASTOR CHARLES WAGNER'S VISIT — HIS OWN STORY OF A TYPICAL AUDIENCE — INCIDENTS OF DR. KLOPSCH'S WORK AMONG THE OUTCASTS TOLD BY ONE WHO KNEW — PRESIDENT TAFT'S VISIT THE CROWNING EVENT — HIS UPLIFTING TALK AS MAN TO MAN — "CHRISTIAN HERALD'S" COMMENT.

EVERY great city has its human drift-wood, its wrecks of men cast up by the tide of misfortune and despair. Hungry of body and starved of soul, both body and soul must be fed for their own salvation and the good of society. The histories of these men are a tragedy. The work of rescue, of reclamation and reformation, must be done by those in whom the spirit of sympathy is joined with practical, everyday common sense.

In all his philanthropic and charitable labors as a comrade to humanity, doing a man's work among men, no chapter shines more brightly in the life-work of Dr. Klopsch than the story of what he did for the human drift-wood of the great city of New York. The means by which he did this was the Bowery Mission.

The history of this remarkable mission is a simple one. It had been the wish of Jerry McAuley, of the Water Street Mission, to establish a similar one on the Bowery. The Rev. A. J. Ruliffson, and Mrs. Ruliffson, engaged in mission work on the East Side, often talked over the subject with Mr. McAuley, and after much prayer and earnest thought, they opened a mission in an old dimly lighted room at No. 14 Bowery. Soon they found it necessary to seek more commodious quarters, and a suitable building was rented at No. 36 Bowery. During the first year Mr. J. Ward Childs was Superintendent, Mr. Ruliffson being President. For fifteen years the work of rescue was carried on in the very center of vice and crime and degradation in America's leading city. To the Bowery drifted the waifs and strays, the wrecks and derelicts of humanity from all parts of the world.

The romantic story of how Dr. Klopsch had his attention first directed to the work of the Mission he never seemed to tire of telling. He had been with Dr. Talmage on his memorable visit to the Holy Land, and on the return trip the party called at Smyrna. On landing they were met by John Parkinson, who at that time was superintendent of an English speaking seaman's mission at Smyrna. They accepted his invitation to visit the mission hall. During the course of the meeting Parkinson "gave his testimony," which was to the effect that many years previously he was a sailor and a low-down, besotted drunkard at that. One evening in New York, thoroughly intoxicated, he staggered into the Bowery Mission, thinking it was one of the many vile concert halls that then were the chief

characteristic of that famous street. He was taken
care of by the mission workers, sobered up, and
became soundly converted to God. For some time
he continued his seafaring life, and wherever he
went he lost no opportunity of telling of the wonderful thing that happened him. In the course of
a few years he became a seaman's missionary and
ultimately was placed in charge of the mission in
Smyrna.

With the death of Superintendent Childs in the
spring of 1895, there came a serious crisis in the history of the Mission. For various reasons its old
managers were unable to continue the work, which
seemed doomed to come under purely secular control.
Its usefulness was imperiled, and the question was
raised whether it would not be well to abandon
the work permanently and close the Mission. At
this juncture some of its friends appealed to Dr.
Klopsch in its behalf, and after a full investigation he became convinced that with new management, more earnest effort, and a full dependence
upon divine approval, the Mission might yet go on
triumphantly. On April 1, 1895, he assumed the
care of the Bowery Mission, with all its responsi-
bilities and its enormous power for good. In describing the scope of the work at that time, *The
Christian Herald* said:

"In every city of large population there are many
men who, having gone down step by step in the
paths of sin, have at last reached a depth beyond
which it would seem impossible to go. They are
the moral ship-wrecks who have been swallowed up

in the maelstrom on whose edges they dallied until hopelessly engulfed. At last, ruined and forsaken, they are cast up like wreckage upon the outer coasts of society to be turned from with loathing by their fellowmen as something too utterly vile for recognition. They have reaped well-nigh the full harvest of their sins, and it would seem that nothing remained but a wretched close to a career so miserable and forlorn. Many of these poor stranded waifs have, by God's mercy, been cast up at the doors of the Bowery Mission. Rejected elsewhere, they have there found a haven of welcome. Their poor clothing and filthy condition have been the cause of other doors being shut in their faces, for even in mission work it is customary to draw the line at those who have fallen so low as to make their very touch contamination. But the Bowery Mission, like a lifeboat on its merciful errand, plunges down to its lowest depths, for by doing so it may bring up some poor sinking fellow mortal into the light of God's love. Are they sick and penniless? It cares for them as tenderly as though they were brothers. Ragged? It is never without a garment for those who need one to shut out the piercing winds of winter. Are they idle and despairing? It aids them in finding employment."

When Dr. Klopsch assumed charge, he had the Mission incorporated. The incorporators were Rev. John Hall, T. DeWitt Talmage, Mrs. Sarah J. Bird, Rev. David J. Burrell, Rev. C. H. Mead, Rev. Josiah Strong, Mrs. Amelia E. Barr, Rev. Louis E. Banks, Henry Edward Rowland, B. Fay Mills, Rev. A. C. Dixon, Rev. Stephen Merritt, Rev. R. S. MacArthur, Rev. J. Wilbur Chapman, and Rev. James Everett King.

There could be no adequate sketch of the Mission without mention of the work of Mrs. Sarah J. Bird, "the Mother of the Bowery Mission," as she was called, who gave up the advantages of wealth and ease to labor among the outcasts of the city. Her many years of devoted service in rescue work form one of the brightest records of Christian effort in the great metropolis. Her Christmas tree, loaded with useful gifts, was for many years an object of delight to the little ones whose lives are usually so joyless. Her addresses to the men and boys were always a powerful means of good.

The Thursday night gatherings of Mrs. Bird, like those she held on Sundays, were invariably crowded. The men who formed her audiences were of all ages, from the young man a little more than a mere stripling, to the aged wanderer whose wrecked life is a record of indulgence and wasted opportunities. Some came from the Bowery lodging houses, others from the streets, which they had walked until foot-sore in the vain search for work. For all there was the same kind of welcome, a cup of steaming coffee and a sandwich to appease the cravings of hunger. Mrs. Bird herself, writing of her work, said:

"Sometimes, as I look down from my platform, I see some poor fellow kneeling and in anguish of soul in front of me. No one but God knows the fight some of these poor fellows are having with temptations from without and from within, and only the mighty power of Jesus to save gives us courage and faith to see these sad discouraged souls struggling for life. These are men who have wandered from God and home. They have come from every city on the face of the earth; if a man becomes engulfed in sin in any part of the world, his ambition is to get to the Bowery. This is the magnet that attracts the restless and vicious wanderer. These men are often brought where they are surrounded by conditions that are beyond control. Parents and friends die, or there are hard fathers and unwise thoughtless mothers; the boy leaves home and is soon stranded in a cheap Bowery lodging house. I give the Gospel invitation to over 40,000 of these lost men every year, many of them men of fine education and birth."

When Dr. Klopsch took charge, Mrs. Bird was active in her work, which has continued uninterruptedly up to the present time. Mr. John H. Wayburn was installed as Superintendent, and the work of the Mission, both on its spiritual and secular side, was broadened in many ways. A free dispensary was inaugurated, new restaurants were provided, where the poor could dine for a nominal sum, and the midnight "bread line" became an established institution. Dr. Klopsch regarded the Mission as a beacon light for lost men, and his appeals for support never failed to set forth what he was seeking to do for these men. A little poem which he circulated reflected this sentiment. One verse ran:

> Throw out the Life-Line across the dark wave,
> There is a brother whom someone should save;
> Somebody's brother! Oh, who, then will dare
> To throw out the Life-Line, his peril to share?

The Mission had some ups and downs, and some changes, and in 1898 suffered a very destructive fire. Then new quarters were obtained and the Mission was located at No. 227 Bowery, where it now is.

In December, 1899, Rev. John G. Hallimond, D.D., was installed as Superintendent amid great enthusiasm. Dr. Hallimond had been connected with the great West London Mission, of which the famous Rev. Hugh Price Hughes was Superintendent. On his arrival in New York he became private secretary to Commander Ballington Booth of the Salvation Army, and was intimately concerned in the social work of the Army. Later he was identified with the Volunteers of America. His experience especially qualified him for the practical rescue work that has been the special sphere of the Bowery Mission.

The work of the Mission was described at the twentieth anniversary in January, 1901, when special exercises were held. The Rev. T. DeWitt Talmage preached a remarkable sermon, and then Superintendent Hallimond reviewed the work. He said:

"Among the rescue missions of the world, the Bowery Mission occupies a thoroughly unique position. Many religious enterprises have been carried on upon a much more extensive scale and have been of a much more pretentious character, but for a protracted and sustained soul-saving work, few institutions in the history of the Christian Church can furnish a record like that of the Bowery Mission. For twenty years it has stood in the darkest section of the city, holding out a helping hand to those who are about to disappear in the black depths of eternal despair. Wonderful as the results have been in the past, the opportunity is now presented for immensely enlarging and strengthening its activities. For twenty years the work has been carried on unostentatiously. It was inaugurated by humble but consecrated people; and all along it has been supported by Christian workers of limited means from all denominations. For the last five years, especially during the time it has been under the auspices of *The Christian Herald,* the funds with two notable exceptions (Dr. Klopsch and Mrs. Bird) have come from a multitude of small contributors all over the United States and Canada — from poor men, themselves redeemed in the Mission; from fathers in the far-away antipodes, sending thank-offerings for the reclamation of their sons. Many a time a tear-stained letter arrives from a sorrowing mother enclosing twenty-five or fifty cents, and asking us to pray for her wandering boy, who, she hopes, may drift into our doors and come under our influence. This is the kind of support the Mission has received during the past twenty years."

The work described by Superintendent Hallimond on the twentieth anniversary has continued since, broadening on the industrial side, and with new fields opened up. It is, however, in the incidents of the Mission from day to day and night to night and year to year that the spirit in which the work is carried on and the rescue and reformation accomplished, as well as the brightening of clouded lives, are shown. There is, for example, Mrs. Bird's

Christmas tree. Then there is the Thanksgiving on the East Side. Here is an extract from a description of an East Side Thanksgiving at the Bowery Mission, by a well-known writer:

"Already a note is in the air telling of the Thanksgiving Dinner to be given at the Bowery Mission for the men who tramp that famous thoroughfare. Here for many years these homeless and hungry men have been bidden to a feast such as many of them never have seen before, much less enjoyed. Turkey and all the 'fixings,' hot coffee, fruit, and big slices of bread in abundance, serve to fill empty stomachs, while words of cheer from the good men and women, who have their hearts in this mission work, fall like dew upon the parched hearts before them.

"I found a great crowd of men of all ages and many nationalities waiting for the doors to be opened. A word, and the crowd made way; a tap, and the door opened. I slipped in and my day at the Bowery Mission had begun. There was a kitchen prayer meeting, and then morning service in the big hall. In the few moments before the meeting began in the hall, Mr. Hallimond told in the most interesting manner, with his heart in the telling, so many things, that I scarcely know where to begin my story, and having begun, know still less where to stop. 'You must see Mother Bird,' he said. I must also meet the quartette, and be introduced to the organist.

"On a platform, facing hundreds of men, I sat with dear Mrs. Bird, who conducted the meeting. The one dominant word was love, heard through prayer, reading of the Scriptures, singing and talking. I was impressed as never before with the common sense of religion. There sat hundreds of them, these men of the Bowery, a story written on each face, many telling of tragic ending, not far off, unless a

helping hand was stretched forth to save. Just here
comes in the practical part of the Bowery Mission, as a hungry man cannot be expected to listen
very patiently to religious teaching or advice, be it
ever so good. He wants something to eat, and he
gets it here — a big cup of hot coffee and a sandwich
so thick that a 'Bowery barker' could hardly open
his jaws wide enough to accommodate it unless the
slices were separated. How many come just for
the coffee and the sandwich, it would be hard to tell,
but that a world of good has been done by this
Mission, and a multitude of men saved from destruction, is a matter of simple fact. How much the hot
coffee may have to do with the preliminary work of
salvation among these poor wayfarers, it matters
not, so that they are comforted sufficiently to even
think one straight wholesome thought.

"The testimonies given by those who have been
saved by the Mission's help being extended to them
when they had not a friend upon earth, must have
made a deep impression upon the men to whom
they were talking. The members of the quartette,
who sang, and others, told their stories, differing
only in detail. They were drunken and miserable,
forsaken by their friends who stuck by them while
a penny was left to treat them, but dropped them
when all was spent. Reduced to the last extremity,
sick, hungry and cold, they had wandered up and
down the Bowery. Discouraged, defiant, hard of
heart, they had drifted into the Mission."

Another incident was of the "bread line." There
was a surprise in store when one cold night Superintendent Hallimond announced that he had ten
cents to present to each man to enable him to procure a night's lodging. This donation, the Superintendent told them, had come from a man who

himself had been on the "bread line" just three or four weeks previously, but who had since become possessed of a small fortune of $1,000. One hundred dollars of this sum he had donated for the relief of such of the "down and outs" as were on the "bread line" on that bitterly cold night.

And then there are the Bowery Mission funerals. Here is an account of one, taken from a New York paper:

A BOWERY MISSION FUNERAL

(From the New York Sun)

Henry McCluskey, an old man who died in the Bowery Mission last Sunday night (Nov. 27), while service was being held, was buried from the Mission yesterday.[1] It is said that he attended every meeting held there for the last five years. On Sunday night the place was so crowded that he had to sit on the stairs leading to the second floor. During the singing of a hymn he fell from the stairs and was found to be dead. McCluskey was a distinguished looking old man. Long before the service began the benches were filled with men. A couple of Salvation Army lassies sat on the platform. Mrs. Sarah J. Bird, or "Mother" Bird, as she is called, who leads many of the Bowery meetings, explained that the funeral would be simple.

"We might have bought him flowers," she said, "but it would have been a mockery. Just these few violets will do."

"If you could only see with a clearer vision," said the Rev. Stephen Merritt after the congregation had sung, "you would find that our dead brother is now at rest in Abraham's bosom. I hope that I will see you all again in a better land. You will all be there, for no black sheep will remain among you. You will be washed whiter than snow."

One of the Mission workers sang, "And when I Think of the

[1] The poor old man, who was destitute, was buried by the Mission.

Home Land my Eyes are Filled with Tears." One of the undertaker's assistants sprinkled Mother Bird's violets upon the casket, and after the congregation had filed past, it was carried away.

Sometimes there are the entertainments provided by those at the other end of the social ladder. There was, for example, one evening in January, 1908, the concert by the members of the Amateur Concert Club, composed exclusively of ladies of the most prominent families in New York society. It was a piteously wet night. Rain and sleet swirled down upon the sidewalks and flooded the gutters, but this was not sufficient to prevent an enormous crowd of men gathering. Very punctually the procession of automobiles arrived and deposited their fair occupants, and the concert began. A physiological student would have found a most engrossing study in the faces of the poor beaten, baffled, discouraged men as they listened. "I saw," said Superintendent Hallimond, "many a lip quiver. When Miss Gallard played on the harp the simple strains of 'Home, Sweet Home,' there were many men who bowed their heads and wept."

The Bowery Mission has attracted visitors from all over the world, not merely curiosity-seekers, but those who feel a real interest in its work, and whose presence offers cheer and hope to the derelicts of humanity. Once it was Countess Adelaide Schimmelmann, the titled evangelist, who told the story of her own life at the German Court.

Then there was Helen Gould, in her noble work of uplifting the unfortunate, who wrote warm words of praise of the Mission. And there were countless other visitors, may of them of national and even international fame.

Perhaps one of the most significant of all the visits was paid by Pastor Charles Wagner, the famous French preacher, whose advocacy of the "Simple Life" appealed so powerfully to President Roosevelt. It was during his visit to New York in the early winter of 1904. He had engagements in the upper part of the city that evening, but he had promised Dr. Klopsch to come to the Mission, and had expressed a desire to see the "bread line." The night was bitterly cold. A little before midnight, when the hall was so full that scarcely another man could be squeezed through the doorway, and the "bread line" had already begun to form, there rolled up a carriage, and from it emerged Dr. Klopsch, quickly followed by Pastor Wagner, Dr. Koenig, and Mr. DeBrunoff. The story of that visit was told by *The Christian Herald:*

"The great majority of our men who heard Charles Wagner the other night, had been seated in the hall for over five hours, waiting for him, as, owing to his numerous engagements, we were unable to announce the exact hour at which he would speak. He had expressed a desire to see our famous "bread line," which begins to form a little after midnight, waiting for the opening of the doors at 1 o'clock, A.M. We, therefore, announced a meeting which would begin at 12 o'clock. Subsequently it was found that he would arrive earlier in the evening, but too late to speak at our ordinary night meeting. Thus it came to pass that on Monday evening, November 28, we held our longest evening meeting on record.

TENEMENT WAIFS AT THE CHILDREN'S HOME, WELCOMING DR. KLOPSCH

"But the men were very patient. A few of the worn-out ones fell asleep, and for once we did not disturb them. The night was a bitterly cold one, so that we could only open the doors and windows for ventilating purposes at short intervals, and, in consequence, the atmosphere was conducive to sleep; but the majority kept bravely awake. The time was pleasantly spent in singing our stirring hymns to the accompaniment of both organ and piano, in testimonies, and in occasional exhortations thrown in by the Superintendent and the regular leader of the evening, Mr. Simon Trenwith, our financial secretary.

"At about 11.30, when the hall was so full that scarcely another man could be squeezed through the doorway, and the "bread line" had already begun to form, there rolled up a carriage, and from it emerged Dr. Klopsch, energetic and happy looking, quickly followed by Pastor Wagner, Dr. Koenig, and M. DeBrunoff.

"It is needless to say that our Bowery crowd scanned most eagerly the face of the famous Paris pastor, when once he had become seated on the platform. A few moments more, and the great audience was on its feet, singing as lustily as though it were just beginning its Sunday morning service the hymn that has become so popular with them, 'Keep Step with the Master.' Then, after a few words of introduction from the Superintendent, the author of "The Simple Life" stood with compressed lips, grasping the brass rail in front of him, face to face with what he afterwards described as the most remarkable audience he had ever addressed. A tear glistened in his eye as he began, and his deep, rich voice trembled with unwonted emotion. He had been eagerly scanning the faces of the men, and now that the time had come for him to speak to them, it seemed as though any language, much less one that he had only mastered within recent months, would utterly fail to convey the wealth of profound sympathy that had suddenly surged into his heart for these suffering brethren of his. But the words came at last, and wonderful words they were. There was no cant, no insincerity, no patronage in this man, who could say, as, surely, they had never heard any one else say so strikingly before, 'I give my love to you. I greet you my brethren — I sympathize with you. I am of the people; I always will be of the people, as I always will be a boy. Tell me what it is that makes you look so sad?' There was something in this that reminded these poor battered and beaten men of what they had heard so many times of One, who, nineteen hundred years ago, was so gladly heard by the common people.

"Charles Wagner did not need to be told that these men had sinned. The marks of the beast were upon them. The badges of servitude to the evil one were prominent on every hand. But the one great fact that seemed to burn itself into his very innermost consciousness was that they were suffering, they were down, they were away from home. Call them back! Tell them that God loves them!

"Oh, how pathetic were the words, 'I am here as your friend. Would that I could press the hand of each one of you. Would that I could press the heart. We need each other — you and I. We have to love each other.

"When Pastor Wagner finished, the audience broke into song again:

> Wonderful words, beautiful words,
> Beautiful words of Life,

and as this appropriate chorus still lingered in the ears of all, Dr. Klopsch rose, and in appropriate terms thanked the great simple-minded, loving-hearted teacher for the message he had brought.

"Then came the first instalment of the breakfast, for it was now close on 1 o'clock. No sooner did the mission workers commence distributing the rolls and coffee than Mr. Wagner made his way down into the midst of the motley crowd. Eager hands were stretched out to him, which he just as eagerly gripped in his big, strong, kindly grasp.

"Guided by Dr. Klopsch, Mr. Wagner and his friends then proceeded through the Mission kitchen to the basement hall, where, by the time they arrived, the great throng of shivering, hungry men were streaming in in one unbroken line. There was little opportunity here for personal intercourse with the men, for it is always a scene of bustling activity, so, after a brief survey of the pathetic scene, Pastor Wagner, greatly moved, ascended to the upper hall again, saying, as he did so, 'A strange sight! A strange night! A strange city!'"

After his return to Europe, Pastor Wagner wrote his own account of his visit to the Bowery Mission and the impression it made upon him. It appeared in his volume entitled "American Impressions." Here is an extract from his story:

"I sat awhile in a sort of soul stupor until, fortunately, the organ began to play, and the people to sing. Then I could observe this accumulation of the dregs of nations. There was not a single woman, but every man bore the marks of defeat; not as though routed in some late battle, and still bewildered by dreadful visions of the fight; but vanquished long ago and too nearly trampled out and annihilated now to remember. Their faces represented types of every country, at the same time showing each of them to be a man without a country. They had fallen without the meshes that enclose the prudent among their fellow countrymen, into the great dragnet of misfortune, and there they lay, victims of their idleness, their drunkenness, their want of character or the brutal circumstances against which the little skiff wherein they had embarked their life was shattered.

"From my place I made them personal visits, observing them carefully, one by one, and among these hundreds of wrecks of men, there was not one bad face. There was diversity under the sordid uniformity of rags; there were bearded men and smooth-faced, bald men and hirsute, and a disproportionate number were one-eyed. By how many different paths had their lives, once fresh and full of hope, come to this downfall, this demolition, that was condensing and confusing them in a dark residue at the bottom of the social alembic? They seemed to me so great in their absolute nothingness, that suddenly the whole of respectable middle-class existence was obscured in their shadow, and some invisible hand removed from me all the store upon which a man ordinarily draws when he speaks to his fellows who have a bed to lie on and a table at which to sit; who carry about them that passport called money, and are animated by the breath of that soul of the social life — credit. Out of sympathy, I felt myself reduced to utter helplessness, to a humanity stript, wounded, and miserable, until I became their equal. And when I rose to call them brothers I saw in the midst of them the spirit of suffering humanity, the Son of Man, who had not where to lay his head. Never was I more deeply conscious of strength from the power to speak in His name; and never had the judgment, at once merciful and inexorable, that He pronounced upon our vanities and the hollowness of our comfortable Christianity, seemed more scathing. That night I learned one of those lessons that fill the soul with grief, with anguish.

"Had these men any knowledge of the preternatural effect they made upon me? Evidently not; but they listened with good-will to what I said aloud, as I listened in silence to their silent speech. Then I stepped down from the platform and begged them to show, by their uplifted hands, who among them spoke English, French or German, the only languages in which I could make myself understood, and I conversed with them individually. Their short biographies, all ending badly, reminded me of a succession of evil tidings, one report after another announcing a new catastrophe.

"As the hour for closing approached, cups of coffee were passed along the ranks, and there was a generous distribution of bread when the men went out. 'Where will they sleep?' I asked myself, as I watched the dark columns disperse in the foggy night; and a vision of them pursued me — a lamentable and distressful vision of them holding before my mind the huge question of vagabondage."

Superintendent Hallimond thus feelingly reviews Dr. Klopsch's noble services in connection with the Mission:

"For fifteen years Dr. Klopsch, by pen and tongue, and through the instrumentality of *The Christian Herald* columns, bravely and enthusiastically upheld the interests of this work. Sometimes under the most disheartening circumstances, as when, for instance, the Mission took fire in March 1898, and eleven lives were lost; but always in the most cheerful, patient and willing manner he bore the heavy burden.

"No one could read the appeals for the Mission which always came from his own pen at Thanksgiving and Christmas times, without realizing how vividly he realized his responsibility in the concern, and with what burning earnestness he watched over its interests. 'If God has prospered you, give a mite to this grand work. It is very near my heart. I pray daily for the men and boys at the Bowery Mission.' Misfortune has overtaken them, disappointment has been their lot, and now in their despair they appeal to the Bowery Mission. We cannot and must not turn them away. While these boys are with us, some, oh, so homesick, we must look after them.' These were some of the characteristic sentences found in his annual letters to the members of his large *Christian Herald* family. They could not, and did not, fail to meet with the generous and wholehearted responses that enabled him and the Mission to carry on the work with such unprecedented success.

"Dr. Klopsch, blessed as he was with such keen business acumen, seemed to realize intuitively, rather than by academic study, the economic conditions that made such a place as the Bowery inevitable. Unconsciously to himself, perhaps, the pressure of these thoughts would force themselves into his appeals. On one occasion he wrote, 'The men and boys of the Bowery are the ambitious sons of reputable parents, who started out with high hopes of making their future in the great city. The peaceful little country town was too slow for them, for at best it seemed to promise but a humdrum existence. Once out in the metropolis of the Western world, they hoped soon to send word to Father and Mother that success had attended their efforts, that they were on their way to a fortune, and in a position to contribute to the comfort of the old folks at home. Unfortunately they did not realize their fond hopes, and now they are ashamed to write home; and while Mother is singing, 'Oh, Where is my Wandering Boy Tonight?' and Father is praying for the return of the prodigal, and sisters are anxiously awaiting his coming, the poor fellow is walking off the heels of his boots in vain search for employment, day by day becoming more and more shabby, until, having lost faith in himself, he is now ashamed to write, ashamed to return.'

"Dr. Klopsch made it his almost invariable custom to attend the Mission, with the members of his family, on Thanksgiving evening. He never failed to manifest the same heart interest in the poor, homeless men gathered together within the hospitable walls of the Mission, that he showed in all his writings. His short, earnest addresses, were always of the most appropriate and helpful character.

'Never despair,' 'Cheer up,' 'It's never too late to mend,' 'God, able to save to the uttermost,' were familiar topics with him, and many a saved man, who has risen from Bowery wretchedness and despair to a rehabilitated manhood, will thank God for the inspiration given him through the words of this able and devoted man.

"It was not only, however, his interest in the outcast men of the Bowery as a *mass*, that characterized Dr. Klopsch. He was one of the busiest of men, but never hesitated, whenever any individual case of need was brought to his attention, to bestow upon it that minute, detailed care which his business associates were so familiar with in *The Christian Herald* office.

"I remember having a very difficult case to deal with. A young professional man came to me for advice and help. It was a sad, pathetic story, a story of sudden temptation, yielding, and — sin. As he proceeded with his relation of it, I felt more and more my own helplessness. The complications were serious, threatening, bewildering. No time was to be lost. His broken-hearted wife and six months old baby were awaiting his return at a neighboring hotel. An officer of the law might at any moment step in and arrest him. The man was desperate and panic-stricken. Very reluctantly I went to Dr. Klopsch. I felt guilty of a sense of unfairness in asking this busy man to accept any share of a burden which properly fell to my lot as superintendent of the Mission, but I was baffled and nervous, so I disturbed him in the midst of a

busy day, unusually so even for him. I repeated
the story to him. He listened patiently, but even
while I talked, that keen intuitive faculty he possessed had gone to the heart of things, and he had
formed his plans. He propounded a few quick,
incisive questions about dates, names, addresses,
etc., all of them pertaining to a far distant city.
Then he sprang to the telephone, and for two hours
kept the wires of the long distance hot, eventually
straightening matters out by assuming a certain
financial liability himself, and sending the young
fellow on his way a free and hopeful man again.

"On one cold, wintry morning Dr. Klopsch
visited the 'bread line.' The poor, shivering, ill-
clad men were trooping in for that hot coffee and
rolls. A respectable looking, but sad-faced old man
stood just within the door, peering eagerly into
the face of each man as he crossed the threshold
and stepped into the light. Dr. Klopsch, scenting
a tragedy, spoke kindly to him, and found that he
was a Father in search of his prodigal son. For
over seven years the boy had been a wanderer from
home. News had come that he was in New York
City and penniless. The man had read of the
'bread line' at the Mission, and had said, 'If my
boy is destitute, that's a very likely place to find
him at,' so he came. Dr. Klopsch stood at the old
man's side during the whole of the breakfast, and
when the line had passed in grim review before them
and the boy was not there, it was he who spoke
comforting words to the disappointed parent. By
that time it was after 2 o'clock in the morning,

but in his characteristically energetic manner he set machinery at work for a thorough inquiry amongst the lodging houses of the Bowery. Within a few hours the search was successful. The lost was found. The Father's heart was gladdened, and an early Sunday morning train took him and the recovered prodigal back to their home in New England.

"A man came to the 'bread line' at another time in an almost unspeakable condition of need. Whilst under the influence of drink he had fallen from a trolley car and had broken his leg. He was taken to Bellevue Hospital, treated, and kept there for a time. The crowded conditions of the city hospital that winter, however, obliged the authorities to discharge him, whilst he still had the plaster cast on his leg, and only able to walk on crutches. There he was, on a bitter winter night, without shelter, without food, without friends, and — a helpless cripple. Such a case, even among the thousands of needy cases clamoring for treatment, demanded special help. Fortunately for the man, Dr. Klopsch was again visiting the Mission. At once he became interested. The man was taken to the Memorial House, an adjunct of the Mission, and cared for many weeks. Then he became an employee and for several years has lived a consistent and useful life amongst his fellow men."

The crowning event in the history of the Mission was the visit of President Taft. It was given to Dr. Klopsch to see, before his life-work ended, this momentous event, the Chief Executive of one of the greatest Christian nations on earth standing before these wrecks of men, speaking to them as man to man, as brother to brother. It was an occasion which was without parallel.

President Taft had heard much of the work of the Bowery Mission in connection with Dr. Klopsch's other philanthropies. He had promised that on the first occasion he would visit it. It was on the night of Monday, December 13, 1909, when, after addressing a mass meeting in Carnegie Hall, he was whirled down in his automobile to the Bowery in the midst of a heavy rain-storm.

The account of the President's visit and of his brief address is taken from *The Christian Herald*.

PRESIDENT TAFT AT THE BOWERY MISSION

A NIGHT VISIT IN A POURING RAIN AND A CHEERING MESSAGE TO THE UNEMPLOYED

Monday, Dec. 13, 1909, will be a memorable day in the history of the Bowery Mission. President Taft, who had been speaking at a mass meeting in Carnegie Hall, at the conclusion of that meeting was whirled downtown in his automobile to the Bowery. The Presidential party, who followed, occupied several Stearns taxicabs, which made most excellent time in spite of the heaviest rain-storm the city had known in many months.

It was nearly 11 o'clock P.M. when they reached the Mission. Uniformed police and detectives in plain clothes guarded all the entrances. Everything, however, was quiet and orderly and the guardians of the peace were themselves deeply interested spectators of the proceedings.

The usual Gospel service was in progress when the autos reached the rear entrance, and when President Taft stepped from his machine he heard the big audience of Bowery men singing the Mission's favorite hymn, "I'm Holding On," to the accompaniment of organ and piano.   As he passed through the hallway and came upon the platform a tremendous burst of applause greeted him, which continued several minutes, the President bowing and smiling to the enthusiastic men before him.

On the platform beside the President were Dr. Louis Klopsch, the President of the Bowery Mission; Rev. Mr. Hallimond, Superintendent; "Mother" Bird, Bishop Darlington of Harrisburg, Dr. Ferdinand Iglehart, Mrs. Klopsch, Mrs. Hallimond, Harry Steele Morrison, and a number of others.

After another "three rousing cheers for the President of the United States," called for by Dr. Klopsch, had been given with an energy and volume of sound that made Mr. Taft's smile broaden, Superintendent Hallimond told the men briefly that their distinguished guest had a message for them.   The President arose and faced the men of the Bowery.   For a moment he seemed to scan the faces individually, then he spoke in a clear and distinct voice, as follows:

"My Friends!   I am just about as much surprised at being here as you are at seeing me.   I had a note from your benefactor, Dr. Klopsch, asking me to come, after the meeting at Carnegie Hall, to the Mission which he has established in the Bowery.

"Now, I have known Dr. Klopsch personally not very long; but I have known him for a long while in the way that perhaps you do, by what he has done.   [Cheers.]

"It has been my fortune in life to be a good deal of a sort of a figurehead.   Some men do the work, while others are figureheads, and nature has developed me in such a way that I fill a pretty good part as a figurehead.   [Cheers.]   So they put me at the head of the Red Cross, and as head of the Red Cross I came to know of the enormous energy and tremendous power for good which Dr. Klopsch exercises through *The Christian Herald* in raising hundreds of thousands of dollars to relieve human suffering wherever it may be in the world.

"And so, when he wrote to ask me to come here, I wasn't exactly advised, except that it was in the Bowery.   I always

had a good deal of curiosity to know the Bowery, and I felt certain that where Dr. Klopsch and the Bowery met, there would
probably be the best part of the Bowery, and so I came here.
[Loud cheering.]

"Now, your Superintendent has been good enough to say
some complimentary things about my coming from Carnegie
Hall down to the Bowery to meet you. I am not conscious of
deserving any credit for it. As I look into your faces I see you
are earnest American citizens. To use a colloquial expression,
some of you are 'down on your luck,' but nevertheless, respon-
sive to the same sentiments of loyalty and patriotism and love
of country, and with the same ideals and aspirations for better
things that are, I hope, shared by every man.

"I am glad to be here, if by being here and saying so I can
convince you that the so-called chasm between you and people
who seem for a time to be more fortunate is not a chasm, and
that there is extending through and between you and them a
deep feeling of sympathy, a deep, earnest desire that you shall
have that equality of opportunity — that means of getting on
your feet, of supporting your family and of earning your liveli-
hood — which we hope every man under the Stars and Stripes
may fully enjoy.

"I am glad to come here and to testify by my presence here
my sympathy with the great work of Dr. Klopsch in this Mission, by which he shall from time to time and constantly —
but not always the same people — help men over hard places;
help over the time when things seem desperate and when it
seems as if the Lord and everybody else have turned against
you, and to help you in those times to believe that there are
people in this world who do sympathize with you, and who
wish to help you to achieve better things.

"I know it is difficult for you to believe that I, who for the
time being am receiving a large salary from the United States,
and living in comfort, can understand or take into my heart
the feeling you may have of desperation, and the sense of
injustice you may have in feeling that you have not had the
chances other men have had. Yet I assure you that in spite

of those seeming differences your fellow-citizens and mine are
not the greedy, oppressive persons some would make you believe; but that more to-day than ever in the history of the
world their hearts are open and their desire to help the needy
and the suffering is greater than it ever was, and is growing
greater every minute.

"Dr. Klopsch is one of those through whom I hope that
thought is being conveyed to you, so that you may not burn
with a sense of injustice, but that you may hope on and struggle
on, made strong in the belief that the future is brighter for you
than before."

At the conclusion of the President's address there was an
outburst of tumultuous applause from the men in the body
of the hall, the visitors' galleries and the platform. He had
touched a deep chord in the breasts of his hearers, and they
felt that every word in this message of cheer and encouragement was spoken from the heart. Then after the applause
had subsided the President and his immediate party rose to
leave the platform. "Good night, boys," said Mr. Taft, waving his hand in kindly greeting to the men. "Good night,
Bill!" came back in a resounding, stentorian chorus. "Merry
Christmas!" he called out as he withdrew after shaking hands
cordially with those on the platform. He did not leave the
Mission building, however, until he had visited the quarters
of the "bread line," on the floor below, and inspected the
arrangements for feeding and comforting the thousands of homeless men and boys who come every midnight to be warmed and
fed at the Bowery Mission.

After his departure, the Gospel meeting in the Mission hall
went on with increased fervor. There was a new warmth in the
"testimonies" that night, a deeper spirituality in the prayers
and a higher note of praise and thankfulness in the hymns.

The police arrangements, under Inspector Hogan and Captain Day, were excellent. Owing to the stormy night there
was no large outside crowd, and the approaches to the Mission, front and rear, were kept clear and well guarded. Never
did President face a better behaved, more enthusiastic or

more loyal audience than did Mr. Taft that night, and his
words of kindness to the poor waifs of the Bowery will never
be forgotten. He is the first National Executive who has set
the example of coming down from his high station, for a single
hour, and mingling with the "down-and-outs," and the men
of the Bowery declare that the visit and the speech together
have inspired them with fresh courage and done them a world
of good.

In an editorial comment, *The Christian Herald*
said of this visit by the President:

"It was a new note which President Taft sounded.
It was a note of cheer and encouragement from the
executive head of this nation. He stepped down
for the moment from the social environment of his
high position to that of the humblest and saddest
of wayfarers. Through his big frame there flows a
warm current of sympathy with suffering and misfortune, and his talk with these men of the Bowery,
social outcasts as they are ranked, gave them a
glimpse of the goodness of his heart and made them
feel that the speaker was first a man, then a President. In the driving December storm he came to
them as a messenger of cheer, telling them that
even when the skies were blackest, and when it
seemed as if everybody had turned against them,
they were not friendless, for there were people who
stood ready to help them to better things.

"This is the real note of the uplift. It is when
we are down and weak with struggling, that we most
need the grasp of the friendly hand to help us upon
our feet. And there can be nothing more eloquent
in this world than such a hand, when it reaches out
at the right moment. It inspires courage, restores

self-respect, gives strength to the weak, makes the battle of adversity less arduous. It was a brave and commendable thing that Mr. Taft did down at the Bowery Mission, and society is his debtor for it. His words and example have done more to close the gap between rich and poor, than anything else that could possibly have happened. In that half hour when he stood face to face with the men of the Bowery, whom he called his 'boys,' we believe he received as much as he gave."

PRESIDENT TAFT ON THE PLATFORM OF THE BOWERY MISSION, NEW YORK

CHAPTER XVI

THE CRY OF THE CHILDREN

HOW THE MONT-LAWN HOME CAME TO BE OPENED IN 1895 — GROWTH OF DR. KLOPSCH'S FAVORITE CHARITY — STREET WAIFS IN THE GREAT CITY — FROM THE SLUMS TO AN EARTHLY PARADISE — A DAY'S DOINGS FOR THE TENEMENT GUESTS DESCRIBED — SATURDAY AFTERNOON ROMPS — WHAT A STRANGER FROM ENGLAND SAW — SONGS OF PRAISE — THE TEMPLE SERVICES — DR. KLOPSCH'S UNIQUE MESSAGE TO YOUTHFUL HEARTS — LESSONS IN PATRIOTISM — DISTINGUISHED VISITORS ON THE FOURTH OF JULY — A CELEBRATION WITHOUT THE FOUNDER — THE CHINESE MINISTER'S TRIBUTE— FUTURE OF MONT-LAWN.

THE cry of the children is a constant one. In a city such as New York, it goes up from the highways and byways, from the crowded tenements in the districts where population is most dense, sometimes with piercing shrillness. To those of generous impulses the call is an irresistible one. To the man who in his measures of relief for the sufferers from massacre and famine in Armenia, in Macedonia, in India, in China, and in Japan thought always of the orphans that must be provided for, it was certain that the waifs of the streets at home would appeal. Dr. Klopsch loved the little ones.

The opportunity for helping tenement children of New York City came early in his philanthropic career. At the conclusion of the New York "food-fund," which was solicited for the aid of the unemployed in the winter of 1893–94, and when there was no further need of relief operations, there was an unexpended balance of $4,900 in the treasury. Since the contributors to the fund numbered several thousand persons, scattered all over the country, who had given sums ranging from twenty-five cents upward, to return their gifts was a practical impossibility. It was suggested to Dr. Klopsch, by one of his associates, that as the winter's work had dealt very largely with the women and children, it would be a logical extension of the same work if the balance could be utilized for the purpose of opening a "Fresh Air Home" in the suburbs, for the little folks of the tenements, who had been subjected to so much privation during the winter.

This suggestion met with immediate approval by Dr. Klopsch. It gave him a long desired opportunity to put into operation an experiment in behalf of neglected city children, which promised to produce salutary results, morally and physically, besides affording the little ones such a pleasure as they never before enjoyed. The Rev. Dr. A. D. Lawrence Jewett, of Nyack, thirty miles up the Hudson, who was in hearty sympathy with the work, generously gave the use of his beautiful estate, known as Mont-Lawn, at a merely nominal rental, for the Children's Home. Some $2,000 was spent on furnishing and general equipment, a matron and helpers were engaged, and in June, 1895, the Home was opened to two hundred tenement children. That year twelve hundred were received. They were selected from the poorest families and no distinctions were made as to creed or nationality.

At the end of the first season, there was a deficit of about $1,000, which Dr. Klopsch personally supplied. Next year he succeeded in interesting many patrons among his readers, and the Home grew apace. It was enlarged and improved from year to year, until there are now five large dormitories, an open-air dining and play building, a beautiful chapel, stables, an artesian well, etc. The whole property is valued at something like $70,000.

Since the Home was started, about forty thousand children have been received at Mont-Lawn, the average stay being ten days each, and the season running ten weeks through the hottest period of the summer. The cost for each child for the season is three dollars. There is a matron with a corps of teachers or caretakers, a dormitory corps, and kitchen and garden help. The Home is maintained by voluntary contributions from people in many states, some of whom have been patrons since its foundation. It was Dr. Klopsch's favorite charity, and he spent the greater part of his summers there romping with the children, directing their games, leading in their exercises, and planning for their welfare and enjoyment.

This is in few words the story of the Children's Home at Mont-Lawn, but it has a thousand variations. Its purpose was best expressed in the first year of its existence, when Dr. Klopsch, in an article in *The Christian Herald*, said:

"There is no pleasure in this world of ours so pure and innocent as that of a little child, no laughter so sweet as that of children, no picture so sad as that of joyless childhood. In all our great cities, and especially in New York, there are thousands upon thousands of little ones whose early years are passed amid surroundings so miserable, unwholesome and vicious, as to augur ominously for their future. Many of them have never seen a Sabbath School, and don't know the name of Jesus, except when they hear it uttered in profanity. Some never even saw a blade of grass, or pulled a flower. Seen for the first time, a wood to them is a wonderland; a smooth lawn a dream of delight. It was of such as this that the poetess Elizabeth Barrett Browning wrote:

> "'Tis the young, young children, O my brothers,
>   They are weeping bitter tears;
>   They are weeping in the playtime of the others,
>   And their sorrow comes with years."

In describing those reached by the missionaries of the "Fresh Air Work," the paper said:

"Those neglected ones are the children of the slums, the tiny waifs, orphans and outcasts, who burrow in the very poorest and dirtiest sections of the city, live sometimes in cellars, or in the farthest removed places of some crazy tenement, or sometimes in the recess of a dock, for the want of a better home. Some of the children have parents who care little what becomes of their offspring, as long as their own animal wants are satisfied. Others are absolute waifs and outcasts, sleeping around on stairways, in cellars, or in wagons, or where they may. A few, though hardly yet in their teens, have taken the first steps in crime, and under the tuition of some low thief, now too old and decrepit to ply his trade himself, are being taught to pick pockets for a living. And this is but a realistic picture of thousands of other children in New York City.

"Tired and starved, in body, mind and soul, their unrelieved lot is poverty and want, suffering and death. They come and go like puny shadows on the dial of time. Not theirs the sweet pleasure of romping in the green fields, or resting in the cool woods. They may never hear the song of birds, nor breathe the sweet incense of flowers. It is this class that *The Christian Herald's* "Fresh Air Workers" seek out in the purlieus of the great city and take to our "Children's Home at Mont-Lawn."

A graphic description was given in one of the newspapers of the preparations for the trip. A summer visitor sat looking across the way from a window in Cooper Union Library, and noticed how children flocked to the Bible House between the hours of 11 and 1. They came in squads of five, six, fifteen, twenty, in charge of older people; or forlorn mites struggled along by themselves; they are evidently children of the poor. Some are laden with fruits and flowers, or bags evidently containing treasures. If the visitor questions a New Yorker, he will be informed that he is watching the initial operations of one of the most interesting and excellent charities of the metropolis. The children thronging into the Bible House are incoming and outgoing guests of *The Christian Herald's* Summer Home for Children at Nyack-on-the-Hudson. The adults in charge are missionaries, who bring them from the tenement districts, or caretakers who conduct them back and forth between the Home and the city. For every detachment of twenty-five children brought back from the Home, a corresponding number is returned. Each child stays ten days. Beneficiaries must be between the ages of five and twelve. Candidates undergo a medical examination, and those showing symptoms of contagious diseases are necessarily excluded, but are told to try again when better.

The trip up the Hudson to Nyack is filled with incidents. Some of the children are almost dumb with joy and amusement, while others are very voluble. "My," said one little girl after landing at Nyack, "but that was a long water." Her knowledge of what a river is was evidently limited to the definition in her geography, and she evidently did not connect it with the real thing.

A day's doings at Mont-Lawn have a never-ending novelty for the little guests from the tenements. The routine begins with the early morning, when the children, waiting, after a refreshing night's sleep, are hungry for breakfast and eager for play. Dormitories are like bee-hives; little folks are busy getting into clothes as quickly as possible, caretakers and older children are helping. At last, with buttons secure, faces washed, heads combed and brushed, they assemble on the lawn in front of the porch. In the doorway stands their house-mother with her hand on the gong. At the first stroke they fall in line; at the second, march off to the tent. Long white tables under the tent are set varied with oatmeal or rice and mugs of rich cream, milk, and many slices of buttered bread. Each little boy and girl takes his or her seat, heads are bowed, little hands are folded, and the children sing their pretty grace, beginning:

> God is great and God is good,
> And we thank Him for our food.

Such they are, poor half-famished little ones. Some who came pinched and pale, too weak and sick even to care for food, are hungry enough now and march and play sturdily. "Teachers"— this is what they elect to call their caretakers — go from table to table replenishing plates and mugs, and serving out numbers of slices of white and brown bread. Breakfast over and rat-a-tat-tat on the drum, they march in review again, and the house-mother standing on the steps asks the children what is the Golden Text. They answer, giving, as they were taught at Sunday School in the chapel, the Golden Text for the week. Every day they say the Text and are bidden to remember it in their play until the passing week brings a new Golden Text, to be graven into their memories and lives.

After the Text, they run off to the swings, the pool, to pluck flowers from the hillsides, to gather berries, to weave daisy chains and oak wreaths, to listen to stories told by wise and loving caretakers, to sing many a happy song, to play many a merry game, until dinner time, and again until evening, when supper comes, and the little chapel service follows, when the children hear short loving talks from the matron and caretakers about their "child king" Jesus, who put it into the hearts of kind friends to send them there; they sing little hymns of praise and thanksgiving, and pray God to make and keep them good, and to bless the dear kind friends who sent them to this beautiful Home.

Cool dormitories, filled with sleepy little folk; teachers and big children help the smaller ones to undress. All say "Our Father," and the little limbs are folded for the night; restless limbs are still, black heads and brown heads lie quiet on white pillows; through open windows sweep winds from the Rockland Hills on one side and the Hudson on the other; moon and stars shine down like a benediction on a placid river and solemn hills. Silence falls on Mont-Lawn. Even the busy caretakers, whose work has seemingly no end, may rest.

Another writer described Mont-Lawn as the "Children's Garden of Eden."

"During the day and night I spent there," she wrote, "I saw many things that made me glad — and alas! much to make one's heart ache. Little wistful faces would look up at me as I paused before a group of boys and girls, some of whom could not speak more than a word or two of English. One little Syrian, in whom I was particularly interested, stood apart from the others, solemnly watching them at their play. I took her by the hand, and going upon the wide veranda, seated myself in a big rocking chair. Taking the forlorn bit of humanity in my arms — she seemed about six years of age — I found that she was very gentle and could understand

English a little. She told me her name was Mary. She lay a long time very still, and I thought she was dozing; it was near sunset, and the air so soft and balmy, I was glad if it would lull her to sleep. The little curly head nestled against me and the long black lashes drooped over the olive cheek when suddenly she looked up, without moving, a glance that showed me she was far from sleeping. 'What do you want, Mary?' I asked. She answered only one word — 'Mama' — but it was enough to show that with beauty all around her and kindness on every hand, she still longed for the only one in the world who was really mother.

"Saturday afternoons, Mr. Klopsch goes up to Mont-Lawn, and then the outdoor games begin in earnest — the bean game, foot races, and various other things, which this man of far-reaching interests seems to enjoy as much as if he were one of the little ones. I could not help thinking, and repeating over and over, 'except ye become as little children.'

"And how the children love the man! When it came time for him to go, they lined up and gave him three rousing cheers. Then after watching him as far down the road as they could see, and waving their handkerchiefs, they suddenly, with one mind, scampered to the high platform at the other side of the house and waited, anxiously watching a turn in the road visible from this point down the mountain side. When the carriage came in sight, more than a mile away, such a cheer as went up from two hundred happy little ones, and such frantic waving of handkerchiefs! And until another turn hid the carriage from us, an answering wave of the white signal of love."

In 1909, C. O. S. Mawson, the English journalist, wrote an article telling "What a Stranger saw at Mont-Lawn." He was greatly impressed with everything he saw. He wrote:

"'I love God and little children.' There are many in this fair land who would unhesitatingly make such an avowal; but how many are there whose love so expresses itself in worthy deeds? When I saw these golden words which adorn the entrance to the Children's Home at Nyack, the voices of three hundred happy children were ringing in my ears; the hillside resounded with a welcome such as falls to the lot of few men; and the genial founder, Dr. Klopsch, flung back the greeting in kind, a veritable boy received in triumph by his play-fellows. His is the part of a foster parent, yet a comrade withal. One look at his face as he beheld his beloved children revealed the love which he bears them — a love which is felt by every child, and to which every child responds.

"Nowhere in the world have I seen such an undertaking as this; the very perfection of the scheme bespeaks an able organizer, as well as a lover of children. Mont-Lawn is not an ordinary institution; rather is it a village of clean and artistic homes, where the members all gather together at one family board, sing and worship in one Temple, and conform to the rules and guidance of one head. 'Health, happiness and harmony' are the watchwords. The children know they are there to be happy, and to radiate happiness around them. They are there for a holiday; a holiday all too brief, but free from every want or sadness. For at least ten days in their young lives their heaven is unclouded, and all seems radiant without and within. Looking at the bright upturned faces, it was hard to believe that these children were of the poorest and most friendless in the metropolis. How quickly fresh air, good food, and happy surroundings transform even the most delicate child!

"What particularly impressed me was the fact that in this vast charitable enterprise the seal of charity in its worldly sense is nowhere visible. The most sensitive child could feel no sense of shame or patronage. For instance, should a child arrive in ragged and wretched clothing, an outfit is provided by the Home, but all semblance of uniformity is conspicuous by its absence. These friendless children (can they indeed be friendless with such a friend?) are virtually at Mont-Lawn as the young guests of *The Christian Herald*.

"The obvious intelligence of the children was most notable. Doubtless their native environment tends to foster this precocity. In our talk, the able and courteous lady superintendent of the Home assured me that not only are the children most intelligent, but as mouldable as wax. Dr. Klopsch rightly instils a spirit of obedience and discipline.

"Still more remarkable is their singing; and it seemed inconceivable that one-third of these clear-voiced singers had only been there one day, and another third but three days. When the children took their places in the beautiful Temple, the crowning gift of the founder, their singing was heard to great advantage. The swing and the go were magnificent. In perfect tune, and with an enthusiasm that no American child ever lacks when singing of his beloved country, they commence the exercises with that patriotic song:

> It matters not where we may roam,
> Or what may be our quest,
> Our own, our dear old native land
> We're sure to love the best.

"At the close of each verse, every child produced a miniature flag and waved it aloft to the time of the rousing chorus. Standing as we were on the platform, facing the young singers, the spectacle was at once affective and inspiring. When the last notes of the organ died away, every right hand was raised, every eye upturned to the outspread stars and stripes, and every voice clearly and proudly proclaimed:

"'I pledge allegiance to my flag, and to the republic for which it stands; one nation indivisible, with liberty and justice for all.'"

The Children's Temple, to which this writer referred, was one of the many improvements which Dr. Klopsch, with the aid of *The Christian Herald* contributions, made at Mont-Lawn. In it are held the Sunday services. They are truly the children of all nations who gather there to worship, and there are those by whom the bright Temple service is looked upon with round-eyed wonder as a mysterious

rite. To all, however, it grows precious with the
association, and the seed which is sown so wisely
and lovingly during the quiet Sunday afternoon
bears out the parable of old — though some fall by
the wayside and among thorns and stony places,
yet others fall into good and fertile soil, which shall
bring forth a glorious harvest in time to come.

"When Dr. Klopsch rises," said a writer telling of
the Temple services, "scores of youthful hearts are
ready for his message — a message unique in its
application to the barren lives of his young auditors.
'Once upon a time,' he begins in the good old way,
'there was in the far-off city of Florence a rare and
beautiful statue. Of spotless and snowy marble the
fair and delicate beauty of the figure was so graceful
in its outline, so full of harmony in its pose, that
every eye which beheld it acknowledged its perfection. There came a day when the people of Florence
were allowed to enter the great gallery of art in
which this gem of sculpture stood.

"'Among the great throng who poured through
the open doors and passed before the wonderful expression of a master's art, there was one small
Florentine girl, dirty and tattered and poor, oh so
poor, with a big beautiful soul that responded greatly
to the beauty which surrounded her. She stood
motionless before the statue, gazing with rapt eyes
at every detail of grace and purity. Then the little
one stole away, turning with dragging feet to her
own squalid home. But she took the memory of the
marble with her in all its immaculate spotlessness,
and her first act was to cleanse her own soiled hands

and face, that they might bear some resemblance to the stately white figure of the Florentine statue.

"'Day by day the little child of poverty crept back to feast her beauty-loving heart upon the master-piece. Day by day, as she returned to her home, she sought to bring the lesson of the statue into her own poor life. The slender little body was pure and clean now, rough boards were scoured, and even the indifferent mother, who regarded the change in her child with astonishment, was moved to effort by her little daughter's great longing to bring into the humble home some reminder of the snowy image which had inspired within her hungry heart a great yearning for cleanliness and grace.

"'That, children, is what we want Mont-Lawn to become to you. May this fair and beautiful domain, in all its shining cleanliness, be to your lives the Florentine statue, from which you shall learn habits of neatness, repose of manner, and both moral and physical grace and charm. When you go home, children, carry with you the memory of the pure white statue, never forgetting that cleanliness and order are lessons well worth learning; that only the hand of the divine Sculptor can make us all glorious within.'"

The Fourth of July is always a great day at Mont-Lawn. The lessons of patriotism, as will be seen from what has been told of the exercises and of the impressions of different visitors, are not limited to a single day. But Independence Day is the culmination. Speakers of note are always glad to volunteer their presence and to tell the little folks what the day has meant in the past and what it should mean in the future.

That there are many races and nationalities among the children who celebrate the independence of the United States will be apparent from what already has been told of them. "How many of you are Germans?" asked Dr. Klopsch on one Fourth of July. Nearly a hundred hands went up. "How many are Italians?" Perhaps twenty-five hands were uplifted. "How many Jewish?" A generous sprinkling of hands followed. "How many Americans?" and now more hands than ever rose. The rest were divided among Irish, Scandinavians, a few Syrians, Hungarians, and one wee dainty little tot, whose name, Annie Yun Toy, would have proclaimed her a tiny human flower of the celestial kingdom, even if her twinkling, beady black eyes had not. But when Dr. Klopsch asked the last question, "How many mean to make noble American men and women?" every arm flew to its highest point. It was a sight at which the pessimist, who stalks abroad, gloomily prophesying the downfall of American institutions, would have hid his face in shame.

At the celebration in 1907, Rear-Admiral Charles D. Sigsbee talked to the little ones. He told them of the progress of our country, the righteous cause of her wars, and the happy and prosperous present. Referring to the encouraging conditions which are giving us the opportunity to educate the children of an immigrant population for the glorious destiny of American citizenship which awaits them, he closed by saying that it was always an inspiration to him, as he traveled over the country, to look into the faces of the children, and to realize that they represented the potential strength of the future. At the close of the exercises, everybody was pleased to receive a cordial handshake from the gallant commander of the *Maine*.

In the celebration of 1908, the visitors were greatly impressed by the flag drill by the children on the big lawn. The salute to the flag was one of the patriotic events of the day, and showed how deeply rooted is the love of country in the heart of even the poorest child. On this occasion one of the speakers was the Rev. David Charles Hughes, father of the distinguished Governor of New York, who gave a brief, but effective talk, which was enjoyed by the grownups, as well as the children.

The last celebration of the Fourth to be chronicled, July 4, 1910, was without the presence of the founder and patron. How greatly he was missed, all can tell, but as was his wish, the patriotic exercises went forward as in the past. Mrs. Klopsch came up from New York and spent the greater part of the day, greatly to the pleasure of all those who loved Mont-Lawn and its founder. During the day she held an almost continuous reception, and at the service of song in the chapel, had a place of honor on the platform. Dr. G. H. Sandison, managing editor of *The Christian Herald*, presided, and introduced as the leading orator of the day Hon. Arthur S. Tompkins, Judge of the Supreme Court, who delivered a stirring and patriotic address on "The Day We Celebrate." The next speaker, Mr. Don O. Shelton,

ADMIRAL SIGSBEE ADDRESSING A FOURTH OF JULY AUDIENCE AT THE CHILDREN'S HOME
MONT-LAWN

president of the National Bible Institute of New York, took as his topic "Our Young Folks," and gave some splendid practical advice to both children and adults. Cynthia Westover Alden, president of the International Sunshine Society, spoke on "Sunshiny Lives" and told her hearers how they might learn to radiate happiness everywhere. Kate Upson Clark, of *The Christian Herald* editorial staff, and well known as an author and lecturer, gave some excellent advice to "Our Girls." Rev. Dr. C. H. Mead kept the children in roars of laughter, and the big folks as well, by his inimitable stories. The one sad task of the day was assigned to Rev. Dr. Ferdinand C. Iglehart, who spoke on "Our Friends Who Have Passed Over." His address was an eloquent tribute to the memory of the late Dr. Louis Klopsch, the founder of Mont-Lawn and the "Children's Friend."

Rear-Admiral Charles D. Sigsbee, who came down from the Catskills specially to visit Mont-Lawn, and who is a popular favorite there, made a brief address, which was greatly enjoyed.

Just as the oratorical programme was about to conclude, a slender man of distinguished mien, clad in a flowing robe of some silken stuff, and with a thoughtful scholarly face, stepped from an open carriage at the entrance gate of Mont-Lawn. He was accompanied by a younger man, dressed in a light summer suit of American make. The visitors were His Excellency Chang Yin Tang, Ambassador of China to the United States, and his son and secretary, Hon. Henry Chang. Minister Chang had come to see the little tenement guests of Mont-Lawn at their holiday exercises. Like his predecessor, Minister Wu Ting Fang, Minister Chang was familiar with the great work done in China by *The Christian Herald* and its readers in relieving suffering during the great famine, and in supporting a large number of orphans who were left parentless and destitute after the famine ended. Minister Chang was introduced to the assemblage and through his secretary made a brief address. He spoke in terms of high commendation of the generous efforts of *The Christian Herald* and its readers in China and other lands and paid a noble tribute to the memory of Dr. Klopsch. He expressed the hope that *The Christian Herald* might go on successfully in its beneficent career of world-wide philanthropy and helpfulness, and that its readers might continue to enjoy the blessings that come to all who strive for the uplift of humanity.

Many of the leading guests were then presented to Minister Chang, who received all most graciously. After watching with deep interest the games and drill of the children on the wide-spreading lawn, he walked over to "Fort Plenty" and stood by, a greatly interested spectator, while the children filed in to take seats for supper. Minister and secretary watched with wide-open eyes the long orderly procession file past and deploy into the different aisles, each group taking seats at its proper table. Then the clear, young voices were raised in the simple little song of thanksgiving and all fell to eating with hearty appetites. Before leaving Mont-Lawn, Minister Chang expressed his appreciation of his experience there in unmeasured terms.

The evening passed quickly with games and music, the Piccaninny Band fairly eclipsing itself in its instrumental efforts. "Twilight tea" was served to the guests where they sat on the porches and the lawn. Then as the shadows fell and the long, perfect summer day drew to a close, a brilliant display of fireworks made beautiful Mont-Lawn luminous for miles around. By eight o'clock the visitors had departed, Matron Hyde had all her little boys and girls in bed in the dormitories, and half an hour later all was quiet at the "Children's Paradise." Sleep reigned over Mont-Lawn.

It was Dr. Klopsch's hope that the Children's Home — his favorite benevolence — might ultimately be endowed, so that it should be beyond any need of annual appeals. Had he lived, he would undoubtedly have accomplished this purpose; but called away from his labors by death, he left the unfinished task as a legacy to those who have been the friends and supporters of this beautiful benevolence for many years, knowing that they would not fail to perpetuate the work he had so lovingly founded and so successfully conducted. Had he been asked to choose, Mont-Lawn would have been the only monument he would have desired. "I Love God and Little Children" was written over its gates by Dr. Klopsch's direction. He put his own best love and service into this beneficent work. He spent there what he used to recall as the most enjoyable days of his life, among the little children. Let Mont-Lawn be his Monument, a permanent institution and a Memorial to his great love for the children of the poor!

Shortly after his death, when the subject of its endowment as a lasting memorial to his memory was brought up by some friends, President Taft, hearing of the matter, spoke to the Rev. J. Wesley Hill in cordial commendation of the Children's Home, and added that if the movement for its endowment were started, he would be glad to be a contributor.

It is confidently hoped that when this generous approval from so high a source is made public, many friends will be found willing to coöperate liberally in the proposed endowment, so that the "Children's Paradise" may be put on a permanent and enduring footing.

CHAPTER XVII

EDITOR AND PUBLISHER

BROAD FIELD OF THE EVANGELICAL NEWSPAPER — THE WEEKLY PULPIT AND OTHER FEATURES — SYMPOSIUMS ON IMPORTANT TOPICS — FAMOUS CONTRIBUTORS — DWIGHT L. MOODY'S GRATITUDE FOR IMPORTANT SERVICES — EDITORIAL ASSOCIATES — "THE CHRISTIAN HERALD'S" SUCCESSFUL CAMPAIGN TO RESTORE THE MOTTO "IN GOD WE TRUST" ON THE NATIONAL COINAGE — ANTI-MORMON AGITATION — SUPPORT OF TEMPERANCE — DR. KLOPSCH'S ORIGINAL METHODS — BELIEF IN PUBLICITY — INTIMATE PERSONAL RELATION WITH SUBSCRIBERS — USEFULNESS AS A PUBLISHER OF GOOD LITERATURE — CIRCULATING THE SCRIPTURES — THE RED LETTER BIBLE.

THE influence of the newspaper for good or evil is universally recognized. Happily on the part of most journals it is exerted for good. Whether the publication be daily, weekly, or monthly, its functions are essentially the same. The field is the world. The sphere of usefulness widens from year to year.

Dr. Klopsch was a born journalist. His intuitive perception of what interests people, of how to reach them in a manner to attract and hold them, of how to interest them in what is going on around and about them; his originality in planning and his ableness in execution made him the ideal head of a great newspaper. That he chose the evangelical field, rather than the secular one, was often the occasion of comment by those who were in control of great daily newspapers. They recognized in him a compeer and they thought that in their own domain he would have found even a broader ground for action. Dr. Klopsch did not share this opinion. He believed that the evangelical newspaper had fully as wide a field as the secular one. It was for him to plow the field, as he sometimes put it, in his own way in order to show that he was not mistaken. He rarely talked about the mission of journalism, but he fulfilled that mission to the utmost.

In the editorial and other features, Dr. Klopsch always aimed at freshness and at attractive treatment of current news events, while seeking at the same time the deeper significance which lay beyond them. He believed in satisfying legitimate curiosity as to what was going on all over the world, particularly new discoveries and progress. He believed also in telling about people who through their own deeds had made themselves interesting. There was always a motive behind the articles which were published, but his preference was, as he often said, that the sermon should preach itself. Of the young folks he was always thoughtful. He believed that good reading for them meant the foundation for wholesome lives and he sought to lay that foundation broad and deep.

The "weekly pulpit" was one of the first features which Dr. Klopsch established and during the lifetime of Dr. T. DeWitt Talmage, his sermons were printed regularly, reaching a vast audience.

After the death of Dr. Talmage, the "weekly pulpit" continued to be filled by other noted divines who have a message, and who are glad to convey it through *The Christian Herald*.

Dr. Klopsch was a believer in getting at other people's opinions. Hence the frequency with which symposiums on various topics appeared. Sometimes they related purely to religious topics; sometimes they centered on secular subjects, but always with a distinct purpose in view of bringing out the moral element in secular affairs. In this way Dr. Klopsch kept his readers in touch with what men of thought were thinking, and of what men of action were doing. One of the symposiums brought the following suggestive letter from Miss Helen Gould:

LYNDHURST, IRVINGTON-ON-HUDSON.

MR. LOUIS KLOPSCH,

Dear Sir: Your letter of October 4th is at hand asking my opinion on the subject "How to make the most of wealth." It is a topic on which I am not well qualified to speak, and I would suggest that you make this same inquiry of some of our leading clergymen whose views would be a great inspiration to us all.

The Christian idea that wealth is a stewardship, or trust, and not to be used for one's personal pleasure alone but for the welfare of others, certainly seems the noblest, and those who have more money or broader culture owe a debt to those who have had fewer opportunities. And there are so many ways in which one can help!

Children, the sick and the aged especially have claims on our attention, and the forms of work for them are numerous, from kindergartens, day nurseries and industrial schools, to "homes" and hospitals. Our institutions for higher education require gifts in order to do their best work, for the tuition fees do not cover the expense of the advantages offered; and certainly such societies as those in our churches, and the Young Women's Christian Association and Young Men's Christian Association deserve our hearty co-operation. The earnest workers who so nobly and lovingly give their lives to promote the welfare of others, give far more than though they had simply made gifts of money, so those who cannot afford to give largely need not feel discouraged on that account.   After all, sympathy and good will may be a greater force than wealth, and we can all extend to others a kindly feeling and courteous consideration that will make life sweeter and better.

Sometimes it seems to me we do not sufficiently realise the good that is done by money that is used in the different industries in giving employment to great numbers of people under the direction of clever men and women; and surely it takes more ability, perseverance and time to successfully manage such an enterprise than to merely make gifts.

You will, I am sure, be sorry you have made the inquiry of me since I have given you so little information, but I think you can easily obtain opinions that will be far more helpful than mine.   Believe me,

Very truly,

HELEN MILLER GOULD.

October 8th, 1900.

The Rev. Charles H. Spurgeon, the famous Baptist preacher of England, who for a generation thrilled the Christian world with his eloquent messages, was a contributor in the early days of *The Christian Herald*.   His sermons were published in its columns until his death in 1892.

The columns of *The Christian Herald* bear evidence to the famous men and women who have been contributors.   Most of these were glad to secure such a medium.   The Rev. Charles M. Sheldon, the author of "In His Steps," was a frequent contributor, both of serials and of short articles.   When Pastor Sheldon began the experiment of printing a daily paper in Topeka, such as he believed Christ would have sanctioned, Dr. Klopsch sent a special representative to Topeka to describe the experiment.

The Rev. Cyrus Townsend Brady contributed some of his stirring fiction. Marion Harland was a regular contributor.

Blind Fanny Crosby, whose sweet hymns have brought consolation to millions of Christian hearts, published many of her hymns for the first time in *The Christian Herald.* On her ninetieth birthday in 1910, a sketch of her appeared.

Mrs. Amelia E. Barr, the writer of wholesome fiction, found place for many of her serial stories.

Florence Morse Kingsley was one of Dr. Klopsch's valued contributors.

Marietta Holley, better known as "Aunt Samantha," brightened its columns by her own humor with its moral tone.

Pastor Charles Wagner also found the medium for reiterating his messages on the "Simple Life" in the columns of *The Christian Herald.* A very interesting story of his visit to Dr. Klopsch, and the story of his own work, was published in November, 1894, in *The Christian Herald.* Some excerpts are made from the article:

"It was a day of bright, sparkling sunshine. New York's principal streets were crowded with gay holiday shoppers, and Broadway was almost impassable, owing to the multitude who thronged the sidewalks and streamed in and out of the stores. Women predominated, and all ages and conditions were represented. The brilliant displays in the shop windows drew in a steady stream of buyers.

"On the same day of the scene above described,

Pastor Wagner entered *The Christian Herald* offices in the Bible House. He came unannounced, his tall, athletic form filling the doorway, and a smile lighting up his ruddy face. The Alsatian is a well-preserved man of fifty-two, broad-shouldered, and with a physique which suggests athletic power. A slight stoop betrays the student. He stood irresolute for a moment.

"'Pardon me,' he began. 'I came to see a gentleman — I quite forget his name — the man who went to India, Finland and Norwegen, to feed those famine people.'

"This unconventional introduction sufficed, and a moment later Pastor Wagner was ensconced in the biggest and easiest leather chair in the editorial sanctum. Warmly greeted by Dr. Klopsch and associates, he began to talk freely of his American visit and his work at home.

"Being asked concerning his work at home, he said: 'It is twenty-three years ago since I began the work on which I am now engaged. My purpose was to present to my own people a clearer view of practical religion, which all might understand, and to bring to them a definite comprehension of the purpose for which we are placed in this world.'"

Ira D. Sankey, Moody's comrade, the song evangelist, was one of Dr. Klopsch's earliest friends, and his contributions appeared in the journal. Dwight L. Moody was one of Dr. Klopsch's most valued and appreciative friends, and his contributions to *The Christian Herald* were most welcome. The great evangelist never forgot the services which Dr. Klopsch so freely rendered to the causes which were dearest to his heart. In 1894, when the Bible Institute at Chicago was in financial straits, Dr.

Klopsch came to the front at once and started the "Moody Gospel Fund," making one of his direct appeals to his readers. He sent a check for $1,000 as the first response to his appeal, and followed it with later contributions, explaining that the fund was being raised to enable the Bible Institute in Chicago to train, educate, and send forth an army of Christian workers among the millions of unevangelized in the cities and towns of America.

"The Bible Institute," said *The Christian Herald,* "is to the world's hosts what the drilling camp is to an army. It trains the raw recruit into the trained soldier. A thrilling national peril may call out thousands of fine men to the national standard, but it would be only courting defeat to lead them immediately like a helpless mob against the enemy. Enthusiasm is not sufficient, as great generals have proven again and again. The recruit must be taught the use of his weapons, must learn how to turn them to account, and how to coöperate with others. In opposing the great adversary of souls, like preparation is needed, as the untrained worker finds to his cost. And to do this effectively, the facilities of the Bible Institute must at once be increased tenfold. It is a campaign in which there is no retreat."

A grateful and encouraging acknowledgment of the first contribution was received from Mr. Moody. It was as follows:

EAST NORTHFIELD, MASS., July 16, 1894.
DEAR MR. KLOPSCH: I beg to acknowledge receipt of your check for $1,000 for the Bible Institute of Chicago. Permit me to thank you for your kindness in allowing *The Christian*

Herald to become the vehicle for presenting to the public the claims of the Institute, and to thank your readers through you for their prompt and generous response to the appeal. To every one of your readers who has contributed to this fund I wish to express my sincere gratitude. They are helping the cause of Christ more than they know. The doors of the Institute are besieged by earnest consecrated intelligent men and women who need only such training as is given in the Institute to become successful soul-winners. This money that comes through you enables us to receive some of them. But there are many others still waiting. For them I appeal. Christ waits for their services, the world waits for their life-giving message. I long to send them forth properly equipped for their work. May I hope that you will continue to receive contributions for the purpose? And may God bless you and your noble journal and your generous readers.

(Signed)   D. L. MOODY.

The Christian Herald continued to raise contributions for the Institute at Chicago, and since that period it has been a constant supporter of the Bible Institute at East Northfield, Mass., coöperating, after the death of Dwight L. Moody, with his son, W. R. Moody. A striking series of unpublished sermons of the great evangelist was published in *The Christian Herald* in the summer of 1910.

In his editorial aides, Dr. Klopsch always had loyal support. For years Dr. B. J. Fernie was one of the associate editors and gave his fervent piety and great industry to the work. Dr. G. H. Sandison, who still continues as the managing editor of the paper, was associated with Dr. Klopsch for twenty years. Mrs. Margaret E. Sangster has almost as long a service. Dr. Ferdinand C. Iglehart was a later and valued addition to the editorial department. In the art department, which was always a feature of the paper because Dr. Klopsch believed that there was no greater educating influence than good pictures, Mr. A. J. Belford presided for years and still remains.

An instance where Dr. Klopsch put *The Christian Herald* to a most effective use by an aggressive campaign was in the demand that the motto, "In God We Trust," be restored to the national coinage. It may be remembered that in 1907, for so-called artistic reasons, the motto was taken off and the coins of the United States appeared without it.

The story of the motto was told in a letter to *The Christian Herald* by C. R. Gehrhart of Lockhaven, Penn. In 1861, President Lincoln appointed Ex-Governor James Pollock of that state, Director of the United States Mint. Governor Pollock had been called "the great Christian Governor of Pennsylvania," as Andrew G. Curtin, who succeeded him, was "the War Governor." He was a ruling elder in the Presbyterian Church for well-nigh a generation. He was a lawyer of eminence, having graduated from Princeton College. He served in Congress and was instrumental in getting the appropriation to build the experimental telegraph line between Baltimore and Washington, which his friend Prof. S. F. B. Morse organized. Mr. Pollock for many years was Sunday School Superintendent of the West Arch Presbyterian Church, Philadelphia. He was President of the Board of Trustees of Lafayette College and President of the American Sunday School Union. Mr. Pollock enjoyed the friendship and confidence of President Lincoln, and there is every reason to believe that the bill which he framed, and which provided for the motto, was approved by Mr. Lincoln. The bill passed both House and Senate by unanimous vote, and until the brief period in 1907, and the early part of 1908, "In God We Trust" appeared on our national coinage.

Dr. Klopsch did not question the motives of those who had been responsible for removing the motto. He simply demanded in the name of the Christian people of America that it be restored. In response to this demand, numerous bills were introduced in Congress for that purpose, and many Congressmen pledged their support. The result was victory for the motto. In March, 1908, the bill for restoring it passed the House of Representatives by a vote of 259 yeas to 5 nays. In the debate, Representative Ellis of South Carolina quoted the following verse on the subject:

> We bowed before the shrine of wealth,
> And, drunk with riches, went astray,
> Restore, O God, the nation's health
> And lead it in the old true way!
> In sorrow, shame and vain regret,
> We plead that thou will spare us yet.

The measure was soon passed by the Senate, and the motto was later restored to the national coinage of the United States.

When the women of America started the agitation against what was considered recognition of plural marriage by allowing a Mormon Representative from Utah to be seated in Congress, *The Christian*

Herald was in full sympathy with them. Its columns were opened to their protests, and a great national movement began, which resulted in triumph for the women, the Mormon Congressman retiring from his seat. In this campaign, *The Christian Herald* secured the legal opinion of the eminent jurist, Ex-Senator George F. Edmunds, regarding the best form for a constitutional amendment, which would meet the vital question.

For the temperance movement in all its forms, *The Christian Herald* was always open. It constantly encouraged every organized effort to grapple with the drink evil, and the Women's Christian Temperance Union and other organizations of wide scope and genuine activity always found support from Dr. Klopsch.

There are other phases of Dr. Klopsch's career as an editor and publisher which give an insight into some of his remarkable characteristics. It was here that his originality, his fertility of invention, his ableness in trying new ideas, found their fullest scope. In his business relations he was noted among the publishers of the country as one who had the executive quality developed to an extraordinary degree. He was a master of men and knew how to use a large force to the best advantage. He constantly invited the submission of new ideas, and it was amusing to note the deftness with which he sifted them out and adapted them to practical uses, never failing to recognize and reward the suggester.

The value of publicity in every proper form was something that Dr. Klopsch keenly appreciated.

He did not believe that a publisher should hide his
light under a bushel, nor that a public man who
served a large constituency, distributed over an
entire continent, should be a recluse. A favorite
motto of his was:

> Do all the good you can,
>   To everybody you can,
>   And tell all the people you can.

This is sound logic and good practical business
philosophy. The result was that his name and work
became known throughout the whole country, and
in many other lands. He did not do this for vain-
glory; it was with him purely a matter of business.
There was no man in the publishing business in
America who was more widely known. From the
farming districts and stock raising ranches in the far
West up to Alaska, up and down through the great
Canadian Northwest, down to the borders of Mexico, and in every state in the Union, his name was
a household word, synonymous with big charitable
enterprises.

Another evidence of his appreciation of the value
of publicity was found in his methods of advertising.
He looked beyond mere monetary results and saw
the advantages to be derived from the impression
made on the public mind, and especially on the
minds of the publishing trade and general advertisers. His advertising broadsides thus had a double
object in view: they brought in subscriptions by
the tens of thousands, and sold innumerable premiums, and they also placed his journal at the top of

the ladder for advertising propaganda, and gave it a high standing among advertisers generally. In the Periodical Publishers' Association, which is composed of the leading weekly and monthly magazines and journals of the United States, Dr. Klopsch was an influential factor. His judgment was highly respected by his associates, who frequently sought his advice.

A trade paper, *Printers' Ink,* in discussing Dr. Klopsch's position, said:

The religious press has no other personal representative who combines evangelical enthusiasm and business methods like Louis Klopsch. Of course that is what we would look for in a man that built up a great newspaper property upon the foundations of the nation's belief in missionaries, and an inherited fondness for universal salvation. He publishes a paper that makes an elementary appeal to the people who believe in the Christian religion. His *clientèle* is the civilized world. The enterprising and progressive paper that seeks new fields must go far abroad. Louis Klopsch has successfully led *The Christian Herald* into that vague pasturage; but, after all, the man is there. Charitable impulses could follow the pulse of the people until they died from self-suffocation. Unless they were directed and aided to a healthful flow, that is what would happen. That is what Louis Klopsch professes to have done. He says, "I apply twentieth century methods to the new necessities of a crowded twentieth century life." His mind deals with great suffering, and he seeks to relieve it by great methods.

Dr. Klopsch himself did not object to being called sensational, when that term was not misunderstood. His views on this point were given in a New York newspaper, which published a symposium at a time when there was much talk about sensationalism in the pulpit. Dr. Klopsch wrote:

"Everything that is in the domain of public morals; everything that makes for or against public virtue; everything that tends to uplift or debase a community, state or nation, is a fitting subject for consideration by the Christian pulpit. Christ himself set the example of wholesome and fearless criticism in his dealings with conditions and events as he found them. He scored the corrupters, the squanderers, the usurers, the selfish rich and the publicans or politicians, as deservedly as he rebuked the scribes and Pharisees.

"The pulpit differs from the press and the public forum in the sense that it is specifically spiritual. It should not lend itself to political methods, nor permit itself to be used for the purpose of any party or faction. If it does so, its influence instantly ceases. To indulge in individual criticism of persons, simply because they happen to be prominent in public affairs or finance, is in the worst possible taste, and wholly out of place in a pulpit. At the same time, the preacher who, in consequence of the liberal gifts or the generous support of the rich, allows himself to become blind to the existence of wrongs that ought to be righted, and evils that should be denounced, is a faithless shepherd, untrue to his high calling, and unworthy the confidence of his people."

In the other aspects of his work as editor and publisher, Dr. Klopsch came into the most intimate relation with those, who, while actual strangers to him, felt that he was not a stranger to them. Men wrote to him for advice about their business affairs, and as to the distribution of funds for benevolent and church purposes; preachers of all denominations addressed him as "Dear Brother Klopsch." Churches carried their troubles to him, and he was a reliable and sagacious adviser.

In his large enterprises outside of *The Christian Herald*, he came in contact with people of high station, not only at home, but also abroad. By sheer force of gravity he came to the front in almost every national and international enterprise of benevolent or humane character. All of these things gave the man and his journal the highest imaginable prestige, and put it upon a pinnacle of popularity as an organ of wide-spread humanitarianism such as no other publication in the world has ever before enjoyed. Yet, with all the publicity and honor and attention that were bestowed upon him, Dr. Klopsch did not overestimate their value, but took them rather as a tribute to the work than to himself. He often expressed his simple gratitude at being chosen as the instrument by which so many of God's people all over the country could work out their plans for the betterment of humanity.

"I am merely the channel," he would say, "through which these good people are working. It is their good hearts and generous hands, supplemented by my head, which is accomplishing these things, and I esteem it a pleasure and a privilege to be so used."

When he had no great enterprises on hand to engross his attention and demand his utmost energies, he would be sure to find in some corner of the daily newspapers, or in some letter received through the mail, a case worthy of attention. It might be some poor family about to be dispossessed, for whom he would offer to pay the rent, or secure new quarters; and he would never omit to send a supply of food from the nearest grocery or bakery. Some old farmer at a distance, about to lose his property, would be succored temporarily and helped to fight out the battle under better auspices. These cases, which were constantly occurring, were merely incidents, as he looked on them, in his business as an editor and publisher.

It would be difficult to estimate the good that Dr. Klopsch did in his publishing business, by supplying good literature at popular prices. Many of the books he issued, either as premiums with *The Christian Herald*, or as separate ventures, have a permanent value and go to make up many a library. His greatest work as a publisher probably was in Bible distribution. Dr. Klopsch, having all his life been an ardent student of the Bible, conceived the idea which took form in the issue of the "Red Letter Bible." This he designed to show, first, the words in the New Testament actually spoken by the Saviour; and second, the prophetic references to Christ in the Old Testament. To carry out this idea, he engaged the services of a number of distinguished Bible scholars, including several leading college professors in this country and abroad. To each of these he wrote explaining the nature of the work, and giving to each a certain part of the books of the Old and New Testaments to mark for the "Red Letter" edition. When the entire Bible was finished, the separate books were then interchanged among these workers, so that each eminent scholar practically went over the entire Bible and annotated the work already done by the others. Many months were occupied in this interchange, but at last the task was accomplished.

The "Red Letter Testament" was produced, and it met with such instant success that soon the entire Bible was put in press. Since then it has been sold all over the world and has been of the greatest assistance to Bible students everywhere. Their Majesties the King and Queen of Sweden made a special acknowledgment of their appreciation of the "Red Letter Testament." An edition of the "Red Letter Testament" was published in German. "Red Letter Bibles" have been issued by various publishing houses in imitation of Dr. Klopsch's original product, and they have met with a large sale.

It is doubtful whether any single agency equalled Dr. Klopsch as a Bible distributor. During his management of *The Christian Herald*, it is estimated that for many years he issued not less than 60,000 Bibles and Testaments annually, both black and red letter. The various Bible societies awarded him the honor of being the one man above all others who helped to make the Bible the most widely read book on the North American continent.

CHAPTER XVIII

THE MAN AND HIS METHODS

MARKS OF GREAT BUSINESS CAPACITY — HOW HIS PHILANTHROPIC CAMPAIGNS
WERE ORGANIZED — WAYS OF COLLECTING FUNDS — MANNER OF DISTRIBU-
TION — A SACRED STEWARDSHIP — DR. KLOPSCH'S INTIMATE PERSONAL RE-
LATIONSHIP WITH RELIEF CONTRIBUTORS — INSTANCES OF QUICK PERCEPTION
— MR. SANDISON'S ACCOUNT OF GOING AHEAD ON FAITH — APPLICATION OF
ABILITY IN HIS OWN AFFAIRS — THINKING IN FIGURES — AN HOUR IN "THE
CHRISTIAN HERALD" OFFICE — ADVICE TO A CONVICT — KINDLY RELATIONS
WITH ASSOCIATES AND EMPLOYEES — IMPRESSIONS OF A FOREIGN VISITOR
— PERSONALITY ANALYZED BY A HINDU JOURNALIST — SUNDAY SCHOOL
ACTIVITIES.

WORKS speak for the man. The wide field of philanthropy covered by Dr. Klopsch's various enterprises could only have been undertaken by a man of the broadest sympathies. He was born into the world to do good — one of the great inspirational forces of his generation. In all he did the evangelical spirit was dominant. Yet his charitable impulses and benevolent instincts were always regulated by sound judgment and common sense.

These qualities were really the marks of great business capacity. Dr. Klopsch was a master of commercial organization. He had the faculty of intuition coupled with extraordinary executive ability. All that he did was regulated by system. The results were shown in the management of his own vast and complicated business and in the management of the campaigns for charity which made him famous.

326

Dr. Klopsch had faith in the goodness of human nature. He knew that the vast majority of people are ever ready to make sacrifices themselves in order to relieve suffering and to make the world better by their own individual effort. But he also realized that, with most people, it is difficult to translate these benevolent instincts into practical operation. What is needed is some one to show the way. Dr. Klopsch was the man who showed the way for those who were ready to do good.

His idea of charity was of the *simplest elementary* sort. It consisted of three things — to feed the hungry, to send or carry aid to the sick, and to spread the Gospel message everywhere. The record of his life-work, as given in the chapters of this book, show some of the deserving causes which enlisted him, and there were many others. He raised money for a large number of weak and struggling schools and churches, benevolent institutions and rescue missions; for evangelistic work; for the dissemination of the Gospel at home and abroad; for indigent homes for children and adults; for Gospel missions in the Cumberland Mountains and the Ozarks, and for a variety of other good causes.

Dr. Klopsch knew that ordinary, conservative methods are not enough to meet great emergencies such as famines, and disasters such as earthquakes. With him, in these matters, to think was to act. He applied literally the French maxim, "Be bold, and evermore be bold," when the emergency arose. Usually he did not wait to have the funds in hand when the need was a pressing one. He would prepare his appeal and then make a contribution in advance, oftentimes a very large sum, but always confident that *The Christian Herald* readers and the others to whom it was addressed would respond. His plan was to make known the situation which required succor; explain the needs so that contributors to relief funds would know just what was asked of them; forward by cable the first remittance, and then begin the work of collection in a systematic way.

In securing funds and in making known distressing situations, he adopted modern methods. He did not hesitate to advertise the distress which it was sought to relieve. The columns of *The Christian Herald* were filled with vivid descriptions. In other religious journals he placed advertisements. Many of these journals, lacking the means themselves of collecting and distributing funds, were glad to coöperate in this manner, knowing that with Dr. Klopsch in control, the philanthropic effort would not go amiss. He also, by means of circulars and leaflets, supplemented the newspaper appeals.

When the stream of contributions was fairly started, more attention would be paid to distribution. Dr. Klopsch, wherever possible, sought himself to see how the work went on. This was the motive of his personal visits during the famine periods to Russia, to Finland, India, Cuba, and Italy. Always he sought the coöperation of the missionaries, who were on the ground, and through them he reached the classes whom he knew that the contributors to *The Christian Herald* funds were most anxious to have reached. The aid of the government officials in Washington, and in the various countries where the distress existed, was always sought and given. Local relief committees and appropriate representatives of foreign governments were enlisted. The Red Cross Society of every country was recognized in his work.

An explanation of the principle which governed the distribution was made in an editorial in answer to an inquiry received from a contributor, who wanted to know how much Dr. Klopsch would distribute while he was among the famine sufferers in Finland.

"I will distribute no money at all," said the editorial. "No one connected with *The Christian Herald* ever undertakes the distribution of funds entrusted to his care for use in any benevolent or missionary field. In every instance — in Cuba, Russia, China, Porto Rico, Armenia and India, as well as now in Finland — the money is invariably administered by missionaries or by representative local resident committees under the supervision of a resident general or central committee which is charged with the relief of suffering.

"Experience in humanitarian work in many lands has convinced *The Christian Herald* that the reputable, intelligent, Christian residents of the country where such work is needed, and where relief monies are to be distributed, are far better qualified to administer such a trust than any outsiders, resident in a distant country. They know the field and the people, and are familiar with their needs; consequently, they are in a position to conduct the distribution of relief in a far more judicious and effective manner than could be possible for the management of *The Christian Herald*, located thousands of miles away."

This principle was always adhered to, but either by his own visits or by sending special commissioners, Dr. Klopsch was able above all things to see that the distribution was properly attended to by the various agencies to which it was entrusted.

In collecting funds, no sum was too small to be received and accounted for. It has been noted how often the dime and the quarter occur in the list of contributions, and of dollar contributions to the funds the totals run up into the hundreds of thousands. The strictest account was kept. Bookkeeping methods were rigorously applied. Dr. Klopsch knew how often funds are apt to be wasted or lost through unwise methods, and he also knew how many persons there are with the very best of intentions, who have no conception of the necessity of strict business methods in everything that relates to charity and philanthropy.

Following this idea, the receipt of funds would be acknowledged in *The Christian Herald*, the state in which the contributor lived being given, but not the residence, so that everyone could see his or her contribution placed on record. Then, when the time came for the fund to be closed, announcement would be made, and later would appear the detailed account of receipts and disbursements, certified by the public accountants who had audited them. Every item of expense of collection and of disbursement would be given in detail, the total receipts, and the purpose for which they were applied. To Dr. Klopsch this was a sacred trust. As the columns of *The Christian Herald* through twenty years of his activities show audited statements of every dollar received and disbursed in the enormous charity campaigns which were conducted. Of more than $700,000 that went to India (exclusive of orphan support), there is a complete account, and also of the more than $600,000 to China, and the other famine and relief movements, which footed up over $3,000,000, which Dr. Klopsch collected and disbursed. The great movements are given fully, but the details are just as complete as for the minor ones.

In all this work, Dr. Klopsch was in the most intimate relation with his subscribers and contributors. His appeals to them were in the nature of a personal message. Each response he looked on as a personal message of confidence to himself. Hence it came that he had not only the confidence of Presidents McKinley, Roosevelt, Taft, and high officials at Washington, and was given marks of royal honor by the Czar of Russia, the Royal families of Denmark and Sweden, the King of England, and the King of Italy; but he earned the gratitude of millions whose sufferings were relieved and of hundreds of thousands who contributed to the relief of those sufferings.

The keen business insight, the native shrewdness, and the marvelous perceptive qualities of Dr. Klopsch were apparent in all his relief work. He saw almost at a glance the situations which were so often pre-

sented to him and which others could resolve only
with slowness. In five minutes he would look at a
question from all points of view, would foresee the
objections and difficulties, and determine whether
they could be overcome. In as short a time he
would decide whether the cause should be helped
or not. Here his common sense came oftenest into
play. Reports would come of distress in some
quarter, with the appeal for relief before the nature
and extent of the suffering was known. That would
be put aside until more light could be had. Another
time he would shake his head, and with a brief
remark, "an unworthy cause," would dismiss the
case which was presented to him. Sometimes he
would remark regretfully, "a good cause, but not
in the right hands."

An instance of Dr. Klopsch's quick perception as
to difficulties was shown when Miss Ellen M. Stone,
the missionary in Macedonia, was kidnapped by the
brigands. Dr. Klopsch canvassed the whole situation. He foresaw the objections which would be
made, and not improperly, to raising the ransom
fund. He realized that it might be made an instrument of blackmail, and he knew that many protests
would go up against encouraging a relief measure
of this kind. But he concluded quickly in his own
mind that in spite of these drawbacks and of the
possible consequences, a real emergency existed and
it would be necessary in order to obtain the release
of Miss Stone to raise the funds for the ransom. So
within ten minutes the telephone in his office was
working, messages were speeding over the country,

and *The Christian Herald* fund was started for the ransom of Miss Stone.

In other cases, his perception of distress that would grow into great proportions was instantaneous. One morning the newspapers contained dispatches intimating that a famine in a far-away land was worse than the previous accounts had stated, was spreading, and that the government of the country itself might require foreign aid. That morning, in Washington, the writer was walking across Lafayette Park when a cabinet member joined him. I had on previous occasions sought and secured on behalf of Dr. Klopsch the coöperation of this official. He had been reading the newspaper dispatches. He remarked, "It looks as though we will have to turn in and help those poor people. I suppose I will find a message from Dr. Klopsch when I reach my office. Have you heard from him?"

Yes, I had heard from him. Dr. Klopsch had read the paper at his early cup of coffee, and at my own breakfast I had got a long-distance telephone message asking me to go to the White House and solicit the coöperation of the President in the relief movement which he proposed to start. The cabinet member, when he reached his office, was not disappointed. There was a message from Dr. Klopsch saying the emergency was great and that he wanted to transmit $10,000 by cable through the State Department to our Consul at the seat of suffering. This famine did grow and became appalling.

Many illustrations of Dr. Klopsch's quickness of perception and action are given by those who were associated with him in his editorial and other work. Mr. Sandison (who was his associate for over twenty years), writing on this subject, says:

"An urgent appeal would be made by missionaries in some remote country for help in an emergency. Such a case would usually require much thought and investigation before any step could be taken. Dr. Klopsch would turn to the telephone, call up the State Department in Washington, or get into communication with the ambassador, or cable direct to the American Minister or Consul-General representing the United States in the country in question, and would soon be in possession of the essential facts, which would convince him that the cause was good and the appeal justified. He would discuss with his associates the amount of relief to be sent, and their counsel would usually be for some moderate sum, but Dr. Klopsch knew his readers better than any other man, and he did nothing by halves. He would cable in such cases a remittance for ten or twenty thousand dollars, with the utmost confidence that the cause would not only prove worthy of such substantial help, but that it was one that would appeal to the sympathy of his constituency. In such emergencies, his intuition and judgment never failed, and his confidence in his readers was abundantly justified. He would simply lay such cases before his readers in plain, unvarnished language, stating that he already had advanced such an amount, and inviting their coöperation. And forthwith the contributions would come rolling in, increasing in volume by every mail. They knew him and trusted him.

"It was a favorite saying of his that he liked to go ahead on faith. What to other men might have seemed like plunging, was to him an exercise of supreme faith in God's blessing resting on all he did. I have seen him on faith send $25,000 as an Easter Offering to stricken India; on faith he sent out sums aggregating many thousands of dollars, often before he had received a dollar by way of contribution to the particular cause he was assisting. His faith was manifested in a courage which permitted him to throw out afar his golden line of help, as Douglas flung out the casket which contained the heart of Bruce into the midst of the foe.

"A striking illustration of the quickness of his actions in such matters occurred in the Cuban relief work among the *reconcentrados*. In conjunction with other members of the committee appointed by President McKinley, he had made many shipments of food and clothing by the regular ship lines, but somehow things did not go to his liking down in Havana. The centers of suffering were not being reached. One morning he left New York and four days later he was in Cuba's capital. It was as he had feared. The relief goods were piling up in warehouses, and the distribution was woefully slow and ineffective. Dr. Klopsch took a carriage and did some record driving in Havana that day. He visited scores of Spanish officials, and his earnest masterful way and the simple appeal he made for the *reconcentrados* in the name of humanity carried the day. The Spanish officials were won over, and within twenty-four hours after his arrival, railroad trains were speeding from Havana in the direction of the suffering districts in the outlying provinces.

"Another illustration was during the India famine. He went out there, and against the protests of the missionaries, he personally visited several of the fever camps. There was food and medicine, yet the people were dying. He saw them lying weak and emaciated on the bare soil. At one of the missions, he got into telegraphic communication with a blanket manufactory, and several of the camps were surprised the next day to find a large consignment of native blankets, which were of great benefit and comfort to the sick. He had ordered thirty thousand blankets at a breakdown price, and said he could have readily used as many more, but could not get them. That quick decision made life easier for thousands of sufferers, and no doubt helped many to recover.

"These are evidences of the broad sympathy and the grasp of an organizing mind in relief and rescue work. But there were other traits which showed his extraordinary qualities of mind in their application to his own business affairs and the great evangelical newspaper which he built up. His active brain could not rest. He used to say that much of his planning was done at home and in the five-minute walk to and from his apartments to his office. But in everything he was systematic.

"Dr. Klopsch had a mind, which, if his bent had taken a little different turn, might have led him to become a mathematician of no mean distinction. He thought in figures. A source of continued amazement to his acquaintances was the rapidity

DR. GEO. H. SANDISON, EDITOR OF *THE CHRISTIAN HERALD*
For Twenty Years Associate of Dr. Klopsch

with which he could mentally compute the cost of material and production, the cost of advertising and other details of a great publishing business. No matter how intricate the business problem, he was equal to it almost without resort to paper and pencil. It was his invariable custom to carry a little memorandum book in the upper pocket of his vest, which was to him an epitome of his entire business. By reference to it, he could instantly compare the conditions of one year, one week, one day, with that of the preceding year at the same season. He was a man of many problems, yet their number did not trouble him. At a single sitting he would sometimes discuss half a dozen different questions and reach a satisfactory conclusion in each case. He had an intuition which led him to do the right thing at the right moment.

"His was an electric personality. It permeated and stimulated all his surroundings. His good nature was infinite, and he could enjoy a joke in the midst of the most pressing affairs. He himself radiated cheerfulness. His comment was sometimes humorous, always incisive and always kindly, but it never missed the point."

An hour in Dr. Klopsch's inner office at *The Christian Herald* was a revelation to those who had not previously known his extraordinary capacity. A mass of correspondence would be before him, some relating to technical matters of the publishing business, some to its purely financial aspect, and much more to various philanthropic and charitable works. He would dictate letter after letter in answer, commenting between times on other subjects. Then there would be the telephone calls, sometimes long-distance and sometimes from within New York City. These he always managed, as he would say, with his ear to the telephone, and his eye to the big table on which was spread out his business.

A stream of visitors would be waiting in the outer office. Almost any day there would be a missionary from some distant land, or a foreign philanthropist who wanted to learn practical lessons from this great master of practical philanthropy. Frequently there would be a high Washington official, or a foreign diplomat sandwiched in between some of the Bowery Mission workers, or the caretakers from Mont-Lawn. Almost certainly there would be a country pastor from some poor struggling church which wanted a little help, that would be given along with very sound advice. Sometimes there would be a distinguished army officer, such as General O. O. Howard, or a naval commander, such as Admiral Sigsbee. The door would open to admit one or two visitors, and a cheery call would come from Dr. Klopsch to the others begging them to wait just a moment longer.

No one was too lowly to be given the privilege of a hearing. Once Dr. Klopsch asked me to excuse him from talking until he had spoken to a man whose presence I had not noticed on entering the office. The man had a haunted look which told his story. I knew in an instant that he was an ex-convict. He whispered his fears to Dr. Klopsch, who spoke out strongly and clearly:

"Nonsense, man, you have nothing to be afraid of. The police are not following you. If you think they are, walk right up to them and tell them who you are. They want you to get work and to lead an honest life, just as much as I do. Now, your room rent in Hoboken is paid for a month. Your breakfast is provided, and here's something for dinner to-day. But don't be afraid to go out again and ask work. I told you nobody is going to molest you. I believe in you and others believe in you."

The man straightened up at once and left the office with a firm step, his fears dispelled. How many times the same thing happened, others who were oftener in the private office can perhaps tell, but I knew that this was not a single instance.

In his relations with his associates and employees, no man could be more kindly or considerate than Dr. Klopsch. Any negligence on their part pained him, and when he spoke of it, it was always with regret. Actual wrong doing distressed him almost beyond expression. Once a girl employee had been brought to him under some accusation. It was a serious case. The proof lay in his hands. A great wave of sorrow for the girl rose within him. He attempted to speak to her reproachfully, and even with severity, but the effort failed. His eyes and throat seemed to fill simultaneously, and he passed over the task to a subordinate, saying huskily, "You deal with her; I can't; but remember, don't do anything that will hurt her rather than help," and this was his invariable attitude towards those who offended against the law or morals. He believed that the best course was to help reform the offender by kindness, rather than utterly to condemn and send the guilty one beyond all hope of reformation.

The impression made by Dr. Klopsch on his visitor who saw him for the first time was always a deep one. Writing of a visit to him, William Durban, in an article in the *British Workman*, gave his impressions as follows:

"There are a few persons whom I never fail to call upon whenever I find myself in the United States. These are amongst the most prominent American friends of humanity, and one of the most conspicuous is Dr. Louis Klopsch, noted for his world-wide travels, his indefatigable philanthropy, his great success as a journalist, and his generosity to the slum children of the vast tenement regions of New York. Dr. Klopsch is an extraordinary personality. He is full of vivacity, is all day long occupied at his office in receiving and answering telephone messages from all parts of his country, with telegrams and letters from every land on earth, yet he is ever cordially willing to talk with a visitor from England over the great and useful schemes dear to his heart, because they contribute to the uplifting of those who need help anywhere in the world."

After describing an interview with Dr. Klopsch, in which some of the relief work was enumerated, Mr. Durban continued:

"I certainly felt that this was a wonderful enumeration of good works attempted and achieved by a single agency brought to bear on the kindhearted-ness of the people of America, but I well knew that there was one particular direction in which the humanitarian enthusiasm of Dr. Klopsch had always been applied with extreme delight. Asking him what was his favorite work, I received the reply which I looked for:

"'I take much pleasure in working amongst poor children. I have for many years been a constant Sunday School teacher, so that I have not neglected the good ordinary means of reaching young minds of different classes. But after all, what is always supremely needed is effort for the poor little neglected boys and girls who swarm in the congested blocks, the terrible tenement quarters into which every year fresh multitudes of poor immigrants rush from the old world to our American shores.'"

A description of the work at Mont-Lawn then followed.

A Hindu journalist, Mr. Saint Nihl Singh, in an account of Dr. Klopsch as an almoner of nations in distress, gave a very vivid picture of his work. Wrote this journalist from far-off India in most perfect English:

"If you have millions at your command, and you are so inclined, you can easily be a philanthropist. But if you are lacking millions, and yet your heart is burning with a desire to relieve distress, to uplift the depressed, how would you go to work and raise the funds to accomplish your great humanitarian tasks that call for stupendous amounts of money?

"You may be interested in the story of a man — Louis Klopsch, of New York, United States of America, who was reared in poverty, who battled hard with adverse circumstances in his struggle to get on in life, but who withal has done such marvelous feats of philanthropy as to more than earn the soubriquet of an almoner of nations in distress. Even to-day he is not a wealthy man, as wealthy men go in America, but he has been instrumental in distributing upwards of $3,000,000 in sixteen years to relieve acute want in various parts of the world. This amount has been made up of the little sums contributed by you and me, and the man has shown an extraordinary genius in first inspiring the people to loosen their purse-strings, and then making the most of their offerings. Herein lies the specific value of Mr. Klopsch's example to the would-be philanthropist who has the ambition to help others, but not the millions wherewith to translate his desire into action.

"The career of Mr. Klopsch is inspiring inasmuch as it shows how a poor boy with little schooling, and without external help, has overcome all difficulties. The average self-made man when he reaches the pinnacle of his ambition, grows glum and self-satisfied. In his materialism he usually forgets his attitude to his less fortunate fellow-beings. Not so with Mr. Klopsch. He looks upon prosperity merely as a means calculated to place him in a position to better serve mankind. While he is a hard-sensed business man, intensely practical, and extremely shrewd, his heart is full of love and concern for suffering humanity. Out of his hard-earned money, he gives freely to the cause of bettering the condition of the luckless people who have not been given a fair show in life. Better still, he devotes the better portion of his time and vitality to persuading others to unite with him in his noble efforts. Being a practical man of business, he sees to it that he neither gives 'not wisely but too well,' nor that red tape in charity shall distress the already distressed. He is accomplishing a great work, and while honored by kings and presidents, remains as unassuming as when he served as an office boy."

Dr. Klopsch, though he did not often appear on the platform, was a very ready speaker. His talks were straightforward and went directly to the point. He was at his best in addressing children. It was this probably which caused him to take so deep an interest all his life in Sunday School work. While still a young man, he engaged in church labor and this continued throughout his life. It has been mentioned that he conducted the Brooklyn Tabernacle Sunday School work for a number of years, during Dr. Talmage's pastorate. He was Sunday School superintendent of the Bedford Street Methodist Episcopal church in New York City, and for several years he conducted the largest Sunday School in America at the great Ocean Grove Methodist Episcopal Camp Meeting with remarkable success.

His father-in-law, the Rev. Stephen Merritt, in some reminiscences of Dr. Klopsch, gives this story of the Sunday School activities:

"He took hold of the Sunday School and soon made it the sweetest, strongest and best Sunday School in the land. His love for children was phenomenal. Perhaps there wasn't a flower that grew in the Fifth Ward, where the Sunday School was located; and there was not a sick child in the ward but every day it had flowers sent to its home to cheer its heart. He knew all the families and was acquainted with all the children, irrespective of denomination, and he was an angel among them. We bought a wagonette, and every Saturday he took a party of children to Central Park with their teachers, where he supplied all their needs, and in the afternoon was one among them. He loved childhood, and childhood more than worshipped him. Wherever the children met him, in the streets, or at their homes, or in the Sunday School, they climbed upon him, and hung on his neck, and loved and cried with joy. He had the heart of a boy and maintained it till his death.''

CHAPTER XIX

A FAITHFUL STEWARDSHIP

WHAT was the secret of Dr. Klopsch's remarkable success in his own peculiar field? Early in his career, he came in contact with a few men who held to the great principle that all wealth is a stewardship, and that a business which has not God in it cannot bring enduring success or satisfaction. He saw that men "sowed beside all waters"; that they honored their Maker with their increase; and that in a quiet and unostentatious way they did what good they could to their fellowmen.

Louis Klopsch did nothing by halves [writes one of his long time editorial associates]. He believed, with all the strength of his forceful nature, that the Lord prospers every really good work that is undertaken for His sake, and with no purpose of personal gain. And so, staking everything upon the issue — his time, his talent, and his means — he resolved that, throughout his whole life thereafter, he would "*Trust in God and take courage.*" He simply took the Lord at His word and went ahead, to the utmost extent of his ability, with every legitimate enterprise on which he entered, whether it was the closing of a contract, the purchase of a new press, the publication of a set of books, the opening of some great relief work, the liquidation of a mission debt, the financing of an evangelistic campaign, or any business matter whatsoever. To him, God was partner, counselor, banker. He never left his office at the close of business until, before he stepped from his room, he had prayed that the efforts of the day might be blessed to God's glory and the benefit of his fellowmen.

And so, keeping in constant touch with the Divine Source of all power and blessing, he found the master-key which opened to him a thousand doors leading to honorable service. He realized that no one can live unto himself; that to take up the cross of the Master means to live for others. He found, too, beyond all doubting, that the Lord takes care of His own work in His own way, not always or often according to our expectation; and he learned patience in waiting for the wondrous unfolding of God's plans. He saw how "all things work together for good to them that love the Lord," and he marveled at the Divine wisdom in the direction of the great missionary and benevolent enterprises he was led to undertake. Ways opened up where there seemed to be nothing but unsurmountable difficulties; powerful friends came to his aid uninvited; famous missionaries, whose names the whole Christian world reverenced, formed themselves into Committees to carry forward his projects; three successive American Presidents publicly approved his work; governments and rulers of mighty nations were his voluntary allies. And God's people in our own land and elsewhere — though few of them had ever seen him — gave him their loving confidence, loaded him with their offerings, and made him their modern "Knight of Mercy" to the world's poor. And while he wondered at it all, he prayed the more and worked the harder, and took courage!

Such was the secret of Dr. Klopsch's success. He literally lived for others. At whatsoever task he set his hand, he worked with all his might, leaving results wholly to Him who alone gives the harvest. "If I do my share," he would often remark, "I never trouble about the rest. That is God's affair, not mine."

The vast scope of Dr. Klopsch's philanthropic and charitable activities and his evangelical creed has been shown in the account given of some of the more notable ones in the preceding chapters. These, however, do not convey a complete idea of the extent of his humanitarian work. Perhaps a better way to exhibit the numerous fields in which his talents were exerted for the benefit of his fellowmen is to recapitulate them.

How faithfully the stewardship was carried out and how the funds collected were applied, may also be shown by the detailed financial statements as made up and certified by the accountants who from time to time audited the accounts. It is a story of the successful financing of some of the greatest relief movements of the present age as well as of the support extended to smaller ones.

The history of the various good causes aided is set forth in the following succinct summary, which is presented in alphabetical form:

ADANA RELIEF WORK. This fund was raised in response to an appeal from the American missionaries after the frightful massacre of Armenians and Mesopotamians by fanatical Moslem tribesmen. Rev. Mr. Trowbridge and a committee of missionaries conducted the relief at several centers, and were assisted by representatives of the French, English, German, and American governments. Thousands were succored. Tents, hospitals, and food supplies were provided.

AFRICAN CHILD REDEMPTION FUND. This is a fund through which missionaries are enabled to secure the consent of heathen parents and guardians to their children being trained under mission auspices. Hundreds of African children have been educated and trained, and many are now working as missionaries among their own people.

AMERICAN BIBLE SOCIETY. This fund extended over several years and was for the purpose of providing Bible distribution at remote missionary points in different countries.

AMERICAN TRACT SOCIETY. This fund also extended over several years and was applied in Gospel work in the United States and territories.

ANY GOOD CAUSE FUND. This is a general fund, supplied by readers of *The Christian Herald* for giving immediate assistance and relief in urgent cases of need, not in New York alone, but throughout the country. It is almost exclusively confined to cases of physical suffering from sickness, hunger, or homelessness. There have been thousands of beneficiaries during the last fifteen years.

ARMENIAN RELIEF FUND. This was raised by *The Christian Herald* immediately after the great massacres of 1896. Thousands of lives were saved and great suffering averted. The Fund also aided many Armenian exiles who arrived destitute in this country.

BEALS, REV. Z. CHARLES, head of the Christian Mission at Wuhu, China, on the Yang-tse River — a very busy missionary section amid a vast heathen population. Mr. Beals has a number of workers under him, and his mission field is a large one. Dr. Klopsch secured many friends for the support of this work.

BOWERY MISSION. This is the oldest spiritual mission for men in the United States. Through Dr. Klopsch's efforts, it was saved from dissolution some eighteen years ago. He raised friends for it in many states, and to their gifts he added many of his own. During the last year of his life, he practically rebuilt the mission house at 227 Bowery. Bowery Mission converts are found in every part of the world, and many other spiritual missions have sprung from its loins.

BREAD-LINE, THE, NEW YORK. For twelve years, Dr. Klopsch raised or supplied funds for the support of the "Bread-line," which every winter feeds 1,200 to 1,800 men and boys nightly in connection with the Bowery Mission. It still continues.

BROWNSVILLE AND WILLIAMSBURG CHRISTIAN MISSION TO THE JEWS. Rev. Adolf Cohn, a converted rabbi, is the head of this mission, which is the largest one of its kind in the United States and doing a very excellent work.

CHARITY SUBSCRIPTIONS TO "THE CHRISTIAN HERALD." This represents subscriptions at a reduced rate, sent in by a number of readers who wish to supply the paper to jails, reformatories, hospitals, almshouses, and similar institutions.

CHINA FAMINE FUND. There were two great famines in China, one in the ancient provinces of Shensi and Shansi, from 1901–06, and another in the provinces along the Grand Canal, from 1906–08. Large contributions were raised by *Christian Herald* readers to relieve the suffering in both of these famines. The first fund was controlled and distributed by a missionary committee at Tientsin, of which Rev. Arthur J. Smith was chairman, and the second by a missionary and civic joint committee at Shanghai. During the second famine, the United States Government placed at the service of Dr. Klopsch two troop ships, the *Buford* and the *Logan*, to convey the food supplies contributed by *Christian Herald* readers to Shanghai.

CHINA ORPHAN FUND. This fund came into operation at the close of the last great famine in China, some years ago, when thousands of orphans were thrown upon the charity of the Christian missionaries. Dr. Klopsch secured individual support of a large number of his readers for some two thousand of these orphans for a period of years, and a number of orphans are still being maintained.

"CHRISTIAN HERALD" AGED INVALID'S CHAIR. A small fund raised for the benefit of an octogenarian Christian widow. An invalid wheel-chair was procured and the balance applied to her support for over a year, until the fund was exhausted.

CHRISTIAN HERALD CHILDREN'S HOME. Dr. Klopsch founded this home at Mont-Lawn, and enlisted the support of patrons throughout the country, who have contributed yearly to it ever since. It is incorporated. It is situated at Mont-Lawn, near Nyack-on-the-Hudson. Forty thousand children of the New York tenements have been sheltered there since the home first opened.

"CHRISTIAN HERALD" GOSPEL HALL. One of our American missionaries in India, in recognition of help during the great India famine, named a mission hall after Dr. Klopsch's paper, and a few readers sent in small contributions in aid of this work.

CREMORNE MISSION. For a number of years, this well-known New York rescue mission for unfortunate women has been assisted by voluntary contributions through *The Christian Herald*.

CUBAN RELIEF WORK. This was undertaken immediately before the outbreak of the Spanish-American war, and through it many thousands of starving *reconcentrados* were relieved.

DOOR OF HOPE. This is the parent rescue mission founded by Mrs. Whittemore, and it has been the mother of some sixty "Doors of Hope" throughout the country. Dr. Klopsch's readers have sent offerings for it for many years.

FINLAND RELIEF WORK. This was carried on during the widespread famine in 1903, following three years of drought. It extended to Lapland and Sweden.

FIVE POINTS' MISSION. Voluntary contributions for its support have been sent through *The Christian Herald* for a number of years.

FOREIGN MISSIONS. A very large proportion of Dr. Klopsch's readers were directly interested in foreign missionary work, and many of them are now individually supporting white and native missionaries in various fields. These contribu-

tions have extended over nearly twenty years and represent
mission work in India, China, Africa, Tibet, Korea, Asiatic
Russia, Armenia, Palestine, Arabia, Persia, Turkey, Labrador, South America, Japan, and other foreign fields.

GRENFELL, DR. WILFRED. The celebrated author, explorer, and
founder of the Labrador Mission. Voluntary offerings for
the support of his work have been sent to *The Christian
Herald* for many years.

HOME MISSIONS. Funds for a number of home missions, denominational and otherwise, were voluntarily contributed
during a period of over more than fifteen years. This represents missions among the Indians in the West and Southwest
and along the border; missions in Alaska; missionary work
in the American Sunday School Union in new sections, etc.

INDIA FAMINE FUND. India, like China, has had several famines. Between the years 1897 and 1901, a large relief fund
was raised through Dr. Klopsch's efforts for these famines,
the distribution of which was under the control of an
interdenominational missionary committee, representing all
the mission centers of India, Bishop J. M. Thoburn being
chairman. Many thousands of lives were saved by this excellent work. Dr. Klopsch visited India during the latter part
of the famine and personally inspected the relief measures
adopted by the missionaries and their helpers. To a large
extent, the missionary work in the early part of the famine
was done in coöperation with the Viceroy's committee.
At over sixty relief centers *Christian Herald* food supplies,
blankets, etc., were given to the sufferers at regular periods.
This was the greatest of all the foreign charities in which
Dr. Klopsch engaged.

INDIA ORPHAN WORK. This represents a branch of the largest
single charitable operation ever undertaken by *The Christian
Herald*. During the two great India famines, Dr. Klopsch
appealed for funds for the sufferers and sent all offerings to
an interdenominational missionary committee, with headquarters at Calcutta and Bombay. When the famine ceased
there were tens of thousands of orphans to care for. He
raised money for over five thousand of these helpless orphans
from individual patrons in the United States, and continued
this support for several years. This orphan fund has now
only a few hundred protégés, and will shortly complete its
work.

INVALID CHILDREN'S HOMES. This represents voluntary contributions to homes for cripples, deaf-mutes, and other invalids in several states, and covers a period of many years.

ITALIAN EARTHQUAKE FUND, raised during the earthquake disaster in that country several years ago, and distributed partly through the American Red Cross, but more largely under the personal supervision of Queen Helena, who organized a "Mothers' and Babies' Fund" which was exclusively supported by *The Christian Herald* during an entire summer.

JANSSEN, REV. F. W. Mr. Janssen is an American missionary at Cebú, Philippine Islands, with a very large parish, which includes over one hundred islands. The readers of *The Christian Herald* supplied him with a mission boat for his work, and with pecuniary help at various times, during the last seven or eight years.

JAPAN FAMINE FUND. This fund was raised by *The Christian Herald* for the relief of the population of the northern provinces of Japan in 1906, where famine had followed successive crop failures. The work was conducted in conjunction with the American missionaries, and with the Japanese Red Cross.

JAPAN ORPHAN FUND. This work was undertaken after the Japanese famine work had closed, and is comparatively small. These orphans of the Japanese famine are housed in two large orphanages at Okayama and Sendai, and are managed by regular committees.

JERRY MCAULEY MISSION. Dr. Klopsch's readers have been interested for many years in the old Water Street Mission and have sent voluntary contributions for its support for years, through his paper.

LEPER COLONY. This colony is located at Surinam, Dutch Guiana, South America, where it was founded several years ago by the Rev. Henry Weiss. Dr. Klopsch's readers took a great deal of interest in it and helped it for a number of years.

LEPERS AT JERUSALEM. The Jerusalem Leper Mission is one of the best charities in the Holy City and contributions sent through *The Christian Herald* have been entrusted to the various American Consuls at Jerusalem, who have seen that they were properly applied.

MARDIN RELIEF WORK. Mardin is in Mesopotamia, and although a considerable distance from Adana, where the chief massacres took place several years ago, it also suffered,

PRESIDENT TAFT, MR. CARNEGIE, AND DR. KLOPSCH AT THE ORGAN DEDICATION
METROPOLITAN TEMPLE, N. Y.

and contributions were distributed through an official missionary committee at Beirut.

MAYESVILLE INDUSTRIAL INSTITUTE. The foundation of this work was largely due to the help extended by *Christian Herald* readers. It is a training school for poor negro boys and girls, and has been in operation for nearly ten years past. It has been called the "second Tuskegee."

MEXICAN FLOOD SUFFERERS. This fund was raised by popular voluntary subscription through *The Christian Herald*, for the sufferers in Monterey province, Mexico, and was distributed by U. S. Consul Gen. Hanna, with the assistance of American missionaries and native officials. It did excellent work.

MINE DISASTER. This represents contributions sent in by Dr. Klopsch's readers immediately after the Cherryville Mine explosion.

MISSIONARY SUBSTITUTES. Over one hundred native missionary evangelists, Bible women, local pastors, etc., are supported direct by individual patrons in the United States, such patrons being readers of *The Christian Herald*. Their contributions for such support are sent quarterly, without diminution. All these substitute missionaries are under the authority of white missionaries.

MOJAVE INDIANS. This represents voluntary contributions in aid of Gospel propagation among these Indians in New Mexico.

ORPHAN BABIES' HOME. This represents voluntary contributions for child orphans in St. Johnland, N. Y., an undenominational work of long standing.

PARIS FLOOD SUFFERERS. These contributions were sent in during the floods in Paris, some time ago. The amount is small, but larger effort was not needed.

PERKINS, REV. AND MRS. JOHN. These are missionaries in Liberia, West Africa, who are doing a very fine missionary work among the native heathen, on undenominational lines.

PRISON GATE MISSION. This mission, started several years ago, has received occasional support from Dr. Klopsch's readers ever since its inception. The money was applied by the prison chaplain, working under a committee, in behalf of discharged convicts who needed help in obtaining work, etc.

PUNDITA RAMABAI, the famous native India missionary woman, whose spiritual and industrial work at Poona has attracted wide-spread attention. Dr. Klopsch met her while in India, and commended her work to his readers, who have helped her for several years past.

RELIEF WORK AMONG THE POOR IN NEW YORK CITY. These operations covered a period of many years, and included assistance rendered to hundreds of families, widows, the sick, the afflicted, and the homeless — people who were outside of the usual channels of organized help.

RICHARDS, REV. E. H. M. E. missionary, of Inhambane, East Africa. Mr. Richards for the last twelve years has conducted a fine mission work among the natives of Zambesia, and his efforts have enlisted the support of a number of *Christian Herald* readers.

SCHMITT, REV. CHRISTIAN, a devoted missionary of Nain, Labrador, one of the most northerly mission points on the globe. His excellent work has interested Dr. Klopsch's readers for several years past.

SHILOH ORPHANAGE OF AUGUSTA, GA. On a special appeal for this worthy work a few contributions were sent in during two or three successive seasons.

SOCIETY OF SOUL WINNERS. This is an active mountain missionary organization, established by Rev. E. O. Guerrant of Wilmore, Ky., among the hills and valleys of the Cumberlands. He has some eighty workers in that neglected region, who have been helped during ten years by the readers of *The Christian Herald*.

SPANISH GOSPEL FUND. Dr. Klopsch printed and circulated many hundred thousands of Gospels in the Spanish language. He began this work during the Spanish-American War, distributing Gospels in the American camps and afterwards among the Cubans, when the war was ended.

STEELE ORPHANAGE. This work was established twelve or fourteen years ago by Mrs. Almira S. Steele, at Chattanooga, among the poor colored waifs, and is a very successful and excellent one. Dr. Klopsch's readers have helped it through all these years.

SUNSHINE HOME FOR BLIND BABIES. This very beautiful work was established by Mrs. Cynthia Westover Alden, in connection with the International Sunshine Society, and has been very popular among *The Christian Herald* readers for the last eight or ten years, who have given something towards its support every year.

VOLUNTEERS OF AMERICA, Maude Ballington Booth's organization. This prison and charity work being commended to *The Christian Herald* readers, some of them have helped it annually.

WESTERN FARMERS' RELIEF FUND. This was a fund raised for the relief of the farmers of Colorado, Dakota, Kansas, and Nebraska, during the terrible drought of 1895. Train loads of supplies were sent and distributed, and Dr. Klopsch personally visited several states, working in conjunction with the Government Relief Commission, of which the Hon. Mr. Ludden was Chairman.

WHITE DOOR MISSION. A rescue work for women in New York, of which Mrs. Margaret Sangster is a patroness. Dr. Klopsch has helped it for many years.

Besides the foregoing, there was a considerable list of minor charities in which Dr. Klopsch took a personal interest, and to which he not only contributed, but induced his readers to give their support. These include: The Daisy Field Home, Englewood, N. J.; Judson Memorial Church, New York; Tennesseetown Mission, Topeka, Kan.; White Rose Home, N. Y.; Miss Mattie Perry's Mission, Elhanan, N. C.; China Inland Mission, Toronto, Can.; National Bible Institute, N. Y.; Sick Babies' Fund, Edgewater, Crèche; Pacific Garden Mission, Chicago; People's Settlement, Fox, N. Y.; Sunday Morning Breakfast Ass'n, Philadelphia; Bethel Mission; China Lepers; (Hinghua) Work among Canadian Indians; Finnish Seamen's Mission; Finnish Mission Ass'n; Lepers in India; Red Cross Society; Kessab Schools (Syria); Taylor University, Mennonite Mission, Turkey; Hope Farm Protectory; Lincoln University; Dean Peck Children's Home; Mrs. Bird's Christmas tree for the East Side, New York; Poor Children's Home Finding Society; Moody Bible Institute; Armenian Orphans, etc. There were many minor charities, individual cases of relief, contributions to worthy causes, assistance rendered to weak churches and missions, temporary help extended to missionaries and pastors, donations to needy communities where storm, or epidemic, or fire had caused distress — these and many other similar cases would swell the list considerably.

SUMMARY OF DR. KLOPSCH'S PRINCIPAL CHARITIES:

Years	Work	Expended
1909–1910	Adana Relief Work, Mesopotamia ..	$13,524.05
1900–1910	American Bible Society	495.66
1900–1910	American Tract Society	252.30

Years	Work	Expended
1906–1910	Rev. Z. Chas. Beals, Missionary,China	$287.36
1907–1910	Brownsville and Williamsburg Christian Mission to the Jews	58.37
1902–1910	Charity Subscriptions	120.75
1902–1910	China Orphan Fund	42,449.23
1909–1910	Aged Invalid's Fund..............	103.29
1909–1910	*Christian Herald* Gospel Hall, India ..	16.00
1900–1910	Cremorne Mission, New York	259.04
1896–1910	Door of Hope, New York	803.07
1901–1910	Five Points' Mission, New York	254.20
1896–1910	Foreign Missions, General	14,975.33
1903–1910	Dr. W. Grenfell, Labrador Mission..	420.02
1897–1910	Home Missions, General	470.06
1897–1910	India Orphan General Fund	557,786.92
1903–1910	Invalid Children's Home	905.82
1908–1909	Italian Earthquake Fund	71,799.98
1909–1910	Japan Orphan Fund	4,168.12
1902–1910	Leper Colony, Surinam, D. W. I. ...	1,027.26
1902–1910	Leper Colony, Jerusalem	86.25
1909	Rev. Dr. John MacDougall	10.00
1906–1909	Mayesville Institute (Colored), S. C..	4,953.78
1897–1910	Jerry McAuley's Mission	1,229.00
1909–1910	Mexican Flood Sufferers	8.350.60
1909–1910	Mine Disaster (Cherryville)	43.85
1910	Mojave Indians	1.00
1907–1910	Okayama Orphanage, Japan	2,542.29
1909–1910	Orphan Babies' Home, Verbank, N. Y.	12.10
1910	Paris Flood Sufferers	14.50
1909	Rev. and Mrs. John Perkins, Missionaries, Liberia, W. A.	266.95
1903–1910	Prison Gate Mission	874.52
1901–1910	Pundita Ramabai, India Mission Work	2,648.99
1904–1910	Relief Work among the Poor, New York City	1,149.50
1907–1910	Rev. C. Schmitt, Missionary, Nain, Labrador	197.00
1901–1910	Society of Soul Winners, Wilmore, Ky.	665.60
1899–1910	Spanish Gospel Fund for Cuban Camps	973.40
1901–1910	Steele Orphanage, Chattanooga, Tenn.	1,079.54
1905–1910	Sunshine Home for Blind Babies	2,103.17
1903–1909	Volunteers of America	207.25
1901–1910	White Door, New York	2,421.61
1895	Western Famine Fund	26,825.40
1904–1910	African Child Redemption Fund (M. E. Missions)	3,990.23

ERNST & ERNST

CERTIFIED PUBLIC ACCOUNTANTS (OHIO)

IMPARTIAL AUDITS-SYSTEMS

NEW YORK   CHICAGO   CLEVELAND

HANOVER BANK B'LD'G   1ST NAT'L B'K B'LD'G   SCHOFIELD B'LD'G

NEW YORK

September 30th, 1910.

Christian Herald,
New York City.

Gentlemen:—

Pursuant to the request of Mrs. Mary M. Klopsch, Executrix of the Estate of Louis Klopsch, deceased, formerly proprietor and editor of the CHRISTIAN HERALD, we have made an examination of the CHARITY FUNDS collected and disbursed by the CHRISTIAN HERALD from the inception of the various accounts down to February 28th, 1910, and submit herewith our report.

The total liability to the various Charities on February 28th, 1910, as shown by the books, amounted to $110,882.31, and is represented by bank balances verified by us. It is made up as follows: Sinking Fund for China Orphans, guaranteeing support for seven years, $78,528.01; Endowment Fund for Children's Home, $25,638.58; Sinking Fund, guaranteeing support for Indian Orphans, $1,241.85; Sinking Fund for Missionary Substitutes, Japanese Orphans and sundry other Charities, $5,474.87. We submit herewith itemized exhibit, pages 5 and 6.

We found that eight funds had been overpaid by the CHRISTIAN HERALD, making a total overdraft of $6,775.79 as evidenced by itemized exhibit page 7.

We have prepared and submit herewith itemized exhibits showing the yearly Receipts and Disbursements on all the Funds appearing open on February 28th, 1910. We also examined a few of the large accounts, which had been closed prior to that date, as evidenced by exhibits pages 93 to 104.

We tested the accounts by checking all the contributions as published in the regular issues of the paper for certain periods, with the cash receipts and other records of the CHRISTIAN HERALD. We found that the disbursements were supported by properly endorsed checks and invoices.

WE HEREBY CERTIFY that we have examined the CHARITY FUND Accounts of the CHRISTIAN HERALD as above outlined, and it is our opinion that all the contributions received have been properly disbursed as shown by the annexed exhibits.

Very truly yours,

Ernst & Ernst
Certified Public Accountants.

Years	Work	Expended
1896–1910	"Any Good Cause" Fund..........	$14,641.97
1907–1910	Rev. F. W. Janssen, Missionary, Cebú, P. I.	5,502.08
1908–1910	Mardin Relief Work, Mesopotamia .	1,773.53
1907–1910	"Missionary Substitutes" in various lands............................	6,369.40
1901–1909	Rev. E. H. Richards, Missionary, Zambesia, E. A.	591.57
1910	Shiloh Orphanage (N. C.)	25.00
1901–1905	China Famine Fund	128,280.68
1906–1907	China Famine Fund	427,323.91
1897–1904	India Famine Fund	732,187.59
1892–1904	Salvation Army...................	1,220.13
1908–1909	Bishop Scott (for redemption of Jasper Grant's Children, W. A.)	408.89
1905–1906	Taylor University, Indiana	427.00
1906	Japan Famine Fund	241,822.80
1907	Bitlis Earthquake, Armenia	429.62
1906–1907	Boer Home Industries, South Africa	657.60
1906–1907	Mrs. E. Pregensen	361.00
1903	Northland (Finland) Famine Fund..	132,681.27
1903	Macedonia Relief Fund	29,474.78
1900	Galveston Relief Fund	2,035.81
1906	San Francisco Earthquake Fund ...	5,000.00
1892–1893	[1] Russian Famine Relief Fund	32,000.00
1896–1898	Armenia Massacre Relief Fund	63,867.98
1898–1899	Relief Work among the Cuban *reconcentrados*	140,587.96
1894–1910	*Christian Herald* Children's Home (14 years and plant)	242,466.46
1896–1910	Bowery Mission, New York (17 years and plant)	364,687.75
1892–1910	[2] Miscellaneous Home Charities (18 years).........................	20,000.00
		$3,365,648.14

[1] In the Russian Relief Work, Dr. Klopsch chartered the Steamship *Leo* and loaded her with flour, medicines, and delicacies for the sick. In the India Famine he sent two steamers, the *Quito* and the *Everett*, to Bombay and Calcutta, with cargoes of foodstuffs. To China he sent food cargoes on the troop-ships *Logan* and *Buford*, the United States Government granting free transportation. To Cuba he sent partial cargoes of food and clothing on the Ward and Mallory lines.

[2] Includes Mine Disasters, Floods, Missions, Rescue Homes, Orphan Homes (White and Black), Prison Missions, Mountain Missions, Evangelism, Gospel Dissemination, Asylums, Hospitals, Invalid Homes, Blind Babies, Bible Societies, Port Missions, etc.

CHAPTER XX

ILLNESS AND DEATH

THE busy life of Dr. Klopsch was lived in the city where all his good works were done under the fullest publicity, yet those who believed in him and followed his leadership should know something more of him. The biographical annals are so simple that they may be briefly told.

He was born in Lubben, near Berlin, Germany, March 26, 1852. His father, Osmar Klopsch, a physician by profession and an ardent believer in republican institutions, had belonged to the revolutionary party of 1848. This meant prosecution at the hands of the Government of that period, and Dr. Osmar Klopsch decided, as so many of his revolutionary compatriots had done, to seek the United States. He came to New York in 1854, bringing the two-year-old boy. The mother had in the meantime died of a pulmonary affection. The father's circumstances were not prosperous, and at an early

358

age Louis Klopsch became self-supporting. He attended the public schools for a while, and then, before his course could be completed, was obliged to leave and take up his struggle with the world. His boyhood was passed in the heart of the city with which his whole life was identified. The story of his early activities, told in the opening chapter, shows the dominating character of the man. He had a purpose from boyhood which he realized.

In 1886 occurred the event which sweetened his whole life. This was his marriage to Mary Merritt, the daughter of the Rev. Stephen Merritt, to whose philanthropic labors young Klopsch had been drawn almost in the beginning of his career. The union was a most happy one. He found a sympathetic helpmate who shared his enthusiasm and who inspired him in his efforts. Four children were born of this union, a daughter and three sons, all of whom survive.

Dr. Klopsch's home life was an ideal one. During the winter he lived in a large apartment in the heart of New York City. Relief from the cares of his business and of his many charitable enterprises was always to be had in the midst of his family. Those who had the privilege of seeing him in the home circle knew how beautiful was the domestic life. There as a husband and father his existence was ideal. His hospitality was broad, knowing no creed or condition of life, and one of his greatest enjoyments was to have a few guests gathered around his table. An evening at the Klopsch home was one never forgotten by those who shared in it.

In the summer, Dr. Klopsch usually lived at Tarry-town-on-the-Hudson. Born and bred a city man, he loved the country. Another reason for his liking for Tarrytown was that it was just across the Hudson River from Mont-Lawn and he could give part of his time to the children for whom his thoughtful care had provided the Home.

All his life, Dr. Klopsch found rest and recreation in a change of surroundings, though hardly of occupation. A vacation as such he did not know. His trips to relieve suffering in foreign lands, or in his own country, he always called his vacations, but they were such only in the sense that he was free from the pressing details of daily work at *The Christian Herald* office. Occasionally he would recuperate by a flying ocean trip, always accompanied by Mrs. Klopsch. He would visit his friends and relatives in Germany, for whom he entertained great affection. Notwithstanding that he had left his native country as a small child, he was always very fond of it. Usually on these trips he would spend a little time in England also. Then would come the return voyage and the planning for new features of *The Christian Herald*, or new works of relief and rescue. The sea trips were a tonic to him. He loved the ocean. Sometimes he would say, when urged to take a long rest, that a voyage across the Atlantic and back was a year's rest to him. But there came a day when the brave worker who had never hesitated at any task was compelled to lay down the burden of his labors. In February, 1910, he was taken ill. The trouble was intestinal and after due examination an immediate operation was decided to be necessary. He was carefully removed to the German Hospital. Dr. Klopsch had no fear of death. He discussed the prospects of the operation calmly, arranged his business affairs, made his will, and in the hour before he was placed under the anæsthetic talked cheerfully and hopefully with Mrs. Klopsch and the other members of his family.

The skill of the surgeons was unable to cope with the disorder. Dr. Klopsch passed away on the morning of March 7, a few days after the operation.

To the world at large, who knew him by reputation, and to innumerable friends, the news of his death came as a shock, for there had been no previous intimation of his serious illness. At once a wave of sorrow swept over many lands that this great-hearted helper of humanity was no more. Spontaneous tributes poured in from every quarter of the globe, while expressions from the pulpit and the press showed how deeply the loss was felt.

President Taft wrote a letter of condolence to Mrs. Klopsch. It voiced the sorrow of the American nation. The President wrote:

THE WHITE HOUSE,
WASHINGTON, March 8, 1910.

MY DEAR MRS. KLOPSCH: I was greatly shocked to note in the newspapers of yesterday that your good husband passed away under the effects of the operation. I have not known him long, but I have known him long enough to know of the good that he has done, the charity that he has encouraged, and the gratitude that he is entitled to from the poor and oppressed. I sincerely hope that the memory of all these things will sustain you in your grief.

Very sincerely yours,

Only a few months previously the President had appointed Dr. Klopsch to be a member of the International Relief Board of the American Red Cross.

The Viceroy of India cabled direct from Calcutta to President Taft:

Please accept on behalf of Indian Empire and convey to his family, sincere condolences on behalf of Louis Klopsch, whose munificent contributions for relief of distress during two severe famines can never be forgotten by the Government and people of India.

The President, replying through Secretary Knox, acknowledged with sincere appreciation the Viceroy's sympathetic telegram and stated that the message had been conveyed to the family.

Baron Uchida, the Japanese Ambassador in Washington, telegraphed to Mrs. Klopsch his grief at her loss.

Miss Mabel Boardman, of the American Red Cross, telegraphed: "His death is a loss to humanity."

The Rev. J. Wilbur Chapman, the evangelist, wrote: "The world has lost a great man and suffering humanity a good friend."

The Rev. Charles M. Sheldon wrote from Topeka: "The loss is extended throughout a large circle. He is a man who will be missed here on earth by very many personal friends, of whom I count myself one."

Baron Ozawa, the head of the Japanese Red Cross Society, cabled from Tokio his deepest sorrow and his sympathy for Mrs. Klopsch.

William R. Moody, head of the Northfield Moody Schools, telegraphed to Mrs. Klopsch: "May the God of all comfort be your solace in this dark hour."

American Consul-General Hanna at Monterey, Mexico, placed the flag over the Consulate at half-mast in honor of the man who had done so much for the flood sufferers. He also telegraphed his sympathy.

Tributes were paid spontaneously at many church services and public gatherings, where men and women were gathered together for worship. On March 7, at 1 o'clock, just twelve hours after Dr. Klopsch had passed away, a large audience of business men assembled in the open air at Wall and Nassau Streets, New York, and listened with deep attention to an address by the Rev. William Wilkinson of Trinity Church (who has become known as "the Bishop of Wall Street") who had been preaching there daily during the Lenten season. It was such an audience as could be gathered together nowhere else in America. Bankers, brokers, clerks, merchants, importers, and men of all sorts and callings were in the assemblage. Pastor Wilkinson among other things said:

"I turn aside from my usual line of subjects to pay my tribute of love and honor to a princely man, who in this city has left his work on earth to take it up where Jesus Christ his Saviour and Master has appointed. Turn to Proverbs 10:28, 29 — 'The hope of the righteous shall be gladness: the way of the Lord is strength to the upright.' There you have the deepest secret of the life of Dr. Klopsch. Born in Germany fifty-eight years ago, he had ever since coming to this land absorbed its very best spirit. He had a clear mind which saw at a glance the abiding from the accidental, the vital from the incidental. He was always swift to act, and these qualities of vision and action made him a very powerful helper in good work. He saw the Living God back of nature; he knew the world was run by law, not chance; that sin was death; that pardon was a joy complete, and that grace was sufficient for every man. This gave a breadth to his thinking, a plan and purpose to his life and his work which charmed kings.

"Dr. Klopsch was at the head of *The Christian Herald*, which has the largest circulation of any religious paper in the world. It is read in every town and city in the United States. Its editor was every day looking, with wide-open eyes, for means of making larger its power for good. He was always anxious to find young men of striking ability and usefulness in the Church and the world. Such men he brought to the attention of his readers. This in the catholic spirit that marked the man throughout, and hence *The Christian Herald* is a mighty power for good.

"This man had the courage of his convictions. He did not stand fawning on men of power, who sought to enslave the people; he did not use words to darken wisdom and halt reform. For a sober

nation he stood; for proper housing of the workers
he pleaded; and his voice was mighty against short
weight and measure, and the adulterating and cor-
nering of the food of the people. He spake with
clarion tones, in words which rang like the notes of
a trumpet calling armies to battle. It is refreshing
and inspiring to meet a man of this class and practice. No prouder plume can be placed on his tomb
than this. It is the prime, it is the first and highest
duty of Christian men in power to work for conditions where every one can educate his powers and
have a fair, open, just opportunity of living in good
conditions. No help is like ability, by the grace of
God, to help one's self and family. There will, however, be times when it is the duty of editors and
preachers to turn aside from considering men who
sell law, men who buy law, who practice the abom-
inable tyranny which oppresses, and also that which
corrupts the people and the Republic! I mean the
time when pestilence, famine, earthquake, great fire,
and flood demand attention. To read what this
man did is to see the soul of the man. The recital
of facts is more thrilling than romance. It takes the
soul at once over a bridge of nineteen hundred historic years, to the synagogue at Nazareth, when
Jesus stood on that never to be forgotten Sabbath
morning and, turning to the sixty-first chapter of
Isaiah, said: 'The Spirit of the Lord is upon me,
because he hath anointed me to preach good tidings
to the meek; he hath sent me to heal the broken-
hearted, to proclaim liberty to the captives; to open
the prison to them that are bound; to comfort all
that mourn that they might be called trees of righteousness, the planting of the Lord, that he might be
glorified.' Dr. Klopsch raised through his paper and
friends and gave to every good work. He asked
others to give also.

"In Wall Street, in its busiest part, at its busiest hour, when men are planning to make money, when all is rush and push and desire, I stop to call your attention to this type of man who had time to pray, to plan, to work, to do good and delight in it. This brought him peace and honor at the last."

At the First Methodist Church, the Rev. Francis Burdette Short made Dr. Klopsch's life-work the theme of a special address:

"The name of Louis Klopsch," he said, "stands for uprightness, integrity, and philanthropy, world-wide and world-honored. He provided bread for the hungry and brought the dying back to life. His name is a blessing to the multitudes, and his memory will ever prove a delight to the nations of the earth.

"He coveted the best gifts. He sought that more excellent way. He struggled to bring his body and talents into these higher laws, the laws that make for uprightness and peace among men. The warm heart that beat in his bosom was made sensitive and sympathetic by the spirit of the Man of Galilee, and he was only happy when he was pouring out his life that other lives might have that more abundant life."

The wide-spread sorrow for the loss of a great and good man, and the deep respect in which he was held, was made manifest at the funeral services. They were held on the morning of Wednesday, March 9, in the Metropolitan Temple, at Seventh Avenue and Fourteenth Street, of which Dr. Klopsch was a valued member. All classes were represented among those who crowded the building, and many hundreds gathered outside unable to gain entrance, where they remained during the entire services. Within the Temple one could note the mingling of the rich and poor, the prosperous business men and humble workers; the men of the Bowery, who had learned to know and love Dr. Klopsch through his Christlike work in the Bowery Mission, and the men of large enterprises, who knew his ability and his commanding worth in the world of affairs. There, too, were the children of the tenements, met to take a last fond look at their kind benefactor and to sing as an appropriate requiem those sweet songs he had loved to hear them sing at the beautiful Children's Home which he founded for them at Mont-Lawn. Ministers of many different denominations, who had been co-workers with him in enterprises for the spiritual and material uplift of humanity, were present. All were drawn by a common impulse to show their respect, honor, and love for one whose life had been freely spent for others.

The Rev. J. Wesley Hill, D.D., pastor of the Temple, led the procession up the aisle to the altar, reciting the service for the dead. He was accompanied by the Rev. Ferdinand C. Iglehart, the Rev. J. M. Buckley, Rev. Wallace McMullen, the Rev. John Hallimond, and several others. After them came the honorary pall-bearers, who were Rear-Admiral Charles D. Sigsbee, O. S. Marden, G. H. Sandison, J. A. Belford, Otto Koenig, P. B. Bromfield, D. A. Nesbit, J. McGee, Dr. F. Schavoir, R. D. Carter, Charles Francis, S. A. Everett, Arthur J. Little, William B. Howland, and J. J. Little. The bearers of the casket followed, and immediately behind it came the members of the family of the deceased: Mrs. Klopsch, Louis Klopsch, Jr., Miss Mary Klopsch, and Merritt Klopsch, all in deep mourning. The immediate relatives of the family brought up the rear. These included the venerable Stephen Merritt and Mrs. Merritt, Mr. and Mrs. Gilbert H. Crawford, Dr. Mary Crawford, Misses Charlotte and Caroline Crawford, Conrad Crawford, Mr. and Mrs. Morris Crawford, Miss Sarah Merritt, and Stephen Merritt, Jr. The casket was deposited in front of the platform, where it was surrounded by great fragrant banks of beautiful flowers, the loving offerings of friends and associates. The superb floral wreath sent from the White House by President and Mrs. Taft was laid upon the casket. Rev. Dr. Hill opened the service by invoking the divine presence and gracious blessing in these words:

"O Thou, who art the 'shadow of a great rock in a weary land,' we come seeking the refuge of Thy love and the shelter of Thy wing. Thou, who hast said, 'Lo, I am with thee alway, even unto the end of the world,' reveal Thyself unto us in the consolations of Thy grace, the comfort of Thy Spirit, and the inspiration of that hope 'which we have as an anchor of the soul, both sure and steadfast, and which entereth into that within the veil, whither the Forerunner is for us entered, even Jesus Christ.' Amen."

The first musical selection was sung by a quartette composed of Mrs. Fugle, soprano; Mrs. Anna Simpson, contralto; Frederick Boynton, tenor; F. Servier, basso, under the direction of Mr. Charles J.

Evans, musical director of the Temple. Mrs. Prue Baird served as the organist. The selection was "Abide With Me."

The Rev. Dr. F. C. Iglehart read Scripture selections from the twenty-third Psalm and the fourteenth chapter of John's Gospel. The children of the Mont-Lawn Home, in the gallery, sang with surprising and melting pathos "The Glory Song."

The Rev. Dr. Hallimond then offered prayer, as follows:

"O God, our Father, Thou hast seen fit to send a great sorrow to our hearts. We cannot understand it. We stagger under the mystery of it. We ask Thee to forgive us if we have shown any hesitation in accepting Thy will, if we have manifested any rebellion of spirit, if any murmuring has momentarily escaped us, forgive us; and oh, help us, because the task is too hard for us in our poor, frail, faltering humanity. Help us to be still and murmur not, to breathe the prayer divinely taught, 'Thy will be done.' In Thy strength, O God, we accept the decree. If it be Thy will that we take the cup, even so, O Father. But, O God, notwithstanding the great weight, the great burden of sorrow which is resting upon us this morning, we cannot keep our hearts from rising in joy and exultation over the achievements of this wonderful life that has just been brought to a close. We praise Thee, O God, for the many and the varied gifts that Thou didst bestow upon Thy servant; for his marvelous business acumen, for his tireless zeal, for his burning enthusiasm, for his patient industry, for the rare example he has afforded us of a man who was able to make money, and yet never thought of spending it in the pursuit of mere personal pleasure or indulgence.

"We praise Thee, O God, for his wide and world-embracing charity. We thank Thee for the virtue of being able to rise and take a broad and comprehensive view of the world's need. We thank Thee for his almost unparalleled resourcefulness. We thank Thee for his indomitable persistency of purpose. We thank Thee for his steadfastness in the truth. We thank Thee for the almost priceless lesson that he has been teaching the Christian community of this land during the last twenty years. We thank Thee, O God, for the great charitable heart of his. We thank Thee that, aided by Thy wisdom and through the instrumentality of an undenominational journal, Thou hast made it possible for him to gather together the scattered fragments, the units, and bind them in a great, united, happy family circle of Christian believers. We thank Thee for the mighty inspiration his personality has been to millions of his fellow creatures in all lands, from kings and princes and presidents down to the poor, homeless wanderers, outcasts, tramps in the Bowery, and the poor little, white-faced children in the tenements.

"We thank Thee, O God, for all that has been accomplished in connection with that wonderful commission which Thou didst place in his hands, of feeding the hungry multitude, so great, so vast, no other man has ever attempted it since Christ Himself fed the five thousand in a desert place. We thank Thee, we praise Thee, that when, in the mysterious workings of Thy providence, any country has been stricken with famine, or with flood, or with earthquake, or pestilence, that his heart instantly throbbed with a Christlike pity, and his hand was the first to be outstretched with the needed help. We thank Thee, O God, for all these lessons. We thank Thee for his comprehensive sympathy. We thank Thee for all the spiritual results that have come to his life, for his triumphs in the various Sabbath Schools with which he has been connected;

for his noble and incessant care of these thousands of city children at Mont-Lawn for so many years. We thank Thee for his readiness to give spiritual help when it has been needed. We thank Thee for the thousands and tens of thousands that have been saved from the degradations of sin by his instrumentality. We thank Thee for the thousands of homes that have been gladdened and strengthened by his personality, reflected on the pages of his paper.

"O God, Thou knowest how thankful we are for this great life that has just been closed. And now we pray, dear heavenly Father, for those that are left behind. We pray earnestly and specially for his widow, this sweet and gracious woman, whose life has been swept by this desolating sorrow. We pray for these dear boys and this daughter in their bitter sorrow, realizing as they do that they have lost the best and stanchest friend. Wearing the chill of their bereavement, they cry out for 'the touch of that vanished hand and the sound of that voice that is still.' O God, wilt Thou comfort them. Comfort them, Father, with Thine own comfort, 'as one whom a mother comforteth.' Wilt Thou comfort this woman and her fatherless children. We pray, as a congregation of Christian believers, that Thou wilt bless and comfort and strengthen that devoted staff in *The Christian Herald* office, who are grieving as no staff ever grieved before, perhaps, for an employer who has gone, and who was just as much a brother and a friend. O God, bless them and help them.

"Do Thou bless the thousands of little children in this great city this morning who are troubled, and who, in their childish sympathy, sorrow, and wonderment, are asking, as they have been doing, 'Shall we never see his face again?' And bless the thousands of orphans in India and Japan and China who don't even yet know of the great loss that has come to them. Bless the poor men in the bread-line to-night who, in addition to all their misery, have this thought: that they have lost their best friend, their benefactor. And we ask Thee, O God, as a congregation, that Thou wilt grant that those great charities of his, and the numberless small charities that he, aided by Thy wisdom and strengthened by Thy strength, was able to inaugurate and carry on for so many years — we pray that they may be carried on by other faithful souls, who are thus called to take his place. And now we pray for ourselves, that we may go from this service back to our God-given spheres of labor with increased devotion for that great cause to which he has given the last full measure of his devotion. We ask it in the name of our Redeemer. Amen."

The quartette sang "Lead, Kindly Light." The Rev. Dr. Wallace MacMullen read the second Scriptural selection from the fifteenth chapter of I. Corinthians.

The voices of the children of the Mont-Lawn Home again rang out in a beautiful hymn, composed of Bible verses, a selection which was a peculiar favorite of Dr. Klopsch.

The Rev. Dr. James M. Buckley, editor of the *Christian Advocate*, of New York, was the next speaker. He said:

"Our Lord Jesus was the most pitiful of all the preachers. He gave the most comprehensive of all the statements. And above them all he stood ready to teach angels as well as men. He pities us today. He knows that 'the spirit is willing, but the flesh is weak.' He knows that those who suffer most excruciatingly may take his prayer, ' Let this cup pass from me.' If it may pass from me, that would be my desire; but not my will, not my will, Thy will.

"President McKinley turned to his invalid wife as he was about to die, and said, as well as he could, 'Our ways are not God's ways, but God's ways are our ways, and we must make them our ways.' There were many paraphrases of that utterance, but that is the idea, and it stands from the beginning until now to all who have faith. Even a little faith in God will go a long distance toward steadying us. As for 'weeping' and 'sorrow,' those who say the Christian ought not to weep or sorrow do not understand the Bible, nor the human heart. Did Christ rebuke the sisters? Did not St. Paul himself say that God sent his friend Epaphroditus, lest he, Paul, should have sorrow upon sorrow? Did not our Lord weep with the sisters?

"Tears are for the earth, and for the Christian who can say, 'There is my son,' calmly looking into the dead face; for the man who can look upon his wife's face calmly, and say, 'That is God's will and it is my will,' there is no death in either heart. We are made so that we may weep rather than dash against the rocks or become absolutely devoid of reason.

"When a poor man dies, his wife has lost her all. When a rich man dies, there are many things left of temporary comfort; but I have never known any difference between the sorrows of the poor and the sorrows of the rich, where the heart is involved — the same miseries, the same trembling, the same looking for a future, and not ready for it. But God makes every promise that the soul desires. The sacred Book is like the contents of a medicine chest. One must not take anything out of the medicine chest at random. Each item fits the exact need at a certain time. And so, here we go through the Book, and we find a promise for every difficulty.

"You will find no definite promise to comfort a

man who has been bereaved of his wife in the Bible,
from one end of it to the other; but where can you
search without finding some great promise for the
widow?   The sublimest figure in all the Bible relates
to the sorrows of the woman who had lost her husband; and the utterances 'I am the Father of the
fatherless' and 'I am the God of the widow' are
given; and God even rises to this tremendous symbol,
'Thy Maker is thy husband.'

"It is not necessary for us to recount in this
presence all that our friend thought, all that he
intended, all that he did.   Long before we came to
this last house, the newspapers of the country had
told of his achievements.   We are here to sympathize;
we are here to reflect upon the great principles of
God, of immortality, of Christ, and of human life.
Let us get a glance today, through faith, into the
fact that God himself requires the whole universe
to carry out his plan.   No Christian dies accidentally.
If he be thrown down before a car and crushed, in
the thought of God it is not an accident.   'Precious
in the sight of the Lord is the death of his saints.'
All deaths could be postponed without a miracle.
God has constantly a connection with our ideas —
the constant stream of our ideas.   If he saw best,
without a miracle he could influence us in thought
not to get under the wall when it is about to fall.
By a mere movement of our faculties God might
cause us to pass away.   We must accept the old religion of the general providence of God.   Who knows
that this death will not awaken thousands to the
consideration that they must prepare to die?   Who
knows it?   There ought to be persons in this house
today who have seen here the pallid features, the
magazine of energy silent and cold.   They should
take it to their hearts that they will be as silent, as
cold, as helpless, and that the time is unknown.

"What caused this man to do these things? No doubt he was pleased with public approbation. Remember there is a marked difference between selfishness and self-love. We are not required by the Golden Rule to love our neighbor more than we love ourselves. We are to love our neighbor as we love ourselves. And we received the honors of his wonderful philanthropic and successful projects, and he had plenty of Scripture for that; for at the end of all the Epistles there is a list of saints and of the good things they have done. It is when a man works for himself exclusively that he is thrown out of heaven. But he loved God and his neighbor. All these things were a part of his religion. Some rejoice in riches, some in political honors, some in scholastic achievements. He preferred to get his highest honor through assisting those that were not so well off in the world as himself.

"Friends, there is a manifest contrast here. You never saw such a contrast. I never saw such a contrast. Every class and condition of humanity may be found here. This magnificent floral decoration on the casket was sent here by the President of the United States. Recognizing the great difficulty of genuine philanthropy, he finds genuine philanthropy in the heart of this man. And these two hundred children — descended from many nations — these two hundred children that have been singing to us here are the children of the poor. Here is fulfilled in this man's life the proverb three thousand years old, 'Seest thou a man diligent in his business? he shall not stand before mean men; he shall stand before kings.' The country comes up in the act of the President and says, 'Well done! Well done!'

"It is read at almost every service, 'Blessed are the dead that die in the Lord; for they shall rest from their labors, and their works do follow them.'

It is beautiful. 'Their works do follow them.' Am I not right in saying that such has been the nature of this man's philanthropy that the immense number of his works have gone before him? It must be so, for they have included life and death.

"And now, what shall we say? Shall we say that there is a mistake? Suppose that he had lingered, as some philanthropists have, until they were so old and imbecile that they were forgotten! And here speaks with great force the value of a life. He was but little poorer, richer than some of the poorest, when he began. He made a life. He made a fortune. He made a great philanthropy of a peculiar kind. It is an honor to meet together in his honor. I shall miss him, but I did not postpone until his death to commend him. After a visit to his institution for the children, I described as well as I could what I saw, what I heard, and, best of all, what I felt. I hope to meet him where there is no disappointment, no heart-breaking surprises. I suggest to his children that the father of Noah, when Noah was born, said, 'These shall comfort us concerning our work and labor of love.'

"Passing one day a most imposing structure in this city devoted to religion, I turned in to hear the sermon, and the sermon was preached from this text to which I have just referred, and the eloquent preacher said, 'In order to carry out the spirit of the name, it is wise for sons and daughters to carry out, as far as possible, the plans of their parents and thus show confidence in them as respects their judgment and their love for them by manifesting it in such a manner.' And so I say to these sons and this daughter: Always have a deep sympathy with your father's principles and spirit and works, and then each day to the last you will be a comfort to your mother and insure yourselves a final meeting where no sepulchral voice is heard.

"There are minor chords. There are major chords. These are minor chords, but as we go forth let us be so powerfully wrought upon by the virtues of a good and successful life that we may feel within our souls ringing 'Onward! Onward, Christian!'"

As a solo Mrs. Simpson sang "Crossing the Bar." Rev. Dr. Hill closed the regular service by pronouncing the benediction: "The grace of our Lord Jesus Christ, the love of God, and the comfort of the Holy Spirit be and abide with you now and evermore. Amen."

Following the formal church service came the beautiful Masonic rite for the dead by members of the Evangelist Lodge, which was listened to with much feeling. The little group of his fellow-members surrounded the casket, and as the rite proceeded, they depositing on the casket their tiny sprays of evergreen, the token of immortality, a thrill went through the church. Past Master T. S. Roane officiated. Later, when the Scottish rite was performed by another delegation of the Masonic Brotherhood, and a single, perfect white rose was laid upon the breast of the dead, every one felt the beautiful appropriateness of the symbol of a pure and upright life. The late Dr. Klopsch was a thirty-second degree Mason. Commander-in-Chief John Lloyd Thomas pronounced a beautiful eulogy.

After this rite had ended, the casket being still open, the congregation was permitted to take a last look at the face of the departed. Solemnly and silently the long line filed past, many lingering as they gazed with streaming eyes. Many wept as they looked upon the familiar lineaments, now lying so white and stately and still.

The little tenement children followed the adults in the line and gazed wonderingly and with tear-dimmed eyes upon the features of their benefactor.

The pall-bearers, in their turn, filed past the casket, and last of all came the family. It was a painful moment and sobs could be heard throughout the church.

After the closing of the casket, the procession was re-formed, the pall-bearers leading. Slowly they came down the aisle to the mournful strains of the "Dead March." It seemed as if the very depths of sorrow and feeling had been touched. At the door, and far up and down the street, were the crowds who had been unable to obtain admittance. The casket was deposited in the hearse, and the family and immediate relatives entered the mourning coaches in waiting, after which the crowd slowly dispersed.

Among those present at the funeral were Mrs. Sarah J. Bird, "the Mother of the Bowery Mission"; Rev. Frank DeWitt Talmage, Rev. Wilbur F. Crafts of Washington, D. C.; Rev. Daniel S. Gregory, D.D.; Rev. William James, Rev. George Sanderson, chaplain of the Tombs; Rev. Dr. J. M. Farrar, Rev. Dr. F. F. Shannon, Rev. Dr. W. J. Peck, Rev. G. S. Avery, Chester Crest; Alderman Caygill, of New York City; Colonel W. H. Cox and Colonel Margitts, of the Salvation Army; Rev. J. M. Conway, Florence Mission; Rev. John Callahan, Hadley Hall; Mr. J. H. Wyburn, Water Street Mission; Mr. Don Shelton, Mr. H. P. Main, Rev. W. T. Twamley, Rev. Franklin S. Babbitt, of Nyack, N. Y., and many other clergymen.

There was a large delegation of editors and publishers of the religious press of the country, and many men prominent in various lines of business who had been personally acquainted with Dr. Klopsch during his busy lifetime.

Dr. Klopsch's remains were conveyed by rail to Tarrytown-on-the-Hudson. Interment took place in the picturesque cemetery at Sleepy Hollow. It was one of his last wishes that his grave should be chosen in a site that would overlook the Hudson and command a view of his dearly loved Children's Home, and that wish will now be faithfully carried out. There he sleeps, until the last trumpet sounds.

CHAPTER XXI

THE VOICE THAT YET SPEAKS

TESTIMONY TO THE ENDURING INFLUENCE OF DR. KLOPSCH'S GOOD WORKS — A SOLDIER OF HUMANITY — MUTUAL CONFIDENCE IN THE "CHRISTIAN HERALD" FAMILY — PUBLIC MEMORIAL MEETING — RABBI MICHELSON'S PRAISE — BISHOP DARLINGTON'S ADDRESS — DR. MARSDEN'S ANALYSIS — A WORD FROM IRVING BACHELLER — DR. HILL'S TALK — JUDGE TOMPKIN'S VIEW — DR. IGLEHART'S STORY — EDITORIAL COMMENT.

WHEN the grave has closed over the mortal remains of a man whose life has been given to the services of others, the last word has not been said. The voice that is silent yet speaks as with a thousand tongues through the good works that go on. Dr. Klopsch had labored for the future as well as for the present. The deep impression he made on his own generation rendered it certain that his influence would continue and endure.

Tributes continued to be paid to his memory, and the insight into his character as a practical philanthropist which they contained showed how abiding was the work that he had done.

"American philanthropy," said the *Baltimore American* in an appreciative editorial, "will not rate the name of any one deserving honor more highly than Dr. Klopsch, whose sphere of distributing charities in time of national or local disaster, in times of scourge, or famine and floods, made him a conspicuous figure the world over. It was not that he himself had such large means that he could

380

magnify his money with his spirit, but it was because in many cases he became the medium through which the offerings of multitudes of persons, rich and poor, were employed in the most serviceable humane ways; yet he himself was a large giver to charities he had founded. Those who rallied to the call of this charitable editor knew that their money would go directly to the object for which it was subscribed. He had developed a genius as an alleviator of wide distress.

"It would only be necessary to recount honors bestowed upon him by foreign rulers and societies in order to secure a list of countries that acknowledged indebtedness to his broad and generous nature. He was a man with a sense of human responsibility that dignifies a generation."

Another journal, the *Milwaukee Free Press*, under the caption of "A Soldier of Humanity," said:

"Dr. Klopsch was an American citizen of German birth whose eager interest in the suffering and afflicted made him active wherever service was to be rendered to humanity. Where disaster reigned, destitution prevailed, and desperation brooded, he became the foremost organizer and distributor of charitable relief.

"Such a task as this, accomplished through the agency of any one man, is a tremendous performance, and the record of Dr. Klopsch is one for legitimate pride, not only as a philanthropist, but for the business judgment shown in organizing and financing these wide-spread relief movements, thus making it possible for every heart which had gone out in sympathy to the desolation and misery of another land to give that emotion practical expression and make it helpful in succoring those in need. Sympathy that so manifests itself is the one touch of nature that makes the whole world kin and more than many Hague Conferences leads men to realize that He hath made of one flesh all the nations upon earth."

A journal devoted more particularly to men of note in business enterprises, *The Press Scrap Book*, in a sympathetic summary of Dr. Klopsch's work, gave this estimate of his character:

"His energy, ability, and determination to succeed overcame every obstacle and commanded the goodwill, respect, and support of all with whom he came in contact. His industry was marvelous and his fidelity to business engagements helped him materially to win his way to higher success.

"One of the beautiful features of his great work was the supreme harmony, the mutual confidence, and Christian love existing between Dr. Klopsch and his readers. Representing an exceptionally intelligent, high-minded, and sincerely religious class of the community, the patrons of *The Christian Herald* were in complete sympathy with Dr. Klopsch in his charitable undertakings, and contributed most generously to the causes indicated as worthy of relief. Dr. Klopsch on his part not only saw that the funds were faithfully and effectively applied to the purpose for which they were contributed, but also gave liberally of his personal means to *The Christian Herald* charities.

"Dr. Klopsch was in earnest, active, inspiring sympathy with every good cause. His advice and fellowship were sought not merely for the sake of material aid, but because of the impetus which he gave to any movement in which he was interested. He possessed the gift of personal magnetism in a wonderful degree, and attracted the devotion and loyalty of all who were associated with him. He possessed in this and other personal attributes some of the characteristics which are peculiar to true greatness, to men marked out as leaders and guides to their fellows. No man in ancient or modern times has done so much as he to establish the fellowship of man, the brotherhood of our common humanity."

Mr. Melville E. Stone, General Manager of the Associated Press, was a personal friend of Dr. Klopsch. He had come into contact with and had personal knowledge of several of Dr. Klopsch's charities, at home and abroad. Mr. Stone was specially struck with the character and value of the work Dr. Klopsch had done in India, and on returning from a tour in the East, he wrote the following letter recording his impressions of that work:

The Associated Press.

GENERAL OFFICE,

195 BROADWAY, NEW YORK CITY.

OCTOBER 4, 1910.

DEAR MR. SANDISON: While in India, it was my good fortune to see something of one phase of the great work done by the late Dr. Klopsch. I have no hesitation in saying that the peculiar kind of work that he did in India was the most effective missionary work that I observed. I think it would be admitted by all that the efforts to convert Moslems or Hindoo adults to our point of view have been pretty barren of results; but at the orphanages at Ajmeer and Cawnpore and other places which I visited, I found a large company of people growing into young manhood and womanhood under conditions of a most promising character.

When the last great famine occurred, a vast number of infant children were orphaned, and would have died at once but for the intervention of Dr. Klopsch. He provided a fund which made it possible to gather these children together, feed and clothe them, and give them a Christian education. They were removed from the sharp prejudices and superstitions which have such a strong governing influence upon their race, and it cannot be but they will be of great value in spreading the cause of Christian civilization throughout Asia.

Sincerely yours,

Melville E. Stone

A feeling tribute was paid by Myrta Lockwood Avary of Georgia, who was on the staff of *The Christian Herald* for several years, and was very active in its sociological and charity labors, especially the "Fresh Air Work" for the tenement children. In memorial verse she wrote:

> At his command
> Corn-bearing ships to famine lands set sail
> Our country's banners flying at the mast.
> Through these poor hands the bread of life has passed
> To starving millions.
> Now, where he lieth in his cerements,
> The kindly thought of thousands weaves a pall,
> Fragrant and fair as were the flowers that bloomed.

And that the children brought him at his call
To spread above him ere he is entombed,
And o'er his grave the shining vail of death
Floats soft and luminous.

Notwithstanding that the funeral services of Dr.
Klopsch had enabled thousands to pay their tributes
of respect, and noted men to give their estimate of
his life, the desire to make further testimonial to the
man and his good works was so universal that it was
found necessary to arrange special memorial services.
These were held in the large auditorium of the New
Masonic Hall on Twenty-fourth Street, New York
City, on the evening of April 14. Rarely has an
audience been in more sympathetic accord with the
great central theme of the occasion which brought
them together. Almost all those present had been
personal friends of Dr. Klopsch, or had been helped
through some personal acts of kindness or through
some of his enormous philanthropies, or had known
of his great public service at home and abroad, and
wished by their presence to join in honoring his
memory.

On the speaker's platform were Mr. William R.
Moody; Dr. J. H. Darlington, Episcopal Bishop of
Harrisburg; Dr. O. S. Marden; Mr. Irving Bacheller;
Rev. John Wesley Hill; Judge Arthur S. Tompkins;
Rev. Wallace MacMullen; Mr. Edwin S. Ives;
Rev. James M. Farrar; Rev. F. C. Iglehart; Rabbi
Michelson; Mr. K. Yamazaki, Consul-General of
Japan; Mrs. Bird, "Mother of the Bowery Mission";
Rev. George Sanderson, chaplain of the Tombs,
and others. This was the order of the service:

OPENING HYMN . . . . .Prof. H. E. Browne, Organist.
"My Faith Looks Up to Thee."
PRAYER. . . . . .Rev. Wallace MacMullen, D.D.
SCRIPTURE READING . . . . .Rev. James M. Farrar, D.D.
READING OF LETTERS. . . . . Mr. Edwin S. Ives.
ADDRESS. . . . . Rabbi Michelson.
MEMORIAL ADDRESS . . . . .Bishop J. H. Darlington.
BIBLE VERSES . . . . Sung by 250 Mont-Lawn Children.
Prof. Noll, of Nyack, at the Organ.
ADDRESS . . . . .Dr. O. S. Marden.
(Representing the Periodical Publishers' Association.)
SINGING . . . ."The Glory Song," by 250 Mont-Lawn Children.
ADDRESS. . . . . Mr. Irving Bacheller.
ADDRESS . . . . Rev. John Wesley Hill.
ADDRESS. . . . . Judge Arthur S. Tompkins.
SINGING. .Bowery Mission Men's Choir.
"It Is Well With My Soul."
ADDRESS. .Mr. K. Yamazaki of Japan.
ADDRESS. . . . . Rev. Dr. Iglehart.
DOXOLOGY. . . . . Prof. Browne, Organ.
BENEDICTION. . . . . .Rev. Stephen Merritt.

Mr. William R. Moody, of Northfield, Mass., head of the Moody Schools, presided. After the opening hymn, Bishop Darlington, of Harrisburg, led in prayer. The Bishop prayed that "the memory of the good man who has gone may make us more zealous in all good works for God and our fellow men, giving us greater love for Christ, a higher idea of duty, and a firmer resolve to stand fast for the righteousness of the saints."

Rev. James M. Farrar, D.D., of Brooklyn, chose as the Scripture reading the first Psalm. Mr. Edwin S. Ives read extracts from a number of letters received from friends in different states, regretting their inability to be present. Governor Hughes of New York sent word by his secretary that "the Governor would have been very glad to attend the memorial service to Dr. Klopsch were it possible for him to do so, as he highly appreciated Dr. Klopsch's services to humanity." Among those who sent letters of regret were Mr. John C. Havemeyer, of Yonkers; Ex-Mayor Charles A. Schieren, Brooklyn; Mr. John Brisben Walker, Mr. L. N. Doubleday, Mrs. M. V. Terhune ("Marion Harland"), Mr. John Lloyd Thomas, Commander Scottish Rite; Mrs. Margaret E. Sangster, Rev. C. H. Mead, Rev. Bernard Peck, and many others.

Rabbi Michelson, of Trenton, was the next speaker. He said in part:

I am a rabbi. I am in charge of a large congregation; the only rabbi of a Jewish community in Trenton. I am Jewish chaplain of the New Jersey State Prison. When I was a boy, I wanted to read something in English which would arouse me and keep me in touch with the highest, the best, and the truest in the spiritual world, and I then turned to *The Christian Herald*, and I saw there and I can feel now as I felt when I read those bright and brilliant and arousing and soothing pages, in which this man had stamped every word and every line and every syllable with his personality. And so I went on studying *The Christian Herald*, and I am reading it today. He who reads it and understands its policy, will walk in the ways of the Lord, I am sure.

I came in touch with another work of his — the Bowery Mission. I think it is possibly the greatest institution of its kind in the world. When Dr. Klopsch spoke there, you will believe me when I say, I was stepping upon holy ground. When I saw many men, weary, heavy-laden, and when I heard the Gospel of the New Testament, I said "blessed," and the Old

Testament, I said "blessed"; and it was Dr. Klopsch who loved it and worked for it.   Our rabbis tell us that the righteous of all nations shall inherit the kingdom of heaven.   Dr. Louis Klopsch was righteous and he was good, and, therefore, though of a different faith, it is my feeling that he will inherit the kingdom of heaven.   Let this be our prayer, that when we shall all meet our Father, we shall see him side by side there as our brother himself.

Bishop J. H. Darlington, who made the principal address, spoke of Dr. Klopsch as the "friend of the whole world, raising millions of money for those hungering unto death.   In any great trouble, such as a famine at the ends of the earth, he would take up that want and be glad to meet it.   It was seizing the opportunities lying around him that made him a genius.   He was a genius in organizing; not in writing or speaking, but in using the things about him which he made into means of vast good.   He discovered Dr. Farrar and his ability to preach to the children, that he might bring them to the feet of the dear Master.

"It is only a short time ago that I was at the Bowery Mission, when it was visited by the President of the United States.   As I stood there, the boys in their rough way gave three cheers for 'Bill and the Bish'; and I thought they were not cheering the right man.   I little thought that night that so soon the end would come to Dr. Klopsch."

The singing of the "Bible Verses" by the children of Mont-Lawn was beautifully rendered, and made a deep impression on the audience.

Chairman Moody then paid a brief, but eloquent, tribute to Dr. Klopsch, as "a Christian great in his deeds, who dared with great daring deeds of magnitude which many would have shrunk from. His sympathy extended beyond geographical barriers, and made him a great foreign missionary in the best sense; a great home missionary in the truest sense, and a loyal and devoted city missionary also."

Dr. O. S. Marden was the next speaker. He represented the publishing interests in which Dr. Klopsch was so active. In the course of his address, he said:

I met Dr. Klopsch last at a banquet in Washington given by the Periodical Association of America, of which he was an officer. The President of the United States was there. Dr. Klopsch sat at my table and seemed to enjoy the occasion as much as any. He was taken ill that very night. I never saw him alive again. He was thought very highly of by the Periodical Association, which represents something like fifty different magazines and periodicals.

Mr. Klopsch started in New York poor, and made his own career, and if all those who have been befriended by him should wish to come to this memorial service, the highway from the Battery to Central Park would be black with the people who have been helped by his marvelous life. More than that, there are probably one hundred thousand people alive tonight who would have starved but for this man's remarkable ability and organizing energy, his far-seeing sagacity and business ability. He founded orphanages all over the world. But right here at home was one of the greatest of his works, as represented by the children here tonight. I never saw a man enter into child-life so absolutely as did Dr. Klopsch. I understand that over forty thousand children from the East Side, poor, pale, many ill, have been taken to the Home upon the Hudson — Mont-Lawn — and had two or three weeks' vacation. Think of it. Over forty thousand children! And who of us can tell how many of these he has saved from going wrong because he befriended them, and how many would have been dead but for this man? If we could ask Dr. Klopsch tonight what gave him the most satisfaction, what do you suppose it would be? He would point to these children, who have been saved and helped, and to the men saved at the Bowery Mission. It is only what we give away that we save. It is only what we render to others that survives death. We cannot carry a penny across the Great River, but we can carry good deeds; and Dr. Klopsch would say that many of the things we appreciate were mere rubbish. And he would give us another lesson — to do our work while we live. We plan to do good works. Men accumulating money, intend to do much for some good purpose; but Dr. Klopsch gave us a lesson in doing good while we live.

Chairman Moody again introduced the children, who sang most sweetly the " Glory Song."

Rev. Wallace MacMullen offered a prayer, after which Chairman Moody introduced Mr. Irving Bacheller, who spoke briefly. He said in part:

"Our friend, whom we honor tonight, preached with bread; he argued with human kindness; he prayed with wheat and corn and forgiveness and generosity. He baptized with soap and water. We call it the modern spirit, but it is really very old. He preached a sermon to the hungry hordes of India — one of the greatest sermons of history. There were a million bushels of wheat in it. Louis Klopsch was essentially a minister and organizer. His desk was his pulpit; *The Christian Herald* the contribution plate; every son of God was his brother. His weekday was as holy as his Sabbath; his counting-room as consecrated as his church; his note-of-hand as sacred as his Bible; his business as clean as his religion. We need more such ministers. At Bradstreet's his rating was perfect, and I fancy in the archives of St. Peter it is quite as good. If every man, woman, and child whom he had befriended in this wide world should lay a flower upon his grave, a mountain of fragrance and beauty would arise thereon."

Mr. Moody introduced Rev. Dr. John Wesley Hill, Metropolitan M. E. Church, New York, who said:

"Last week, in conversation with President Taft in Washington, with reference to the rare qualities and the phenomenal achievements of our departed friend, our President declared that his late visit to the Bowery Mission was one of the most inspiring and delightful events of his life. Then, pausing for a moment, he said: 'Tell me about the Mission. Will it stand?' I said: 'It truly will. It has been so organized and established that it must enlarge and increase and more and more fulfil the vision which its founder had concerning it.' Then the President said: 'I have heard that Dr. Klopsch founded a Children's Home somewhere. Where is it? Tell me about it.' I told him about it; and then he asked what sort of a memorial would be established to the memory of this great and good man. I told him that an effort had already been projected by the friends of Dr. Klopsch to endow the Children's Home. 'Well,' he said, as I left him, 'keep me advised as to that movement, for when the time comes, I want to send my check as my personal tribute to the character and achievements of Dr. Louis Klopsch.'

"We are too near his memory to fully appreciate his greatness. One must stand back from the mountain in order to behold its magnitude. We shall not forget him. There are moments when he seems far removed from us. But I think he has only stepped around the corner."

Judge Arthur S. Tompkins, of Nyack, N. Y., made a speech that deeply impressed the meeting. He said in part:

Coming from the summer home of Dr. Klopsch, and the scene of his splendid work for the children whom he loved and served, I count it a very great privilege to have a little part in this appropriate memorial service. In his death, countless thousands into whose lives he brought sunshine and cheer and hope, have lost a loving and generous friend, and the world has lost one of its big men, and one of its great benefactors. Few men have touched so many hearts and influenced so many lives for good. His was a world-wide love, as broad as the continent and as deep and intense as the needs of his fellow men. His genius and capacity for great enterprises, his business acumen, his fertility of resources, his energy and courage and enthusiasm enabled him to overcome every obstacle, and surmount every difficulty, and solve every problem, and achieve singular success in every undertaking, and enabled him to do works of charity and benevolence and philanthropy that have startled and amazed the world. And tonight the world is better and sweeter and purer, and heaven is richer because he lived and loved and wrought. The Christlike spirit that has made this the very golden age of philanthropy and benevolence was exemplified in the life of our friend. What must be his reward for all the activities of mind and heart and means; for the spiritual and moral and physical well-being of men and women all the world over? There is no arithmetic by which his benefactions can be counted. The sum total of his kindly deeds and his charitable acts will never be known this side eternity. But we rejoice that the great works that he inaugurated are to continue. Truly, his labors, his works do follow him. He sowed harvests that coming generations will reap. He started some streams of work and influence that will flow on and on forever.

The Bowery Mission Choir then sang "It Is Well With My Soul," the audience singing the chorus.

Rev. Ferdinand C. Iglehart was the last speaker. He said Dr. Klopsch was most Christlike in his love for children. At Mont-Lawn they climbed upon him, put their arms about his neck, and kissed him, and he was happy, and young; and they were happy because he was with them. The speaker happened to be in Washington just a few days after the death of Dr. Klopsch. "President Taft asked me about the institutions which had been founded, and I told him that his family and those he had gathered about him in his institutions promised to continue the beautiful work he had done. The great ones of the earth knew and honored him; the men in the 'bread line' worshiped him; the children loved him. 'Bury me in Sleepy Hollow,' he said when he lay dying, 'so that I can look out upon Mont-Lawn.' It was the apple of his eye, and on fair days the children can look out upon Sleepy Hollow and see the grave of their benefactor. And so long as there shall ring the merry laugh of childhood; so long as there shall be the appreciation of the true, the beautiful, the good, the heroic in human conduct, so long will this man live in the hearts and interests of our countrymen."

After the singing of the Doxology, Chairman Moody asked the Rev. Stephen Merritt to pronounce the benediction.

Commenting on the memorial meeting, *The Christian Herald* said:

"It was a graceful and spontaneous tribute that was paid to the memory of Dr. Klopsch by the gathering of professional and business men and women in New York on April 14. Through all the addresses there ran a note of deep and sincere admiration for the character and work of the man, who through his far-reaching benevolences, and aided by a great army of godly people, had been the means of doing so much good to others. Men of every denomination and every station in life, from President down to the humblest citizen, had been impressed with the value of that work to humanity, and by speech or message they freely expressed their views on the subject. Over all else in the universal estimation was Dr. Klopsch's love for the children, and the majority of the speakers showed this by their eloquent appreciation of the orphanage work, and of the helpful and benevolent influence of the Children's Home at Mont-Lawn, which Dr. Klopsch founded, and where forty thousand little children of the poor have been summer guests in the last fifteen years. Over the gates of Mont-Lawn he inscribed the words of Froebel — 'I love God and Little Children' — and this furnished the real keynote of his life-work, although it had many other ramifications. This latest public expression of approval must be exceedingly grateful to all those who have coöperated with him in his various charities."

Tributes continued to be paid to the good works of Dr. Klopsch by the press, the pulpit, and by the great multitude of those who had been the beneficiaries of his philanthropy, and of those who had by their contributions made it possible. From far-off lands, weeks and months after the last tributes had been paid here, came messages of condolence and of loving appreciation. Missionaries and natives were represented in these tokens of respect and sympathy; thousands of orphans, whom he had been the means of supporting and training, were represented too. And still later, the Gospel workers in the world's remotest parts — in Tibet, in the South Pacific Archipelago, in Labrador and the frozen Arctic — sent letters that glowed with love and admiration for their friend, and expressed sincerest sorrow for the loss they had sustained in his departure. All recognized the characteristics which made him a world almoner, a man with the most intense sympathy for his fellow man. Impulsive and enthusiastic, he was a true knight of charity, for whom the world was a field for the practical exercise of sympathy and kindness, and to whom all men, whatever their color, race, or religion, were his brothers, and none so poor, so low, or so fallen as to be unworthy of kindness or incapable of gratitude. A twentieth century captain of philanthropy, his good deeds did not end with his life. From the secluded grave on the banks of the Hudson, the voice of him who in his lifetime did so much to uplift and encourage humanity yet speaks.